The Philosophy of History

Also available from Continuum:

Philosophy of the Social Sciences, Robert C. Bishop

The Philosophy of History

An Introduction

Mark Day

continuum

Continuum International Publishing Group
The Tower Building   80 Maiden Lane, Suite 704
11 York Road   New York, NY 10038
London SE1 7NX

British Library Cataloguing-in-Publication Data
A catalogue record for this book is available from the British Library.

ISBN: HB: 0-8264-8847-1
       978-0-8264-8847-3
    PB: 0-8264-8848-X
       978-0-8264-8848-0

Library of Congress Cataloging-in-Publication Data
Day, Mark.
   The Philosophy of History: an introduction / Mark Day.
      p.   cm.
   Includes bibliographical references.
   ISBN 978-0-8264-8847-3 – ISBN 978-0-8264-8848-0   1. History–Philosophy.
2. History–Methodology.   3. History–Study and teaching.   I. Title.

   D16.8.D32 2008
   901–dc22
                                    2007027824

Typeset by Aptara Books Ltd.
Printed and bound in Great Britain by The Cromwell Press, Trowbridge, Wiltshire.

To Kim

Contents

Part IV: FROM INTERPRETATION TO DISCOURSE

Part V: TRUTH AND REALITY

Figures and tables

Figures

Tables

Preface

In this book I aim to provide the reader with an understanding of the central philosophical topics required to reflect upon the study of history: evidence, knowledge, explanation, interpretation, language, time, truth. That list is not so different to that of W. H. Walsh in his classic Introduction, published in 1951. And yet so much has changed since then. I hope in what follows to have brought the philosophers of history available to Walsh – Hegel, Oakeshott, Collingwood, Hempel, Dray – into contact with the revolutions in thought that the last 60 years have produced. So I privilege Bayesianism, the new epistemology of testimony, Structuralism, macrosociology, Social Constructivism, dialogical hermeneutics, postmodernism, and more: a motley array of approaches that between them can illuminate historical practice. My aim is to introduce these and other approaches in a way that requires no prior knowledge on the part of the reader, but which moves beyond an elementary level. My intended audience is undergraduates with some experience of philosophy, postgraduates and also professional historians. As this is a *philosophy* of history I privilege argument, in the criticism and critical development of the approaches introduced.

The book is divided into five parts, each with two or three chapters. In the first part, I focus on the relationship between the historian and the evidence, asking how the historian's account is justified by that evidence. The next three parts compare different ways of understanding the historical past. In Part II I examine a scientific approach to history, focusing especially on the relation between general theories and those particular past happenings that tend to be of most interest to most historians. One aim in these chapters is to detach the debate concerning the relations between history and science from that concerning the outdated positivist understanding of science. In Part III I consider historical interpretation, in particular Collingwood's intriguing claim that the historian must re-enact the past in their own mind. In Part IV the debate moves from interpretation to discourse via two ideas: that interpretation is a matter of entering into dialogue with the past, and that interpretation is a matter of applying rhetorical forms to the past. Finally, in Part V I tackle a variety of arguments impugning historical truth: that we haven't got it, that we couldn't have it, or that we create it.

A few terminological preliminaries are necessary. The most important concerns 'philosophy of history' itself. There are two senses of that phrase in contemporary currency. The first implies a way of looking at the past, exemplified in such grand-scale histories as Hegel's and Marx's. This sort of philosophy of history has been distinguished by the prefix 'substantive', or less charitably, 'speculative'. This is *not* the sense in which this book is a philosophy of history (not least because this activity is better regarded not as philosophy, but as a certain way of doing history). In the second sense, 'philosophy of history' is an examination of what historians, as historians, do and what they produce (most especially, historical writing). It has been distinguished by the prefix 'analytic', which illegitimately ties the enterprise to a certain style of philosophy – analytic philosophy – which I do not restrict myself to in what follows, and which in any case is, in the twenty-first century, somewhat out of favour. The second sense of philosophy of history and that, pursued in this book, is better characterized as an extension of history's examination of itself. The aim is to make *more* explicit the theories and presuppositions that are already embedded in historical practice, and which historical self-reflection to some extent recognizes.

A second ambiguity, potentially the source of confusion, lies in the term 'history'. The past is history; the study of that past is also history. (Indeed, the double meaning of 'philosophy of history' can be understood as resulting from the double meaning of 'history'.) It has been suggested that matters be clarified by distinguishing firmly between history as past, and *historiography* as the study of the past. Consequently, one suggestion is that the area for which this book is an Introduction be renamed the philosophy of historiography. However, not only is that a rather unwieldy neologism, but it wrongly implies that all history is a matter of writing. So I stick with both the 'philosophy of history', and also with the traditional double meaning of 'history'; I use 'historiography' to refer to history-as-study only where confusion might otherwise result.

I have avoided gendered language where possible by using the sometimes awkward technique of pluralizing. No solution is perfect, given our linguistic heritage. I have dispensed with 'an historian' in favour of 'a historian', the former seeming to me to be needlessly old fashioned.

Finally, I note for the reader's benefit the importance of the forthcoming *Blackwell Companion to the Philosophy of History and Historiography*. At the time of completing this book, the Blackwell Companion was not yet published. However, having had some acquaintance with both the overall plan of that work, and with certain of the chapters to be featured therein, I fully expect it to be a valuable resource for research into the philosophy of history. I would hope that this shorter Introduction and that more extensive survey of topics would complement each other well in mapping the terrain of contemporary philosophy of history.

Part I
EVIDENCE OF THE PAST

An introduction to historical practice

Chapter Outline

1. The past in the present

At the heart of historical study is the attempt to further knowledge of the human past on the basis of evidence available to the present. That critical reasoning from the evidence – what I shall call historical reasoning – will be the topic of Chapters 2 and 3. But before unearthing the specifics of historical reasoning, it will be useful to situate the philosophical enquiry within the broader edifice of historical study: its preconditions, its purposes, and its forms of production.

We are all historians in so far as we critically approach the past; just as we are all philosophers in so far as we critically approach our beliefs about, say, morality. (A critical approach to the past implies a critical use of evidence; the recognition that testimony and memory can deceive, and that good evidence may not superficially be apparent as such.[1]) But before the critical gaze arrives, we are all already and unavoidably bound up with the past. The past makes you who you are: your parents' meeting and conceiving *you*; your culture with its accumulated knowledge, art and technology; your own past decisions, actions and mistakes. You have many memories of the past, both distinctly recalled and the habitual, without which life would surely be impossible. Given a little experience, you can observe the present world in a past-directed way. You see the remains of a tree struck by lightening, scars on another's body, the grave of a Victorian industrialist, Neolithic earthworks.

As Michael Oakeshott (1933) insisted, there are different ways of observing the present world: in terms of its human history, as well as in terms of the scientific laws that shape it, and of how we can act upon it.[2] I look across the Porter valley, near my home. I can observe the geological effects of the river's course, and the habitation which varies depending upon proximity to the water source. That is to observe the scene scientifically. I can wonder whether it would be possible to canoe or row down the river: that is to observe it practically. Finally, I can see a watermill, from the river's distant past, and the remains of a picnic, from its recent past. In this last way, I observe the present scene historically.

In questioning the present world, we learn about the past and so answer our questions about the present. By such questioning we make explicit our understanding of the dependence of present upon past, and thus permit a more critical history. Questioning that involves the past is hard to avoid for the inquisitive mind and still reflects a much broader activity than the history found in history books, schools and universities. I encourage you to consider your own examples. Mine would include: 'Why does the Sheffield General Cemetery (on the Porter Brook) contain both an Anglican and a non-conformist chapel, in starkly different architectural styles?', 'Why is Sheffield's commercial centre so much smaller compared to similarly populated English cities?', 'Why does our society value "classical" music so highly, when most people listen to it relatively infrequently?', 'Why do I, by and large, prefer jazz music to classical music?' To answer past-directed questions we need evidence.

Historical evidence is wonderfully varied. Items (plates, coins, bones) are found or unearthed. Our everyday human landscape (field boundaries, routes of rights of way, cemeteries) is critically examined. Any part of the present world could potentially be evidence for the past, in so far as the two are causally related (or indeed related in other pertinent ways: see Chapter 2). But we must, of course, be able to use that evidence: the ashes of a letter are related to the history of that letter, yet we cannot use the evidence in the form that it now is to infer anything about what was written. We should set up no *a priori*[3] limits about what sort of evidence can or cannot be used. Yet no close acquaintance with historical reasoning is required to locate the sorts of evidence that *tend* to be most useful to historians. Objects that have persisted from the past to the present, without change or with only gradual and knowable deterioration, provide one sort of evidence, commonly studied by archaeologists. Still more important to history is evidence which is linguistic. The living are questioned orally, the interview format allowing the historian the unique opportunity and unique danger of moulding their evidence. Data in the form of lists or tables (of economic activity, of births and deaths, of book consumption) are a mine to be plundered in ways undreamt of by their creators. And at the heart of most historians' reasoning are written accounts: memoirs, chronicles, letters, orders, minutes and legal records.

2. The professionalization of history

The past and present are connected in epistemology (a word stemming from the Greek 'episteme', meaning knowledge). In order to know the past, one must use what is available in the present. And in order to understand the present, one must turn to the past. Despite these deep and unavoidable connections, the professionalization of history is a relatively recent development.

Since the nineteenth century, history has become a subject for specialists, usually and increasingly located in universities, disseminating their findings to peers, students, and, sometimes, to wider society. History has become a profession with explicit and sometimes sophisticated methods, with exacting criteria for success, requiring both thorough training and diligence of research. (Just as have other subjects which were formerly fit for the inquisitive amateur – the dilettante – including philosophy, economics, chemistry.) Diligence is found in abundance in the figure who, with remarkable unanimity, historians have hailed as the father of professional history, the Prussian Leopold van Ranke. Ranke's early career was built upon a tireless immersion in seemingly vast, untapped archives:

> The cafés stay open until 2:00 or 3:00 am, and the theatre often does not close until 1:30. Then one dines. Not I, naturally. I hurry into bed, since I would like to be at the Palazzo Barberini by 7:00 the next morning. There I use a room belonging to the librarian, which receives the north wind; my manuscripts are piled up there. My scribe arrives soon after I do, and slips in with a 'Ben levato' [Good morning] at the door. The librarian's servant, or the servant's wife, appears before me, and offers me their services with the usual 'Occorre niente?'
>
> (Quoted by Grafton 1997: 36, taken from Ranke's *Das Briefwerk*)

Given that Ranke has had huge influence on subsequent professional history, to which the aforementioned hailing attests, it is worth beginning our characterization of contemporary historical practice by highlighting six elements of Ranke's methodology. (This is not to say that Ranke was the original innovator in all of the following; arguably he was so for none. One strong influence on Ranke's theory was Humboldt's essay 'On the historian's task' (Humboldt 1967). Rather, Ranke extended, exemplified, and instilled in the wider profession the following methodology.)

(1) As the first sentence of this chapter suggests, Ranke's influence in placing evidence at the heart of historical study should be regarded as of primary importance. Indeed, one form of evidence above all others was valued: the archive, that depository of material written by past authors, our exteriorized collective memory. (Recent work in the philosophy of mind suggests that we treat such a term entirely literally. See Clark (1997: 201).) Memory latent, yet not consciously recalled: the task of the historian following Ranke was to bring these documents to consciousness. Ranke expanded the range of historical evidence through a geographical exploration of the archives of Europe, his growing reputation permitting access to yet more documents in Prussia, Austria, Venice and the Papacy. (Grafton (1997: 50–3) well describes Ranke's role of explorer-historian.) The archives provide evidence that is of special value, the primary sources. These transport the historian directly back to the past that the documents describe and of which they were a part, permitting the historian knowledge of that past without the accretion of subsequent interpretation and tradition.

(2) Just as memory is not always reliable, so no historian should suppose that they can learn the truth of what happened simply by believing the authors of primary sources. The foremost realization of the serious historian is that primary sources must be criticized: they must be compared one against the other, must be treated with suspicion, and be used to infer more than the authors intended to disclose. The critical treatment of archival evidence is the topic for Chapters 2 and 3.

(3) Ranke's influence extended beyond his treatment of sources, to the embodiment of a more general orthodoxy of historical practice that has been called 'historism'. In what has become the most quoted, and the most contested, claim in the philosophy of history, Ranke maintained that historians write history 'wie es eigentlich gewesen', usually translated 'as it really happened' (Ranke 1824). The demand[4] requires further elaboration before it can be taken to be particularly informative. One can gain some appreciation of Ranke's sense of

the phrase by locating what it was that Ranke was concerned to avoid. The first contrast is with the Romantic histories of Ranke's time, of which Thomas Carlyle on the end of Robespierre in the French Revolution may be taken as exemplary:

> The Death-tumbrils [carts], with their motley Batch of Outlaws, some Twenty-three or so, from Maximilian Robespierre, to Mayor Fleuriot and Simon the Cordwainer, roll on. All eyes are on Robespierre's Tumbril where he, his jaw bound in dirty linen, with his half-dead Brother and half-dead Henriot, lie shattered . . . At the foot of the scaffold, they stretched him out on the ground till his turn came. Lifted aloft his eyes again opened; caught the bloody axe. Samson wrenched the coat off him; wrenched the dirty linen from his jaw: the jaw fell powerless, there burst from him a cry; hideous to hear and see. Samson, thou canst not be too quick!
>
> (1842: III 242–3)[5]

The historian should be responsible to the sources, not embellishing with detail that could not possibly be known.

(4) A second element of Ranke's historism was his privileging of the concrete historical phenomenon over the abstraction of the scientist's systematizing. A second contrast for Ranke's historism is therefore provided by those histories which are overly abstract. Contemporary scientific abstraction will be the topic of Chapter 4; suffice, at this point, to state that the scientist seeks general laws which explain the particular historical happenings. In Ranke's day, abstraction was most clearly the hallmark of the philosophical approach to history (also called 'speculative philosophy of history', a phrase examined in the Introduction to this book). Hegel's works dominated this field; of particular relevance are his *Phenomenology of Spirit* (1977/1807) and *Philosophy of World History* (1956/1840). Hegel's history traced the development of the concept of freedom, from the ancient Orient, through the Greek and Roman worlds, the French Revolution, and to the modern Prussian state of which Hegel was a subject. This *a priori* structure governed resultant historical study, dictating what was to be included and to what end. Such an approach got history back to front: for Ranke, the sources must come first, the continuity after.

The privileging of concrete over abstract remains unchallenged in mainstream historical practice. Commenting on an example of so-called 'cliometric' history, Fogel and Engerman's history of slavery (1995/1974), Peter Novick comments that

Historians who wanted to know the basis for Robert Fogel and Stanley Engerman's conclusion that slaves were only moderately exploited were told that the answer was

$$E_x = \frac{B}{\sum_{t=0}^{n} \frac{\lambda_t(\alpha_1 P_{ct} Q_t L_t^{-1})}{(1+i)^t}}$$

The dust jacket of a recent work in intellectual history carried the prediction by Mark Poster that 'no historian who reads and comprehends this work will ever write in the same way again.' The promise (or threat) was limited by the qualifying 'and comprehends'.

(1999/1988: 588)

Very amusing. I wonder whether there is any other professional subject in which criticism of another's work would be permissible simply on the basis that it used a theoretical approach that is hard to understand.

(5) It has been suggested that Ranke's 'wie es eigentlich gewesen' be understood not, as it has usually been, as an exhortation to a rather dry fact-collecting exercise, but as gesturing towards a study which went beyond mere appearances. George Iggers claims that 'eigentlich' is better understood as invoking what 'properly' or 'essentially' took place, not just what 'actually' did (Iggers 1974: II 459). Ranke called the historian 'to rise ... from the investigation and contemplation of the particular to a general view of events and to the recognition of their objectively existing relatedness' (Ranke 1973: 23). Yet this was in no way to be confused with history by abstraction. The relation that Ranke referred to was *narrative*. Not the irresponsible narrative of those Romantic historians who wrote too similarly to the novelist, but the historian's integrative narrative.

In short, the Romantic historian should be praised for the vividness of their writing in bringing the past to life, but condemned for their lack of restraint with the truth. The scientific historian should be praised for their concern to base history on the evidence, but condemned for their insistence on explaining by abstract concepts and universal theories. The *a priori* historian should be praised for their discovery of a fundamental unity in the historical past, but condemned for its cursory use of evidence, and total disregard for detailed archival evidence.

(6) Not every feature of Ranke's own historical approach was adhered to by subsequent historians. We have seen a gradual liberalization of many constraints embodied in Ranke's work. His exclusive focus on written evidence,

the archive, was overturned in the use of visual evidence by one of Ranke's students, Johan Huizinga. As I have implied, the scope of evidence has since grown still broader; an achievement for which the genuinely inter-disciplinary Annales school must take much credit. Marc Bloch's insistence that one could infer from features of our present landscape is one of the most striking examples of that extension. Not only evidence, but also topic has broadened: Ranke's near exclusive focus on political and religious history, in which states were the central actors, was in the twentieth century gradually discarded.

3. Relations with the past

Why did Ranke have the influence that he did? His undoubted skill and enthusiasm notwithstanding, the question is particularly pertinent given that one can legitimately question his originality in both critical historical reasoning, and 'historism' more generally.[6] A partial answer can be found in Ranke's educational methodology. He taught his students – among whom Georg Waitz, Jacob Burkhardt and Huizinga were to become influential historians in their own right – by training them to read and criticize the archival documents. And this dissemination relied on the newly created Prussian university system, well organized and yet permitting of academically critical approaches. The work of the professional historian is therefore dependent on elements of their social context. In this section I develop this idea to sketch the ways in which the critical epistemic relationship with the past is bound up in other relations with the past: preservative, dialogic and practical. (In Chapter 9 I expand upon the first two of those relations with the past; in Chapter 12 upon the third.)

Preservative

The historian depends upon a preservative relation with the past, by their memory, by externalized memory in archives, and by oral testimony. Ranke's conclusions were drawn from written evidence found in archives. And though historians have since been able to utilize many other sorts of evidence, the archive remains central to historical reasoning. The existence of archives depend on contingent features of our society: in particular, that institutions persist across the centuries. Until the development of stable states, churches, educational establishments and charities, this condition was not met. Not all documents survive; while the critical historian takes that fact into account when inferring their account, some parts of the past will nonetheless be rendered unreachable.

The historian depends not only on preserved knowledge, but on preserved methods, as indeed the importance of Ranke's educational innovations demonstrates. Ranke himself was well placed with regard to wider intellectual innovation achieved in the eighteenth and early nineteenth centuries. Aviezer Tucker (2004: Chapter 2) stresses the reliance of the nineteenth-century historiographical revolution upon earlier innovation in biblical criticism, classical criticism, and comparative linguistics. The work of Friedrich Wolf and others encouraged the critical examination of ancient texts, examining features of the writing so as to infer the approximate date and possible authorship of those texts. The work of Franz Bopp and others encouraged the examination of the development of different languages, so as to infer their origins as common or diverse.

Dialogic

Historians can be regarded as taking part in a dialogue not only with their contemporaries, but with the enquiries produced by past historians. Previous historical enquiry sets the challenges that must be met by contemporary historians. Gaps in those histories should be filled. Previous historical accounts should be challenged by showing how the new account can better account for present evidence (see Chapter 3), or more intelligibly tell what happened. And even where prior histories are not to be remedied or challenged in any way, they must be acknowledged and 'engaged'. The demand that one engage with other work on the same topic is common to all humanities (including, in this context, philosophy), and interestingly different to the corresponding demand in the sciences. The scientist should know enough about previous attempts to not repeat what has already been tried unless confirmation of those results is the aim. The humanist should more explicitly situate their own developments in the context of previous attempts and disagreements.

Practical

The past can be used. It is a truism that we have a variety of purposes in studying the past. One motivation for the professional historian is to secure the continuation of their career by publishing their work in the form of a paper in a journal whose audience is primarily their professional peers, or a monologue whose audience might further encompass the relevant university student and even the general public. Other uses of past study are of broader interest. One of the virtues of history is the way that the historian's findings bear upon our understanding of the present, whether or not it was the historian's explicit intention to draw those connections. We can use knowledge of the past to understand the present by comparison with the relevant past. The traditional insistence that people – but especially politicians – 'learn from the past' can be taken as the demand to locate past events that are either the same in relevant respects to, or are analogous to, present events of particular practical interest.

One of the most natural ways to understand the present (as the examples at the start of this chapter suggest) is to sketch some narrative that opens with some significant past event, and terminates in the now. That narrative can serve not only to explain the present, but to constitute it by founding an identity with the past. Thus did nineteenth-century history establish the nations of Europe by telling a story that connects some founding event – a battle, the life of a great leader, or the production of some momentous cultural or artistic work – with the resultant *nation*. We *are* Germans, communists, Jews, members of the liberal democratic world; we are not only the *product* of those pasts. One can understand the present in *contrast* to the past, as well as or instead of in connection with the past. Robert Darnton's (1985) examination of the humour found by eighteenth-century workers in their conduct of 'The Great Cat Massacre' (in the essay of that title to be examined in Chapter 8) throws into relief our own standards of morality and of humour. More generally, to study any thinker more distant than a couple of hundred years is not only to be cast into a world that is to some extent alien, but is also to be made aware of features of our own thought that we would otherwise not explicitly recognize.

To what extent does the emphasis on the social and practical context of the historian stand in tension to Ranke's 'wie es eigentlich gewesen'? We should not assume that there need be any tension. Social context can be required for historical knowledge, but the justification of that knowledge be nonetheless independent of that context. And the supporter of historical truth need not insist that the past be studied purely 'for its own sake': the attitude of the scholar and the products of their research should be independently evaluated. I may work on a maths problem out of boredom, because I have been told to, because I am fascinated by maths, or because it will help me make lots of money; but whichever of these is the case will not affect in the least the correctness of the answer that I produce. At any rate, these are distinctions that are useful to bear in mind, pending the more detailed assessment to be undertaken in the last chapter.

4. Forms of historical production

I have introduced the methodology of contemporary history, and its situation within societal structures and demands. I would like to conclude this introductory examination with the finished historical product. Typically, this is in the form of the written word, the monograph, journal paper, or textbook; just as (and it is surely no co-incidence) the fundamental evidence for historians is also the written word. It is history practiced as historiography that I focus on in the bulk of the discussion to come; and for that reason alone it is valuable to be reminded of the ways that history need not be constrained to writing, and what consequences follow from that observation. History is often presented via the spoken word: in person in schools and universities, recorded on the radio or television. And it is presented symbolically, yet not linguistically, through maps and diagrams (one of my favourite history books since childhood has been *The Times Atlas of World History* (1989)). These forms of historical production do not, to my mind, raise any substantive philosophical issues over and above those of historiography. However, two other forms – history as object and history as picture – do, and so deserve more attention.

Artefacts are historical evidence, but are also history themselves in so far as they are presented (in museums, say) so as to enable us to understand the past. That presentation will include text – an explanation of the artefact's context and use – but it is important to realize that the artefact itself has an epistemic effect over and above the accompanying text. In *So Many Ways to Begin*, Jon McGregor describes his protagonist's response to why he enjoyed museums:

> It seemed perfectly natural to him, to be amazed by the physical presence of history, to be able to stand in front of an ancient object and be awed by its reach across time. A thumbprint in a piece of prehistoric pottery. The chipped edge of a Viking battle-axe, and the shattered remains of a human skull. The scribbled designs for the world's first steam engine, spotted with candlewax and stained with jam.
>
> (2006: 37)

Eelco Runia (2006) adopted a similar tone in his more philosophical exploration of the importance of the 'Presence' of the past. That presence is to be understood in terms of metonymy: the linguistic trope that substitutes an attribute of x for x itself. Crucially, that substitution creates a discontinuity, such that the description becomes 'out of place'. Runia's central example is 'the gall bladder in room 615 doesn't want to eat', which places in jarring proximity the language of reductionist medicine of the body, and holistic care of the person. Metonymy can, suggests Runia, be applied to objects as well as words. In this way the historical artefact is best regarded not as evidence but as an object out of context, out of place, bringing us into jarring proximity with the past. Runia applies this account not only to artefacts, but to monuments:

> It should be remarked that while a modern monument *presents* a past event in the here and now, it can hardly be said to *represent* it. A monument like the Berlin Holocaust Memorial is a repository of what haunts the place of the present, a refuge for what has always (or at least since the event in question took place) been there. It is closer to a relic than to a painted, written, or sculpted pictorial account of what happened – though, of course, it differs from a relic in the sense that presence is transferred to a new, and willfully made, object. So, whereas pre-modern, metaphorical monuments are primarily engaged in a transfer of *meaning*, modern metonymical monuments concentrate on a transfer of *presence*.
>
> (Runia 2006: 17)

History as picture (either still or moving) – historiophoty, to use Hayden White's neologism – also raises intriguing issues. History in this form is extremely popular, reaching a wide audience as film – which will be the focus in what follows – painting, photo, documentary and (to stretch the category a little further) theatre and re-enactment. And it is surely popular for good reason. For most contemporary audiences pictorial history tends to outdo historiography not only in engaging the viewer's emotions and holding their interest, but in providing a sense of the sensory and emotional experience of those who were there.

It is obvious that there can be better or worse historical films, just as there is good and bad historical writing. The interesting question is whether the form itself has an effect on the outcome. There have been objections to the use of film in the presentation of history (Jarvie (1978) in particular, while Rosenstone (1988) and White (1988) are at best dubious of history on film). It is often claimed that history on film is insufficiently objective, governed as it is by the director's wishes and overall vision, and the (presumed) audience's demand for an exciting, action-packed movie crammed into a not overly long finished product. Still, one might doubt how different the predicament is to that facing the historiographer, who also has 'wishes', 'a vision' and an audience (albeit a potentially quite different kind of audience). Two better criticisms do stand.

(i) History on film is insufficiently interpretative, given the relative difficulty in adopting techniques that are so easy to employ in a written account of the past. The presentation and integration of multiple perspectives, the explicit criticism of sources (of particular relevance to the oral testimony typically provided in documentary film), the criticism and engagement with other historical interpretations and the explicit defence of one's own: it would take a patient audience to put up with too much of that in a historical film. Without the written word it is difficult to present extended chains of reasoning, references to evidence and other work, and large bodies of evidence. Any historical film that was intended to take a place in historical debate would, in practice, have to be supplemented by historiography.

(ii) History on film is necessarily additive to the evidence. In order to present a persuasive narrative, the film must be continuous, showing *something* even where the evidence warrants no sure inference. And detail in a film is unavoidable, even where the evidence omits it; in Richard Attenborough's film, Gandhi's conductor must have a face; in Joseph Vilsmaier's film, the background to the battle for the Stalingrad tractor works must be detailed, marked with explosions here, rather than there. We might take a stern line in response to this criticism, at least for films that do genuinely purport to be history rather than some form of historical fiction, by insisting on the use of actual footage and photos. Such representation raises the hope that one can achieve a more literal copy of the past. Yet there are familiar rebuffs to this hope found in the most basic texts in film and photography studies: a standpoint has been chosen to record the photo or film, someone has chosen to record this event, but not another, the images are later arranged or spliced together in certain ways with certain ends in mind. All those observations undermine the assumption that the use of actual footage guarantees evidential warrant. Rosenstone (1988: 1179–80) provides us with the example of a film of a gun firing, and then a shell landing. There is no doubt that the footage was authentic. But, contrary to the suggestion implicit in the finished film, the shell that lands will not have been that which was fired by the gun depicted in the previous frame.

Beginning in the next chapter, we shall re-focus our attention on historiography, which, on the basis of the above criticisms, can be appreciated as occupying its pre-eminent position in the historical profession for good reason. This introduction has, I hope, contextualized the work of the critical historiographer, though it is true that it has started many paths of thought and finished few. In the next chapter we shall make further progress on one particularly central issue: what it is for the historian to reason from the evidence.

Further reading and study questions

Bentley, M. (1999) *Modern Historiography: An Introduction*. London: Routledge. Chapters 2 to 4 are relevant to the material of this chapter; but the whole (short) book is recommended more generally as the best introductory history of modern historiography.

Grafton, A. (1997) *The Footnote: A Curious History*. Harvard: Harvard University Press. Chapters 1 to 3 provide a flavoursome account of Ranke's life and work.

Tucker, A. (2004) *Our Knowledge of the Past: A Philosophy of Historiography*. Cambridge: Cambridge University Press. Chapter 2 presents an interesting reconstruction of the nineteenth-century historiographical revolution.

(a) What are the major elements of a Rankean approach to history? In your experience, are those elements present in contemporary historical practice?

(b) Should one be suspicious of a history which is explicitly intended to shed light on the historian's present? If so, why?

(c) To what extent is the historian's *type of evidence* connected to their *subject matter* and to their *methodology*? Specifically, in the case of Ranke, could one claim that there was influence between his evidence (archival), his subject matter (politics) and his methodology (narrative)?

2 Historical methodology

Chapter Outline

1. Scissors and paste

In this chapter, I begin to focus attention on what will be taken to be the central task of the philosophy of history: describing and critiquing the ability of historiography to bring us understanding of the past on the basis of evidentially justified claims. I first flesh out a simple view of historical reasoning, for which we can use R. G. Collingwood's label of 'scissors and paste history'. Later in the chapter I attempt a reasonably detailed description of contemporary historical reasoning, by examining how historians understand that activity. For that self-understanding, I rely on two sources: training manuals for students of history, and peer reviews of professional historiography. Finally, I argue that to regard historical reasoning only in the ways considered to that point leaves open important philosophical questions, in particular *why* historians reason as they do. This argument sets the scene for the more overtly technical accounts of historical reasoning considered in the next chapter.

'Scissors and paste' was Roger Collingwood's term for the historical use of the sources that preceded, and fell short of, critical history. (See, in particular, 'Historical evidence' in Collingwood (1994). Collingwood's positive account of historical reasoning and understanding will be provided in Chapter 7.) To

Collingwood's 'scissors-and-paste man', history is the collection of memories that are transmitted to the historian by the testimony of the sources. The historian's role is to cut those elements of testimony that they think pertinent to their topic, pasting them in to the historical account so as to produce a pleasingly continuous narrative. Such an approach was challenged by the Rankean revolution in historical scholarship, though Collingwood, writing in the 1920s and 1930s, believed that scissors and paste history had not yet been decisively routed. Though no serious historian today will recommend it, an examination of precisely where scissors and paste goes wrong is instructive, for the criticism serves to suggest what it is to reason from the evidence.

Scissors and paste – hereafter designated by the acronym SAP – does have its attractions. In particular, it suggests its own justification, in so far as it relies on the fundamental role of memory in knowing the past, and testimony in disseminating those memories to other people. Nonetheless, Collingwood was right to reject the methodology. To criticize SAP, we shall follow Collingwood in distinguishing between two versions of the doctrine. 'Basic SAP', or 'the common sense theory' (Collingwood 1994: 234–5) has it that a witness observes, remembers, testifies and is believed and transcribed by the historian. It is obvious that proto-SAP doesn't provide a sufficient[1] methodological criterion, since not all testimony should be believed. In general, we do not (and should not) believe those who could not have known about the event or topic which they purport to describe. Beyond that, we tend to distrust those who have good reason to lie or distort; in particular, those who have an incentive to make their own actions appear sympathetic, heroic, or otherwise praiseworthy. Let us then move swiftly on to more viable varieties of SAP, which we might call 'critical SAP'.

Critical SAP takes on board the observation that not all testimony should be believed (Collingwood 1994: 257–9). Historians omit some sources, on the basis both of the sort of legitimate suspicion suggested above, and because in any case sources sometimes contradict. Indeed, one could shift the balance from trusting a source except where one has a reason to doubt it, to holding the source in abeyance until one has positively established its credibility. It is in this movement towards greater criticism, towards greater scepticism (in the everyday sense of the word), that Collingwood links the change in historical language from 'authorities' to 'sources'. The sources remain the historian's raw material, but material that no longer has automatic jurisdiction over the historian. 'Historical reasoning' is more prominent in the more critical versions of SAP, such reasoning being required to justify the inclusion of any part of a historical account. We are some distance from the original idea of SAP that sources are simply selected and copied; since according to the critical version of SAP the knowledge concerning reliability of one source must be gained through other evidence. The latter evidence is not therefore used in SAP fashion, but must be intelligently *applied*.

Still, Collingwood rightly charges even the most refined version of SAP with missing the point of critical history. The key to critical history is not so much that one critically *excludes* testimony, as that one reasons from the evidence to produce statements about the past that are *in addition* to anything testified. The historian includes in their account passages which cannot be found in any source. And that 'additional' material should not be regarded as mere commentary on the main body of source-derived material, for the most substantive of historical conclusions are not found 'ready made' in the testimonies. Collingwood dramatizes this objection with a challenge:

> If any reader still thinks that history as practiced today is a scissors-and-paste affair, and is willing to go to a little trouble in order to settle the question, let him take the history of Greece down to the end of the Peloponnesian War, which I mention as an example peculiarly favourable to himself because Herodotus and Thucydides have here maintained the position of 'authorities' to a quite peculiar degree, and compare in detail the account of it given by Grote [written c. 1850] with that given in the *Cambridge Ancient History* [written c. 1930]. Let him mark in each book every sentence of which he can find the original in Herodotus or Thucydides; and by the time he is through with the job he will have learnt something about how historical method has changed in the last hundred years.
>
> (1994/1946: 260–1)

In what ways do historians supplement what is provided in testimony? Most simply, there is historical evidence which is not testimonial. Primary sources include not only accounts of what the author or other people did, but such writing as orders, letters, ideological or religious theses. Such sources do not describe a further event but are, so to speak, bound up in that which they are evidence for. (Or better: such sources are expressive, not descriptive. The letters of European statesmen and ambassadors in the summer of 1914 express their intentions, they do not describe them; Papal bulls and Luther's 95 Theses express, rather than describe, the author's religious beliefs.) One could seek to account for the use of such sources, while remaining within a broadly SAP framework, by maintaining that the historian is justified in claiming x in so far as a credible source contains x. Such an account would seek to characterize historical reasoning in something like Anthony Grafton's memorable phrase: 'the text persuades, the [foot]notes prove' (1997: 15). (This sort of position has also been saddled with the names 'naive empiricism' (naivety rarely being regarded as a virtue in scholarly circles), and 'positivism'. I would counsel caution in applying the latter term, pending my explication in Chapter 4.)

But historical evidence goes beyond writing of any kind, and with that observation any version of SAP becomes untenable. I have already mentioned objects that persist from the past: pottery, parchments, trees, skulls. And features of the present world may, with more ingenuity, provide evidence for what is past: landscapes, soil composition, the material remains of a crime scene. But those points have already been made in Chapter 1; the demonstration of the failings of SAP is a simple extension to make. A more interesting mistake made by SAP concerns the treatment of testimonial evidence. It is supposed that where testimony is not true, it is thereby worthless. The recognition that this is not so is identified by the recommendation that one use the sources as 'witnesses in spite of themselves'. Much can be learnt from a source that contains nothing but falsehoods.

Collingwood's example of the detective-historian who investigates the murder of John Doe (1994: 266–74) is written so as to make this very point. On receipt of the rector's daughter's confession that she was the murderer, Collingwood's ideal detective-historian rejects its truth and yet (contrary to the SAP methodology) learns from it. 'Why is she telling a lie? Because she is shielding someone. Whom is she shielding? Either her father or her young man. Is it her father? No; fancy the rector! Therefore it is her young man' (1994: 270). Admittedly, Collingwood's dismissal of the rector as a possible suspect is anything but critical; nonetheless, this weakness is not due to the transgression of the boundaries of SAP. (An example of inference from false evidence that relies upon an actual historical source can be found in John Milligan's (1979) analysis of a letter written in the Civil War, which I discuss in the next chapter.)

Further, historians are able to infer not only from true testimony, and from false testimony ('why is she telling a lie?'), but even from testimonial silence. Luisa Passerini has stressed the importance of listening for silences in oral testimony, asking why the topic is being passed over (potentially being 'evidence of a scar'). With regard to written evidence, one example stems from our possession of plentiful written material relating to the bureaucracy of the Holocaust, though with an absence of mention of the final purpose to which those objects and actions were directed. We should, contrary to Holocaust deniers, infer from this silence a desire to hide that final purpose; it is a further and interesting question why that desire was felt.

2. Rules of historical reasoning

I have already made it clear that any serious contemporary historian would regard SAP, and the varieties of 'naive empiricism' which are its family relations, as travesties of historical reasoning. So what *is* the methodology that historians typically take to govern their practice?

Before describing the rules of historical reasoning in more detail, a brief note on my methodology. By examining what is recommended, praised and criticized, we can arrive at an approximation of the rules which govern the production of historical writing. For while one can't infer a norm[2] simply from observing what is and is not done – since people get things wrong ignorantly, negligently, and deliberately – the inference of a norm from others' recommendations and *responses* to what is and is not done is more plausible.[3] I have used 'historiographical manuals' – those books written for the student of history, and in particular postgraduate or PhD students of departments of history[4] – to elucidate the method of source criticism. I have used peer review of professional historiographical monographs to investigate wider rules governing the practice.

From historiographical manuals we gain the appreciation that the historical practice has, at its heart, the Rankean method of source criticism. All historiographical claims should be based on the sources, where that relationship rules out none of the inferences that I have already suggested create such problems for SAP. What follows are five points concerning the use of sources, each of which is consistently emphasized by pedagogical material of the above kind.

(1) In common with Ranke's approach, the historian should prioritize primary sources, though should nonetheless be critical of these sources.
(2) Criticism of sources is two-fold: not only with regard to the claims of those sources concerning their intended topic, but with regard to the implicit claims of those sources concerning themselves. The second sort of criticism is the investigation into the document's authenticity, established by asking whether the author could have written it, whether they could have been where they claimed to be, whether the paper, authorial style and handwriting permit the truth of the

self-proclamation of the author. (So far we have not departed from critical SAP.)

(3)   Source criticism is extended beyond the establishment of the identity of the author, to so-called 'internal' features of the source: the author's aim, their ideological background and their intended audience. It is assumed that knowledge of these facts will aid the historian's use of the source. (Exemplification of this point has already been suggested, in the case where the historian would be wise to find out whether the author had reason to lie, and why they might have done so.)

(4)   Source criticism should also trace the path connecting the source with the historian, asking why it has survived and in the form that it has. (A claim which will be emphasized in 'Unwinding the spool' in Chapter 3.)

(5)   The historian is warned not to depend too much on a single document, but rather to utilize a wide range of evidence. This warning is to some extent implicit in the demand for source criticism, since it is obvious that no serious source criticism can proceed without employing knowledge gained from *other* sources.

Historiographical manuals tend to emphasize the rules of source criticism. Peer reviews tend to emphasize different rules that govern historiography. We can suppose that the former are regarded as more basic, in terms of both difficulty and perhaps importance.

3. Peer reviews

Every contemporary academic professional must undergo the review of their books by their peers. Historiographical reviews provide a wonderful way to find out what historians demand of each other, and hence (barring hypocrisy) from themselves. This collection serves to fill out the skeletal account of historical method suggested via the overview of Ranke's work, in Chapter 1, and to focus attention on historical method in the early twenty-first century. In Table 2.1 I summarize the results of a survey of reviews found in the October 2006 edition of *The American Historical Review* (1133–72).

In my survey, I examined each review of historical monograph or collection of historical papers, noting and categorizing each claim of praise of criticism found therein. I did not take note of very general comments, such as that the book was 'fascinating', or that the argument was 'not persuasive'. In the

Table 2.1 Peer review comments

Comment made in peer review	Positive or negative	Number of reviews that praise	Number of reviews that criticize	Further coverage in this book
THE THESIS				
raising issues of more general relevance	positive	2		
raising issues of relevance to our own time	positive	3		Chapters 9 and 12
bold thesis	positive	2	1	
RELATION TO PREVIOUS STUDY				
supplementing gaps in previous historiography	positive	3		Chapters 9 and 10
tying together previous historiography	positive	2		Chapters 9 and 10
rethinking previous historiographical approaches	positive	3	1	
overly partisan with regard to previous historiography	negative		1	
uncritical or inappropriate application of work of other historians or theorists	negative		3	
SELECTION AND OMISSION				
temporally and/or thematically wide ranging account	positive	5		Chapters 3, 6 and 10
comparative approach	positive	2		Chapter 5
examining case(s) usually overlooked	positive	2		
digression rather than unified argument	negative		2	
omitting investigation of a relevant topic	negative		7	Chapters 6 and 9
(of the cases counted above, those in which the omitted topic was causally relevant to what the historian did include:)	(negative)		(3)	
overlooking the variety and/or detail of the subject matter	negative	2	3	Chapters 5 and 6
sketchy treatment of some topic or part of the story	negative		3	
ETHICAL EVALUATION				
balanced account	positive	1		Chapter 9
morally critical	positive	1	1	Chapter 9
uncritical of actor's motives	negative		1	Chapter 8

Table 2.1 (*Cont.*)

Comment made in peer review	Positive or negative	Number of reviews that praise	Number of reviews that criticize	Further coverage in this book
EVIDENCE AND ARGUMENT				
wide variety of sources used	positive	3	1	Chapter 3
careful use of statistics	positive	2		Chapter 4
authorship of source incorrectly attributed	negative		1	
central thesis unsubstantiated	negative		3	
unsupported assertion	negative		2	Chapter 3
unnecessary interpretative complexity	negative		1	Chapters 8 and 9
general claim made with insufficient evidence	negative		1	Chapter 4
EXPLANATION AND NARRATIVE				
situation within wider temporal and social context	positive	2		
intelligent handling of complex interaction between elements	positive	7		Chapters 6 and 10
narrative excellence	positive	3		Chapter 10
flair in applying theory	positive	1		
internal incompatibility (contradictory sources not reconciled, contradictory claims made)	negative		1	Chapters 3 and 12
causation over and above correlation not demonstrated	negative		1	Chapters 5 and 6
no detailed support for efficacy of claimed process	negative		1	Chapter 6
the claimed full determination not demonstrated (rather than mere partial determination)	negative		1	Chapters 4, 5 and 6
STYLISTIC				
presentation clear, not jargon filled	positive	6	3	
beautiful and telling phraseology	positive	2		Chapter 10
entertaining vignettes, engaging examples	positive	2		
literary flourishes obscure	negative		1	Chapter 10
confusing non-chronological presentation	negative		1	Chapter 10
repetition of claims	negative		3	

respective columns of the table, I first paraphrase the reviewer's comment, so as to be able to treat more than one individual comment as falling under a common kind. I then state whether that comment is positive (approving) or negative (disapproving): the attitude is usually obvious from the comment, though not in all cases. I provide a count of the number of times that that kind of comment is made, both in the context of praise, and of criticism. (Thus, a positive comment is praise, and when inverted, is criticism. A negative comment is criticism, and when inverted, is praise.) Finally, for those comments which are more philosophically interesting, or complex, I offer a reference to those later parts of the book which specifically develop those philosophical topics.

I included implicit approval and disapproval, where the implication was clear (one need not simply record explicit uses of 'good' and 'bad', for we rely on the shared ability to judge evaluation nested in more subtle claims). I organized the praise and criticism into my own categories, to aid understanding of the connection between reviews. These activities obviously required judgement, and it would be remarkable if another's attempt to perform the same task with the same materials did not produce a different result. My source materials did not simply 'speak for themselves'; no sources do. (One example is 'narrative excellence', which on the basis of such praise as 'presenting a convincing story', I take to be primarily of explanatory relevance rather than stylistic.) And, given that there are thousands of reviews produced every year, I cannot argue that the following survey will necessarily be representative of the whole. Nonetheless, a useful picture of contemporary historiography is acquired by collectively examining some 50 reviews.

Though mindful that there may be truth in the idea that different sorts of historiography calls for different rules, I venture to note those issues that are most often mentioned, with a view to guessing those virtues most highly prized in historical accounts. The following stand out. The historical account should be temporally and thematically wide ranging. It should omit little of relevance, so long as digression from the main theme is avoided. It should not overlook the complexity and variety in its subject matter. It should weave its elements together sensitively and intelligently. Finally – the most common issue noted – a historiographical account should be clear and jargon free.

If I may be given license to boil down the findings still further, one might give the following advice: *maximize scope of material covered while ensuring unity; and maximize precision while ensuring clarity.* I will return to this pair of historiographical virtues in the next chapter.

4. A philosophical approach to historical reasoning

Is philosophical enquiry into historical reasoning concluded by producing a list of rules which historians agree upon? It is not, for four reasons. First, the rules must be unpacked. What is it to integrate one's material into a convincing whole? What is it for historiography to 'fit', 'be consistent with' or 'be developed on the basis of' the sources? And what are these sources, anyway?

Second, we will face methodological disagreement between historians that requires resolution. While my description thus far suggests broad agreement among historians, it is possible – even to be expected – that once the rules are given more determinate content, disagreement will come into view. In that case, I suggest that only a philosophical enquiry of the sort pursued in the remainder of the book will allow us to properly compare those differences (either by arguing for the superiority of one conception over another, or for their fundamental compatibility).

Third, rules in any case can conflict. Indeed, conflict will be the usual lot of the historian, not the exception, so long as the methodological rules are not restricted in application. To take one example: if source A exhibits the virtue of providing unintended testimony about event e, and source B exhibits the virtue of being produced temporally closer to event e, and yet A and B disagree, which should the historian believe?

Finally, even if the foregoing concerns were to be solved (or ignored) we would still be left with the question of what justifies the rules. Why should historians follow these rules, rather than following Keith Jenkins' advice that one can 'see history as being (logically) anything you want it to be' (2003/1991: 13)? It is not, one presumes, accidental that these rules rather than a different, or even opposite, set of rules are taught and enforced. Is it possible to make explicit their justification? I propose to tackle the last of these questions head on, in an examination of the *purpose* of historical reasoning that will lay the ground for consideration of the other questions.

Historical reasoning is the way it is because of material relations between the past and present. Those relations underpin the point of historical reasoning: to arrive at truths about the past. In order to make clear the connection between evidence and truth, consider examples in which 'evidence' is used in a rather different way than it has been to this point; in what one might call an *external* manner. Events or properties can be evidence for other events or properties, external to anyone's knowledge of that relation. A lit match is evidence for oxygen, the microwave background evidence for the Big Bang, the lack of mention of the Donation of Constantine in documents between 400 and 700CE evidence that the Donation is not genuine. Those evidential connections hold in so far as the first feature or event is connected in the appropriate way to the second.

A lit match is evidence for oxygen, since all matches require oxygen to light. We can express that claim in terms of a counterfactual: if there had been no oxygen, the match wouldn't have lit. The lack of relevant mention of the Donation of Constantine suggests a corresponding counterfactual: if the Donation had been genuine, it would have been mentioned in those documents. Given that it was not so mentioned, we should conclude that it was not genuine (i.e. was composed at a later date than it purports to originate from). Those counterfactuals are either correct or incorrect, independent of whether anyone formulates or believes them. If, as historians, we know the correct and relevant counterfactuals then present evidence will indeed lead us to past truth.

Evidential connections, and the counterfactuals with which they can be expressed, are built upon relations of dependency in the world. Causal dependence is one relevant type of dependence, and one which I discuss in Chapter 5: effects depend on causes, and so are evidence for those causes. There are other relations of dependence that are also evidentially relevant, including theoretical dependence (being affected by gravity depends upon having non-zero mass, thus the former is evidence for the latter), and perhaps even logical dependence (being square depends upon being quadrilateral, thus in a certain sense the former is evidence for the latter). Nor need the evidential relation be temporally later-to-earlier. The relation can be one of synchronicity: if Sheffield and Leeds always vote the same way, then Sheffield's vote is evidence for Leeds' vote. Or it could be earlier-to-later, in the case where one thing always follows another (the use of evidential connections in this way is called prediction).

This idea of external evidential relations not only makes clear the connection between evidence and past truth, but immediately suggests applications to historical reasoning. Consider, for example, the issue of biased sources. Bias need not be an insuperable difficulty to the intelligent historian (as Elton usefully demonstrates, in Elton and Fogel 1983: 86–7). Yet it sometimes is a hindrance, and this can be expressed in terms of evidential dependence. The (maximally) biased report is not dependent upon the event in question, but only on the author's interests. A biased report is therefore less useful with regard to the event reported, just as a camera with a red filter will afford us less information about the original colour of the scene. Yet this external perspective only provides the bare bones of a philosophical approach to evidence. What it leaves aside is the vital question of how the evidence is *internalized*. How should the evidence impinge upon our beliefs; equivalently, how are we to know whether the counterfactuals we propose and presuppose are correct? External evidential connection needs to be connected to justification of belief. We can make a start on that connection by noting the general requirement that

> *E is evidence for B if and only if B is more justified given E and B^n than by B^n alone*

(In this schema, 'E' is the purported evidence, 'B' the historical belief, and 'B^n' the historian's other beliefs, or 'background' beliefs.) In the next chapter I provide two, overlapping, ways to understand in more detail the relation between evidence and justification.

5. Primary sources

Before examining inferential justification in any detail, I want to conclude this chapter by focusing on one vital element of the typical historian's methodological self-conception that has so far remained under the radar. The 'primary source' is vital to scissors and paste history, but is also the only building block from that picture that is usually taken to be equally essential for its successor, genuinely critical history. Let us, therefore, ask the simple question: on what basis is a source designated either 'primary' or 'secondary'? I begin by noting what historians have to say about the distinction, of which the following pedagogical passage is typical:[5]

> Whether conducting research in the social sciences, humanities (especially history), arts, or natural sciences, the ability to distinguish between primary and secondary source material is essential. Basically, this distinction illustrates the degree to which the author of a piece is removed from the actual event being described, informing the reader as to whether the author is reporting impressions *first hand* (or is first to record these immediately following an event), or conveying the experiences and opinions of others – that is, *second hand*.
>
> [Primary sources] are contemporary accounts of an event, written by someone who experienced or witnessed the event in question. These original documents (i.e. they are not about another document or account) are

often diaries, letters, memoirs, journals, speeches, manuscripts, interviews and other such unpublished works. They may also include published pieces such as newspaper or magazine articles (as long as they are written soon after the fact and not as historical accounts), photographs, audio or video recordings, research reports in the natural or social sciences, or original literary or theatrical works.

The function of [secondary sources] is to interpret primary sources, and so can be described as at least one step removed from the event or phenomenon under review. Secondary source materials, then, interpret, assign values to, conjecture upon, and draw conclusions about the events reported in primary sources. These are usually in the form of published works such as journal articles or books, but may include radio or television documentaries, or conference proceedings.

Notice the multifarious marks of primacy that are suggested in connecting the source (let us call it 's') and the event being described or reported (that I shall designate 'e'). s should not be temporally removed from e; s should report e 'first hand'; s should be written by one who witnessed or experienced the event; s should not be about another document or account; s should not be written as 'an historical account'; s should not interpret, assign values to, nor draw conclusions from e. Let us restrict this list to a more manageable trio of criteria. The first criterion is that s is produced without temporal remove from e. The second criterion is that s is not about another source. The third criterion is that s is written by a witness of e; in other words, is a first-hand account. With those distinctions in place, we can consider the primary/secondary distinction more critically.

The third suggestion – that a primary source must be written by a witness – does not apply to all putatively primary sources. The criterion is only appropriate to sources which are descriptions, and I have already argued that these are only a portion of what are recognized as the historian's primary sources. (That comment does, however, leave open the possibility that being a first-hand witness is sufficient, if not necessary, for primacy of source.) The second suggestion – that a primary source should not be about another source – does not quite get things right either. For most historiography – so-called 'secondary sources' – does not so much write *about* the 'primary sources' as *use* the latter in writing about the event, e. This is particularly clear where sources are used as evidence 'in spite of themselves', inference drawn from silences and untruths. The first suggestion – that a primary source must be temporally proximate to the event in question – doesn't fare much better. Consider the Inquisition

Register of Jacques Fournier, Bishop of Pamiers in what is now southern France from 1318 to 1325. This piece of evidence is well known due to Emmanuel Le Roy Ladurie's use of it to infer features of the daily lives of the Catalan peasants from whom the defendants were drawn (Le Roy Ladurie 1990/1978). The Register is surely a primary source, if any item deserves that name. Yet it was written some 18 years after the events reported (Boyle 1981).

The point of the foregoing comments is not that we find it hard to give necessary and sufficient conditions for – an analysis of – some concept. Rather, I would draw the conclusion that there are different conceptions behind the typical intuitions about source primacy; different conceptions, indeed, of the historical enterprise itself. The most prominent conception of source primacy remains in the tradition of SAP. Primary sources are themselves *about* something else, that part of the past which the historian is interested in: in the philosophical jargon, such evidence exhibits the property of *intentionality*. The criterion of minimum temporal remove suggests a second idea, more congenial to critical history: that primary sources are those which are *evidentially reliable*. This distinction explains the ambivalence we feel about certain sources which are intentionally direct, yet most likely not reliable: memoirs written after many years, for example (see also Marwick 1970: 134–5).[6]

In the next chapter, I begin by following through the second of these suggestions, in the context of accounting for the critical relation between justification and evidence. But, by the end of that chapter, I shall not recommend that the historian's understanding of primary source be purged of its intentional relation with the past. In coming to that realisation, we shall temper Collingwood's critique of scissors and paste history.

Further reading and study questions

Collingwood, R. G. (1994) J. Dussen (ed.), *The Idea of History*. Oxford: Oxford University Press (originally 1946). Two papers in the epilegomena to that work – 'The historical imagination' and 'Historical evidence' – are essential reading with regard to what 'critical history' amounts to.

Howell, M. C. and Prevenier, W. (2001) *From Reliable Sources: An Introduction to Historical Methods*. New York: Cornell University Press. In Chapters 1 and 2, Howell and Prevenier make one of the better attempts to explain, in detail, what source criticism consists of.

Milligan, J. (1979) 'The treatment of an historical source', in *History and Theory* 18, 177–96. A particularly clear example of how the historian criticizes, and infers from, a single historical source; in Milligan's example, a letter written by a federal naval officer in the American Civil War.

(a) What is scissors and paste history? Could it ever provide an appropriate methodology for history?

(b) What is the best characterization of a source's *primacy*? *If* there is no good characterization, is 'primary source' a term best avoided?

(c) Consider the example that a lit match is evidence for oxygen. What difficulties will be faced by an attempt to apply a similar sort of reasoning to the justification of historical claims by evidence?

Reasoning from the evidence

3

Chapter Outline

1. Bayesianism

The philosophical task, then, is to account for what I have called 'historical reasoning': the justification of historical claim by evidence that is at the heart of the historian's enterprise. We have seen that one object or event provides evidence for another in so far as there is a worldly dependence of the right sort between those two objects or events. But how do historians find out about those connections, and how should those attempts themselves be described? In this chapter I present two approaches to evidential justification: Bayesianism (founded on the probabilistic theorem developed by the eighteenth-century Presbyterian minister and mathematician Thomas Bayes), and explanationism. Both are applied in other fields, notably in describing the inferences made by natural scientists, but are sufficiently flexible to provide promising guides to historical reasoning. I shall conclude that the two models, while different, are not incompatible and indeed can both be used to jointly illuminate aspects of historical reasoning. Bayesianism provides a more generally applicable understanding, but explanationism usually sheds more light on the specifics of historical methodology. (On the terminology used in this chapter:

'H is justified by E' is equivalent to 'E can be used to infer H', and also to 'E confirms H'.)

Bayesianism is built upon two claims. First, belief should be proportional to strength of evidence. More fully, a rational enquirer updates the strength of their belief in a hypothesis in accordance with their acceptance of the evidential support for that hypothesis. The second claim provides Bayesianism with its distinctive descriptive bite, and requires introduction. The evidential support for the hypothesis is proportional to the extent that the hypothesis implies, or predicts, that evidence. I shall first express Bayesianism more fully. I will then motivate it with historical examples.

Bayesianism tends to be formulated in terms of equations linking (hypothetical) beliefs with a certain quantitative probability. In these equations, '1' is the value given to a perfectly justified (we might call it a verified) belief, and '0' given to a perfectly unjustified (we might call it a falsified) belief. Two warnings regarding this numerical attribution can be found in a footnote.[1] It is helpful to be aware of the typical Bayesian terminology used to express these equations. *Priors* express the probability of the belief in hypothesis H before the new evidence is in. H is only 'conditional upon' (represented by the symbol '|') the historian's previous, or background, beliefs. The prior is therefore written (H|B). *Posteriors* express the probability of belief in the hypothesis once the new evidence, E, has been considered, and are written (H|E&B). *Likelihoods* express the probability of belief in the evidence, given the assumption that the hypothesis is true, and are written (E|H&B). 'Likelihood' can be regarded as a measure of how well the hypothesis predicts the evidence. (The use of 'likelihood' in this restricted sense potentially invites confusion, since the term could be employed in a more casual sense to mean the probability of any belief. Nonetheless, to avoid confusion, I follow the established literature in restricting the use of 'likelihood' to the narrower sense.) In addition, under some explications of Bayesianism, we need a measure of belief in the prior probability of the evidence itself, written (E|B). This expresses the probability of the evidence in the event of remaining perfectly agnostic over the truth of the hypothesis.

Now for the Bayesian equations themselves. The first equation is applicable to the assessment of a single hypothesis, the second to the comparison of two hypotheses, H and H*.

B1: (H|E&B) = (H&B).(E|H&B)/(E|B)

or Hypothesis posterior equals the product of hypothesis prior and evidential likelihood, divided by evidential prior

$$\text{B2:} \quad \frac{(H|E\&B)}{(H^*|E\&B)} = \frac{(H\&B).(E|H\&B)}{(H^*\&B).(E|H^*\&B)}$$

B2 has certain advantages, and so will provide the focus for the remaining discussion. To focus on comparative (or competitive) confirmation brings Bayesianism into line with certain intuitions concerning evidential reasoning. Note that the Bayesian treats a lot of beliefs as evidence for another: indeed *any* belief which raises the probability of the second. That permissiveness doesn't accord with typical attribution.[2] For example, the belief that Milosevic died raises the probability of the belief that Milosevic committed suicide. But is the former evidence for the latter? Does the former justify the latter? (Perhaps your intuitions lead you to answer in the affirmative. In which case, perhaps a more ridiculous example would be more persuasive: the belief that Milosevic died raises the probability of the belief that Milosevic was squashed by a meteorite. But is the former really evidence for the latter?) The Bayesian who insists upon the relevance of hypothesis competition (and therefore the centrality of equation B2) can respond by requiring for confirmation not simply increase in probability of hypothesis, but a comparative raise in probability with respect to contextually appropriate competing hypotheses. In this case, we would do well to assume such competing hypotheses as that Milosevic died by another's hand, and that he died by natural causes. Given that the belief that Milosevic died does not raise the probability of the suicide hypothesis relative to these competitors, Bayesianism falls into line with the original intuition.

Bayesianism is particularly informative when applied to beliefs which depend upon statistical probabilities. Consider the predicament of a jury asked to weigh the evidence provided by a DNA match between suspect and murder weapon.[3] Let H_1 be the hypothesis of suspect S's guilt, H_2 of S's innocence. The relevant statistical probabilities are the following: (i) where the subject is innocent, the *likelihood* of a match is 1 in 30 million (a statistic based upon claims concerning the precision of DNA matching). (ii) Where a subject is guilty, the *likelihood* of a match is therefore $(1-1/30$ million$)$, or as near to 1 as makes no difference. (iii) The *prior* probability of guilt depends on the number of possible suspects; let us suppose 1 in 300,000 in a murder with a city of that population. (iv) The *prior* probability of innocence is correspondingly 299,999 in 300,000. The jury is being asked to weigh the posterior evidential impact of a DNA match between S and the murder weapon in order to decide between innocence and guilt, our hypotheses H_1 and H_2. It is a simple matter to plug the above figures into equation B2, and thereby to discover that the evidence makes S's guilt 100 times more likely than S's innocence.

Historical reasoning does not usually depend upon such a clear statistical basis, but that does not necessarily obviate the value of Bayesianism. Consider an example mentioned by Aviezer Tucker (2004: 113), in the context of his own defence and application of a Bayesian approach to historical reasoning. Historians are faced with the task of deciding whether the belief that central American pyramids predated Columbus is evidence for there having been much earlier contact between the Mediterranean and the Americas.[4] The historian must weigh the evidential value of the fact that there are pyramids in both the Mediterranean and in pre-1492 central America, to the hypothesis H_3 that there were Mediterranean visitors to central America (long) before Columbus. The *prior* probability of H_3 – Columbus was not the first Mediterranean visitor – we might suppose to be much lower than the *prior* of hypothesis H_4 – Columbus was the first Mediterranean visitor (as we'll see, an exact figure isn't necessary). The *likelihood* of the evidence given H_3 is high, given a likely connection between contact and technological sharing. The most interesting assessment concerns the *likelihood* of the evidence given H_4 (that Columbus was the first Mediterranean visitor). A vital consideration in estimating this likelihood is that pyramids are a unique solution to the building of large structures without advanced engineering techniques. Given that background knowledge, we should estimate $E|H_4\&B$ as high, roughly as high as $E|H_3\&B$. Our judgement, in other words, is that pyramids are to be expected in societies with a need or want for large structures but without advanced engineering techniques, whether or not there is contact with other pyramid-producing societies. In that case, the *posterior* probabilities aren't different to the priors: the fact that pyramids are to be found in central America as well as the Mediterranean pre-1492 is not evidence for pre-Columbus contact.

2. The limitations of Bayesianism

Bayesianism is a philosophy that operates at a high level of abstraction; therein lies its appeal and its limitation. Though I hope that the above examples suggest possible historical uses for Bayesian reasoning, the adoption of Bayesianism as a philosophical position does not require that historians consciously approach their reasoning in Bayesian terms. Indeed, it is plausible to regard more specific rules of historical reasoning (such as those unearthed in Chapter 2) as being context-specific instances of the more general Bayesian norm. In the example of the Mesoamerican pyramids, the rule concerns the relevance of types of problem faced by actors of the past, viz: 'the plausibility that two innovations are the expression of a single generic solution to a general problem undermines the claim that those innovations are evidence of mutual influence'. And to take one example from rules of historical reasoning already mentioned, the Bayesian will interpret the familiar rule that testimony is less valuable when it serves the testifiers' interests, in terms of the truistic (if perhaps depressing) background belief that when it is in your interests for others to believe H, you are more likely to tell them that H is true. In all cases, historical rules are regarded as attempts to use background beliefs to judge the likelihood of the evidence, given the hypotheses under question.

It is not controversial (among philosophers) that Bayesianism describes a necessary constraint on our inferential practices, historical reasoning included. The most common argument given for this necessity is in terms of the practical consequences of adopting a system of beliefs that does not meet the Bayesian requirement. As Frank Ramsey first demonstrated in the 1920s, it can be demonstrated that if the beliefs of such a system were regarded as propensities to bet on certain outcomes, then those beliefs would be subject to a 'Dutch Book', wherein they who held those beliefs would lose no matter what the outcome. But the extent to which Bayesianism provides a *full description and justification* of those practices is a matter of debate. Let's distinguish between more and less ambitious versions of the doctrine, which I respectively designate by the terms 'maximal' and 'minimal' Bayesianism. Minimal Bayesianism imposes the demand that we update our beliefs in some way such that equations B1 and/or B2 hold. As a number of writers have pointed out, this constraint can be understood in a similar way to the constraint of deductive consistency.[5]

Deductive consistency is a requirement upon our set of beliefs, though we can demonstrate how minimal that requirement is in two ways. First, the criterion of deductive consistency alone can be used to demand that one of two inconsistent beliefs be rejected; though cannot be used to prefer one or the other. Second, the criterion of deductive consistency alone can be used to arrive at the idea of deductive entailment, the hypothetical demand that if one belief entails a second, then one should believe the second if one believes the first. One epistemic position is thereby ruled out – a belief in the first but not the second – but no guide is given as to *whether* the first should be believed.

Of course, none of this is a problem with deductive consistency: we simply don't expect those rules to govern our beliefs in any more substantive way. But if Bayesianism is no more central to historical reasoning than deductive consistency, then it would be fair to say that it provides only the most minimal foundation for an understanding of historical practice.

Maximal Bayesianism would add three claims:

(i)   The posterior value corresponds to our actual acceptance of hypotheses.
(ii) The prior and likelihood values are capable of objective correctness.
(iii) Bayesianism provides a sufficient model with which the theorist can describe and justify historical reasoning.

I will here briefly expand upon the first claim; in the remaining discussion I privilege the second and third. To the Bayesian, a belief is never conclusively proven by the evidence. This flies in the face of our usual practice in accepting and rejecting beliefs. When forming beliefs, we weigh evidence only up to the point at which we have made up our mind whether to accept or reject. Continuing to weigh evidence implies *not having a belief* on the subject one way or the other. And when to stop weighing evidence cannot itself be an evidential matter, but must depend on the subject's pragmatic situation (Owens 2000: 25–7). If that is the case, then the Bayesian posterior does not correspond to our actual epistemic practices. Further, we do – at least in a good many cases – believe with subjective certainty, not only with a measure of probability. My feeling, which I suppose most share, is that I am certain of some things about the past, but not strictly certain about anything in the future. The Bayesian picture cannot justify such definitive, closed-minded attitudes.

The second claim suggests a standard issue discussed in the Bayesian literature: the implausibility of claiming that *priors* can be objectively assessed. The consensus is twofold: traditional attempts to objectively ground priors fail[6], at any rate when assessing hypotheses that do not involve objective chances (for example, the sort of case where one is asked the probability of drawing a red ball from an urn containing three red and six white). Yet (second) the subjectivity of most priors need not unduly concern us so long as we appreciate the temporally extended nature of evidential reasoning. For, so long as today's prior is yesterday's posterior, evidence will have played an appropriate role in setting the priors for a sufficiently well-developed chain of question and hypothesis. To explain: two people who initially assign different degrees of belief to H will, on the basis of the Bayesian equations, update that belief differently on the basis of the same evidence. Imagine that the first person rates H as likely, the second as unlikely. Positive confirmation of H would lead the first person to raise their belief a little, but the second to raise it a lot. Negative confirmation would lead the first person to lower their belief greatly, but the second to reduce it only a little. The net effect of common evidence is to bring the two estimations closer together.

Less attention tends to be paid to the possibility of objective correctness of the *likelihood* values; yet this possibility should not be taken for granted in historical reasoning. Likelihood values are most tractable where clear statistical regularities are available, as in the example of DNA matching. Historians would consider themselves fortunate to have a similar basis for their reasoning, and certainly do not limit that reasoning to such propitious circumstances. In order to account for the extensive remainder, I suggest that we need to consider the connections between explaining and inferring.

And that raises the general challenge implied by the third listed feature of maximal Bayesianism. Whether Bayesianism can provide a sufficient model for understanding historical reasoning of course depends on what kind of understanding we want, and what precisely we want to understand. Perhaps no Bayesian has claimed that all aspects of historical reasoning are comprehensible solely in Bayesian terms, though Aviezer Tucker comes close: 'Bayesian analysis can explain most of what historians do and how they reach a ... consensus on determined historiography' (2004: 139). The best way to challenge this claim is to present an alternative: inference as explanation.

3. Explanation and inference

Where Bayesianism would have us compare probabilities given the evidence, explanationism asks that we explain the evidence. Explanationism at its most ambitious is the claim that to infer H from E requires explaining E by H. The more modest version of explanationism, which is all that I attempt to defend, is the claim that explanation of E by H is typically required for, and is a guide to, the inference of H from E. Most examples of historical reasoning suggest an easy fit into the explanationist pattern. One notorious historiographical debate of the past decade concerns the status of the claim that ordinary Germans in the Second World War were 'willing executioners' of the Jews, gypsies, communists and other victims of the Nazi holocaust (the phrase is Goldhagen's (1996), who answers in the affirmative; Browning (1996) is representative of those who oppose Goldhagen's thesis). The explanationist interprets the debate as a matter of whether the 'willing executioner' hypothesis or the structural coercion hypothesis best explains the evidence provided by German behaviour.

It is worth pausing to highlight how surprising the explanationist claim should be to a certain natural understanding of historical reasoning. Much of twentieth-century philosophy of history (and here I refer primarily to the hey-day of analytic philosophy of history, between the 1950s and 1970s) proceeded on the assumption that inference of the historical facts came first, and explanation was a subsequent matter of connecting those facts. The former operation was largely ignored by philosophers, attention being focused on the latter, either in assessment of the Deductive-Nomological model of explanation (see Chapter 4) or, from the 1970s, of a narrative understanding of explanation. It is a valuable consequence of the explanationist account of inference that this rigid two-step picture of historical practice is eroded. Explanation is a part of historical reasoning from the start. Inference from the evidence can be just as active, just as theoretical, as the explanation of past events, trends and activities.[7]

It is therefore unsurprising that the same issues have tended to emerge both in the discussion of historical explanation, and of historical inference or reasoning. One example is provided by Collingwood's theory that the historian must re-enact the thoughts of those they are studying (discussed in Chapters 7 and 8). The re-enactment theory tended to be taken as a position in the philosophy of explanation, to be opposed to the Deductive-Nomological theory. A few, including Leon Goldstein (1972), maintained that the re-enactment theory should be regarded as a position in the philosophy of inference; amounting to the claim that to infer past action the historian was required to re-enact the thought behind that action. Given the explanationist account of inference here developed, I think that we can see why neither of these appropriations of Collingwood's theory has to be rejected.

Still, those readers who are familiar with the tangled paths taken by debates over historical explanation might regard with fear, not hope, the expansion of a role for explanation to historical reasoning. There has been little unanimity over any philosophy of historical explanation, even if usual historical explanatory practice has tended to remain undisturbed by such meta-disagreement. Despite this patchy record, I believe that explanation continues to be an important topic for the philosopher of history, and so in one way or another permeates much of the remainder of this book. But at this point of the debate we don't need to assume much at all about historical explanation in order to put to work explanationism as an account of historical reasoning. All that needs to be assumed about historical explanation here are the following three features:

(1) Explanation provides a central motivation for the suggestion of hypotheses, discovery of evidence and criticism of opposing hypotheses.
(2) Explanations trace the causal history of that which they explain.
(3) Explanations are better or worse partly with respect to explanatory virtues.

The first feature focuses attention on which existing hypotheses are tested, how new hypotheses are arrived at, and which evidence is considered. To use the distinction familiar to philosophers of science: these are all issues pertaining to the context of discovery, rather than the context of justification. Bayesianism doesn't tell us much about the context of discovery; explanationism does. (Though Bayesianism might tell us something, even if not much: first, hypotheses with a probability higher than competing hypotheses but still close to zero are presumably prime candidates for testing. Second, only evidence which one suspects to be relevant to the probability of plausible hypotheses will be considered.)

We *challenge hypotheses* by discovering, emphasizing or re-interpreting some evidence which it appears a rival hypothesis can not explain. Gananath Obeyesekere (1992) and Marshall Sahlins (1995) have conducted a historiographical debate over the supposed apotheosis of Captain James Cook by Hawaiian islanders following Cook's voyage to the islands in 1779. That argument is motivated by challenges to explain evidence. For example, Obeyesekere asks Sahlins to explain why, if the Hawaiians thought of Captain Cook as a god, did the Hawaiian priests not prostrate themselves before him, and instead make Cook prostrate himself before the image of the god Ku? (Obeyesekere 1992: 64). The *search for new evidence* usually has an explanatory focus: to find evidence which one hypothesis explains well, but the competing hypothesis does not. And the relationship moves in the opposite direction: *hypotheses are proposed* which would, if true, well explain the evidence. If one distinctively historical way of explaining is to construct a narrative (as will be cautiously argued in Chapter 10), then we should not be surprised that the typical historian's response to a set of evidence is to imagine a plausible story that unifies that set.

4. Unwinding the spool

The second feature of historical explanation assumed in the previous section is that explanations trace the causal history of what is explained (no commitment need yet be made regarding the philosophy of causation; I take up that topic in Chapter 5). Tracing the history of the evidence is equivalent (if less poetic) to Bloch's insistence that historians 'unwind the film spool' of history: 'in the film which [the historian] is examining, only the last picture remains quite clear. In order to reconstruct the faded features of the others, it behoves him first to unwind the spool in the opposite direction from that in which the pictures were taken.' (2004: 46). The emphasis on the history of the evidence also fits well with the rules of source criticism unearthed in Chapter 2; a fit that I shall argue for by reference to the following historiographical example.

Leonard Boyle (1981) criticized Ladurie's use of the Fournier Register in the latter's *Montaillou*. Some of Boyle's criticisms can be understood as justified by the underlying norm that one use the causal history of the evidence to arrive at historical inference from that evidence. Here are three examples.

(1) We know that only one volume of the Register now survives in the Vatican; three have been lost. Boyle criticizes Ladurie's suggestion that the village priest Pierre Clergue went to prison and 'was silent to the end', on the basis that the fact that two thirds of the original Register is missing provides a plausible alternative explanation. That alternative would explain the absence of Clergue's comments not as due to Clergue's silence, but as due to those comments being transcribed in the lost volumes. Even if Boyle's alternative explanation is no stronger than Ladurie's, a successful inference requires a correspondingly better explanation than a competing inference, and on that basis Ladurie's suggestion is unjustified.

(2) We know that the Register was written between 10 and 25 years after the events reported, and that witnesses were usually held together for some time prior to being questioned. The temporal gap suggests that any explanation would have to take into account the likelihood of retrospective addition by the witnesses. The opportunity to confer prior to questioning suggests that any explanation should expect some degree of collusion between the witnesses, thereby diminishing the value of multiple witnesses. By unwinding the spool, we cast doubt on the credibility of witness offered by those reported in the Register. (The

question of testimonial corroboration and collusion is addressed more fully in Chapter 11.)

(3)   We can trace the history of the evidence back to the intentions of those who produced it.[8] Such so-called 'internal' source criticism encourages us, in this case, to explain a witness' pious portrayal of themselves as due to the obvious benefit of keeping on the right side of the Inquisition. We can be ready, however, to expect a greater truthfulness from accounts of non-religious everyday life, in so far as the witnesses won't usually have anything to gain by distorting their understanding of that life.

It is apparent that even though the foregoing example was intended to highlight the importance of an explanatory attitude to evidence, the fact that consideration of likelihood is ineliminable strongly suggests the underlying compatibility between explanationism and Bayesianism. That compatibility is brought out in a pleasing way in a second example: the evidence provided by a letter apparently written in 1863 by a certain C. R. Ellet, a Federal officer. This letter is introduced and assessed by John Milligan (1979).

In the letter to a member of his family, Ellet mentions that he overheard some of highest ranking Union officers – Sherman, Grant and Porter – alluding to a plot to overthrow the Government at Washington. The falsity of those claims is readily apparent, given the absence of any other evidence for a plot of that sort. Bayesianism can provide more substance to that imputation of falsehood, as follows. Compare the prior of background probability that there was a plot (very low) to the prior probability that there was no plot (very high). Next, compare the likelihood of the evidence given that there was a plot to the likelihood of the evidence given no plot. We might grant that the former is high: if there had been a plot of this sort, it is likely that Ellet would have reported it. Still, for Ellet's report to be plausible, the evidential likelihood given plot would have to be much higher than the evidential likelihood given no plot (if this claim is not obvious, I urge you to turn back to the Bayesian equation B2). But it is not, for we can treat the evidence as likely even had there not been a plot. That's because we know that there was good reason for Ellet to invent the outlandish claim of a high-level Unionist plot.

At this point explanatory considerations come to the fore, both in substantiating the last of these Bayesian terms, but also in understanding the letter independent of its truth value. This is source criticism: the use of other evidence to explain the history of the letter, and so to infer both 'external' features of authorial person, date and place, and 'internal' features of what the author intended, what they understood, and what they wanted. In the case of the letter in question, the falsehood is explained by the writer's having been a 19-year-old man with the responsibility of leading a Union naval squadron; a squadron that was in effect a family concern rather than a part of the regular Unionist army, a squadron that had recently suffered a painful reverse, the blame for which the writer felt sure was to be pinned solely on himself by the aforementioned high-ranking Unionist leadership. In using other evidence to explain Ellet's letter in this way, we thereby obtain in that letter additional evidence that bears on historical understanding of the tensions between professional and amateur in the Union army; the nature of personal ambition in the civil war; and the uneven loyalty of Unionist armed forces to civilian leadership.

5. Explanatory virtues

I think that the clearest argument for explanationism as an account of historical reasoning will proceed via an idea of explanatory virtue. To motivate the introduction of explanatory virtue, let us focus on a condition so far unexamined: that of a 'best explanation'. Peter Lipton, in his defence of the parallel explanationist understanding of the inferences made by natural scientists, makes a valuable distinction. In judging which of two explanations is the 'best', we may choose the 'likeliest' explanation, or the 'loveliest' explanation (Lipton 2004: Chapter 4). The likeliest explanation of E is that which is most probably true; the loveliest explanation of E that which would, if true, provide the most understanding of E. If the explanationist jumps straight to the former notion, it will be difficult to claim that anything but decoration is added to a straightforward Bayesianism. But to move first to lovely explanations, and to then infer the likely from the lovely, accords a substantive role to explanatory consideration.

Lovely explanations are those which embody explanatory virtues. What are those virtues, and where might they enter into historical reasoning? I shall argue that we need to recognize the privileged nature of explanations that are *consilient* (those which unify disparate evidence) and *precise*. These are the very virtues that emerged from the study of peer reviews of historical monographs, presented in Chapter 2.

Recall the Bayesian 'problem of the priors'. One way to dramatize that problem for the natural scientist is to point out that any number of hypotheses can be constructed to fit the evidence to date, and for that reason no specific prior hypothesis can be said to possess a definite and objective value. A finite number of data points permits an indefinite number of equations. We normally see only one 'line of best fit', but that restriction is not straightforwardly implied by the data. Some means of restriction is required, and indeed can be seen to be employed in our evidential reasoning. The explanatory virtue of consilience looks particularly appropriate in accounting for that restriction.

To turn to historical reasoning: we initially value a hypothesis (or suggestion) to the extent that it is consilient. A (more) consilient account is one which unifies evidence by relying on fewer independent elements (than other competing hypotheses). The line of best fit requires an equation with fewer independent terms. The historical hypothesis also accounts for evidence with fewer independent elements, often through the device of so-called 'colligatory' terms: 'Renaissance', 'Industrial Revolution', 'Hapsburg expansion' (a category of historical language that receives specific attention in Chapter 10). Contrast a consilient historical account with one that manifests the opposite vice: such a history would be disconnected – wherein each piece of evidence is explained separately – and ad hoc – such that explanatorily independent principles are introduced on a case-by-case basis. The consilient historical account is not always preferred (one example of consilient yet often distrusted accounts is metanarrative, discussed in Chapter 10). My claim is rather that we generally do favour such accounts, and that the way to account for such a preference is by introducing considerations of explanatory consilience into judgements regarding the Bayesian prior.[9]

So much for the problem of the priors. A similar but less discussed issue for Bayesianism lies in the (sadly non-alliterative) 'problem of the likelihoods'. How should we account for the judgement of evidential likelihood (on the assumption that the hypothesis is true)? If deductive grounds are available, the task is straightforward. For example, if one's background knowledge contains the law 'all corrupt regimes lead to revolutions', then the likelihood of the evidence of revolution given the hypothesis of there having been a corrupt regime can be deduced as being 1. And, more generally, where there is a statistical law stating that E follows H in x per cent of cases, one may assign the likelihood $E|H$ as $x/100$. But laws of this kind are not to be found in historical reasoning (a claim substantiated in Chapter 4). An additional problem for a deductive notion of likelihood can be found in a footnote.[10] An explanationist approach to likelihood would have us consider the extent to which the hypothesis explains the evidence.

More substantively, an explanationist approach to evidential likelihood suggests the relevance of the virtue of precision. A precise explanation is, compared to its competitor(s), more complete – fewer gaps in the causal history – and more accurate. Typically in historical reasoning, and as demonstrated in the two examples of the previous section, one would prefer a detailed narrative of evidential provenance from the hypothesis. A Bayesian theory untouched by considerations of explanatory virtue would be unable to account for this preference. To illustrate with a toy example: compare the more precise hypothesis 'there were four Cathars in Montaillou in 1310' with the more general 'there were a few Cathars in Montaillou in 1310'. In terms of statistical likelihood alone, there is no potential evidence that is more likely given the former than the latter, but plenty of potential evidence that is more likely given the latter than the former. Yet, intuitively, we could imagine evidence which would make us prefer the former over the latter. To account for that preference, we need to recognize the additional virtue of precise explanation.

6. The preservation of testimony

The final section of this chapter provides a counter-balance to the inferential accounts of historical reasoning so far considered. The material here developed also paves the way for a *dialogic* approach to historical understanding, to be considered in Chapter 9.

As I reported in Chapter 2, Collingwood insisted that the historian approach testimonial evidence critically. The critical historian is not credulous: they don't believe everything reported. Further, the critical historian rejects the bivalent view of testimonial evidence as something that should either be believed, or rejected as worthless. Testimonial evidence is evidence like any other, which can be used as the basis for a variety of inferences; the right questions, and other beliefs, permitting. The critical view of testimony, however, leads us into a problem that has recently received rather a lot of philosophical attention:[11] that all knowledge, including historical knowledge, relies on a large base of *uncritically accepted* testimony. The fundamental claim is a simple one: that the vast majority of beliefs that anyone – and specifically, any historian – holds depends to some degree upon testimony that the recipient themselves cannot demonstrate to be reliable. Testimonial acceptance is (to use the name for this philosophical position) a 'non-reductive' sort of knowledge. In particular, testimony is not reducible to the perceptual knowledge of the recipient of testimony. Non-reductivism shares with scissors-and-paste history the idea that the historian must recognize authorities; that historians cannot, as Collingwood demands, make sure that 'all the pieces of evidence' are 'observed by himself' (1994: 280). But non-reductivism need not insist, with scissors-and-paste history, that the words of those authorities are written into the history books. The claim, rather, is that what is written into one's books will be justified, in part, by uncritical acceptance of some authority.

The clearest argument concerns the Bayesian treatment of testimony, so it is that which I specifically critique in substantiating non-reductivism. The Bayesian apparatus, as we have seen in this chapter, deals in the probabilistic relationship between hypothesis and evidence. If we are deciding whether to believe a witness or documentary source, the hypothesis is that the source is true. The Bayesian equations would therefore have us consider which makes the testimonial evidence more likely: that the source was true, or that it was not. That decision might be based on knowledge of the particular case. We might judge that testimony is more likely given the falsity of that testimony, than given its truth, if we have an alternative explanation for that testimony. Such was the case with regard to Ellet's letter. Where a witness has a proven track record and we have no reason to doubt their word, we would conclude the opposite. Finally, the judgement might be based on corroborating testimony.

But in many cases, none of these options are available; and yet we still accept the testimony. To insist that a piece of reasoning such as that mentioned in the previous paragraph *must* be present, if testimony is to be accepted is, says Coady,

> at odds with the phenomenology of *learning*. In our ordinary dealings with others we gather information without this concern for inferring the acceptability of communications from premises about the honesty, reliability, probability, etc., of our communicants. I ring up the telephone company on being unable to locate my bill and am told by an anonymous voice that it comes to $165 and is due on 15 June. No thought of determining the veracity and reliability of the witness occurs to me nor, given that the total is within tolerable limits, does the balancing of probabilities figure in my acceptance.
>
> (1992: 143)

And let no one overlook the extent of our dependence on testimony:

> many of us have never seen a baby born, nor have most of us examined the circulation of the blood nor the actual geography of the world nor any fair sample of the laws of the land, nor have we made the observations that lie behind our knowledge that the lights in the sky are heavenly bodies immensely distant . . .
>
> (1992: 82)

Turning to historical knowledge, we can ask which of us has conducted the study of evidence required to substantiate even the existence and major deeds of a list of well-known historical figures (Homer, Aristotle, Caesar, Christ, Muhammad, Charlemagne, Suleiman the Magnificent, Adam Smith, Karl Marx ...). As Coady rightly points out, historians *learn*, as well as critically enquiring. Of course, not everything we learn is right, and in demonstrating that it is not we reason in the critical way already indicated. But it is a mistake to think that because critical reasoning can show testimony to be unreliable, the reliability of all testimony must be critically established (Coady 1992: 97).

In the remainder of this section I consider possible responses to testimonial non-reductivism. The first response meets the non-reductivist head-on. It might be hard to avoid uncritical reliance on another's testimony, but no one promised that critical history would be easy. Collingwood reluctantly acquiesces to the idea that 'there may be cases in which, as perhaps in some cases of memory, our acceptance of such testimony may go beyond mere belief and deserve the name of knowledge'. Yet 'it can never be historical knowledge' (1994/1946: 257). One can only argue by example that historical knowledge *can* be founded upon the uncritical acceptance of testimony. So what better example to use than one of Collingwood's own, expressly designed with the intention of proving that a chain of inference may be conducted without the uncritical acceptance of testimony: 'who shot John Doe?' (Collingwood 1994/1946: 266–74). Coady (1992: 240–4) has no trouble in pointing out that even in a bespoke example such as this, uncritical acceptance of testimony is presupposed at a number of places in the detective-historian's line of reasoning. From the rectory parlourmaid he learns that the suspect's shoes were muddy in the morning, and most probably also the vital fact that there was no mud in the study. From 'the Yard' he learns that the suspect was a blackmailer. And from unnamed sources, he learns that the suspect was a medical student, that there was a thunderstorm between 12 and 1 and so on and so on. In short, Collingwood's explicit methodology is unfeasible, a fact which Collingwood appears not to have noticed due to the very pervasiveness of our everyday reliance on testimony.

A second response is to suppose that testimony might be established as being generally reliable, even though no specific line of reasoning might be possible to support a particular case. One would, if this is correct, need to be able to establish a general statistical justification: that people usually tell the truth, therefore it is likely that this witness is telling the truth. David Hume explicitly defends our reliance on testimony in this way:

> our assurance in any argument of this kind [from testimony] is derived from
> no other principle than our observation of the veracity of human testimony,
> and of the usual conformity of facts to the reports of witnesses.
>
> (1977/1748: 74)

A statistical justification of this sort is inductive, in so far as the premises render the conclusion likely, though not certain. That alone need not be problematic, since we have already accepted that all historical reasoning is inductive rather than deductive. But successful inductive arguments must meet certain standards, which do not seem to be met in the case of the inductive justification of testimony. Induction is necessary where we cannot observe every member of a set of items, yet still wish to draw conclusions either about the set as a whole or about members of the set not yet observed. Those conclusions are justified only in so far as the members of the set that we have observed are a sufficiently representative sample of the whole, a demand that usually requires observation of a large sample of the whole (how large the sample needs to be will depend on the variation of the whole). Yet this requirement has manifestly not been met in the case of judging testimony. We haven't been acquainted with a representative sample of the living and the dead; still less have we checked for ourselves a representative sample of their claims.

What should we conclude from the fact that uncritical acceptance of some testimony is unavoidable? One suggestion is that testimony is somehow foundational to the historian, evidence that simply cannot be denied (Pompa 1990: 197; Anscombe 1973: 4). But why should we accord testimony a foundational role rather than any other sort of evidential link? This question is especially pressing given that we found it impossible to demonstrate the reliability of testimony in general. To take a silly example: why not believe that the connection between present temperature and temperature in the past is a foundational evidential connection, requiring no further justification, and yet permitting conclusions to be drawn about the past? The best response is to claim that testimony, properly considered, is not evidence at all (a position developed particularly clearly by David Owens (2000: Chapter 11)).

Testimony is not evidence that provides justification, but is a means of transferring justification. The same goes for memory and (if we buy into the notion, as I believe we should) external memory in the form of lists, books, libraries and the internet. Indeed, the non-reductionist argument is arguably more irresistible with regard to memory. One need only imagine the untenable position of one who attempts to run a proof without granting themselves any justification based on earlier, remembered stages of that proof. And if one is to attempt to establish the reliability of memory without assuming the hypothesis, failure would be guaranteed so long as the attempt took time. Each should be regarded as a means of transferring existing justification, not creating justification afresh.

It helps to clarify this idea by realising that something can be essential for our acquisition of a belief, yet be no part of the justification for that belief. In order for me to reach a mathematical conclusion, I need to see figures on a page, or perhaps hear words spoken to me. Perception is essential, yet the justification of the conclusion does not depend on perception (and certainly not on my being able to demonstrate that my perception is reliable). Were I to consider the conclusion again a day later, then my recall of the belief in the conclusion's validity would rely upon memory. In this case, a reliable memory is necessary for me to correctly believe the conclusion, though once again the justification is the original argument, not an inference from the reliability of my memory. So it is with testimony: if I tell you the conclusion, the justification is the original argument. It does not require you to prove that I am a reliable witness, because the testimony is the vehicle of transmission, not the means of justification. We can go further: if the justification of my belief concerning the conclusion to the argument is yesterday's reasoning, then it seems that I can be justified in believing the conclusion today even if I have since forgotten the premises. And you can be justified in believing the conclusion even if you never knew the premises. If these claims are correct, then a fundamental principle of Enlightenment epistemology has been undermined: that the justification for my beliefs must be (at least potentially) available to me, now. (A further consequence of these claims is that we undermine the belief that all historical evidence is, fundamentally, present evidence. If justification is a matter of providing evidence, and given that chains of justification need not terminate in the present, then not all evidential chains need terminate in the present. I make use of this conclusion in Chapter 11.)

To conclude discussion of testimony requires us to consider whether there is conflict between the two proposals – that historians (sometimes) be critical with regard to testimony, and that historians (sometimes) accept testimony uncritically. They need not conflict, since neither proposal is universally recommendable. But the issue is rather more complicated than that simple response suggests. The two attitudes cannot be held entirely separately. We can read a report in two ways: by attempting to work out what has brought the writer to state what they have, and by attending to what the writer writes about, and so learning from that writing. The first way is to focus on the writing as evidence, the second to focus on the writing as the transmission of knowledge. But of course, the intelligent reader entwines the two attitudes. The discussion so far has enabled us to state this issue. To resolve it, we need to consider the place of dialogue, as we shall in Chapter 9.

Further reading and study questions

Coady, C. A. J. (1992) *Testimony: A Philosophical Study*. Oxford: Clarendon Press. A readable book that reinvigorated philosophical enquiry into the epistemology of testimony. Chapters 1, 4, 8, 10, 11 and 13 are recommended.

Dawid, P. (2002) 'Bayes's theorem and weighing evidence by juries', in R. Swinburne (ed.) *Bayes's theorem: Proceedings of the British Academy*, 71–90. Oxford: Oxford University Press. A careful application of Bayesian principles to real-life cases of legal reasoning.

Howson, C. and P. Urbach (2007) *Scientific Reasoning: The Bayesian Method*. Chicago: Open Court (originally 1989). A readable introduction to Bayesianism.

Lipton, P. (2004) *Inference to the Best Explanation*. London: Routledge (originally 1991). In Chapter 4, Lipton unpacks the slogan 'inference to the best explanation'. In Chapter 7 (of the second edition only), Lipton compares his account of inference to the Bayesian.

Tucker, A. (2004) *Our Knowledge of the Past: A Philosophy of Historiography*. Cambridge: Cambridge University Press. Chapter 3 presents Tucker's central arguments for a Bayesian approach to historical reasoning.

(a) Work through an example of Bayesian reasoning by attributing values to the relevant terms in the Bayesian equation B2. Either take your own example of competing hypotheses with regard to a piece of evidence, or assess the following:

'The Donation of Constantine is evidence for the hypothesis that Emperor Constantine granted the Papacy dominion over the Western Roman Empire.'

(b) To what extent can historical practice be seen to follow a two-stage demand: 'first, find the facts, second explain those facts'?

(c) Is it plausible to suppose that Collingwood might have rephrased his story of 'who shot John Doe?' such that the detective-historian need not uncritically rely on the testimony of others at any point?

Part II
HISTORY AS SCIENCE

Abstraction and laws $\boxed{4}$

1. What's so great about science?

Science is the pre-eminent form of intellectual practice, having dethroned other traditional kinds of understanding. Philosophers have largely followed Locke's demand that they become science's under-labourers; religion is treated as an anachronism, forced into the epistemic (if not yet the political) shadows. Should historians regard their own discipline as a science? Should they even seek to bend that discipline, so that its fit with other sciences might be made more apparent, and that it might enjoy the fruits of scientific progress? That question has been central to philosophical discussion concerning history, exercising both philosophers and historians since the start of science's meteoric rise.

'Naturalism' is, in this context, the thesis that history is by and large a science; and that, to the extent that it isn't a science, it should be made into one. (An alternative title for naturalism, though with solely negative connotations, is 'scientism'.) The naturalistic picture is that science is fundamentally unified; there is no sharp divide between natural and social sciences, between Naturwissenschaft and Geistwissenschaft. (The possibility of such a divide is what permits anti-naturalists like Collingwood to describe good historical practice as 'scientific'.) In order to assess naturalism, we need to know what it is that makes a practice scientific. Furthermore, the naturalist owes a justification for their position: they owe an account of what is so great about science.[1]

Scientific belief is justified by evidence alone. Not necessarily experimental evidence: history joins astronomy and volcanology in being an evidentially founded but non-experimental discipline. Application of the evidence criterion to history isn't contentious: we do not find theorists arguing that history should be written in contravention of the evidence. Nonetheless, to ask *how and to what extent* the evidence should guide historical accounts does permit substantive debate. The anti-naturalist might suggest that historical evidence is typically of a radically different kind to scientific evidence, and that inference from that evidence requires a correspondingly divergent method. Such suggestions occupy the bulk of Part III. The extent to which historical accounts are constrained by the evidence invites consideration of the question of underdetermination (Chapter 12). It may be that historical accounts are determined by the evidence to a significantly lesser extent than are scientific accounts; in particular, in so far as those historical accounts are interpretative, or narrative.

The scientific project is to use the evidence in order to bring understanding of the world around us. That understanding is permitted by describing, observing, and manipulating the world in terms of properties that are both general and (typically) abstract. Progress in scientific theorizing occurs when the evidence is better accounted for in terms of a new, or altered, theory: in such cases we might want to claim that scientists closer approach the truth. The evidence for phlogiston theory, for example, was re-explained by Robert Boyle's employment of the contemporary notion of oxidation. One way that a theory can constitute an improvement is if it is more general; if it has greater scope than the previous theory. Thus we might understand Boyle's own gas laws to be a single manifestation of the more general atomic theory of gases, and Newtonian laws of motion as a special case of Einstein's more general laws.

In addition to the inter-twined virtues of the scientific approach already outlined – evidential support and cognitive scope – one cannot help but notice the practical aspect of scientific achievement. Technological innovation over the past four centuries in such fields as medicine, farming, structural engineering and electronics has radically altered all of our daily lives. The general theories that scientists produce make possible prediction and control of the natural world. (That is not to say that one should adopt a pragmatic *definition* for scientific achievement: there is genuine understanding brought without guarantee of practical application by such fields as fractal mathematics, or from investigation into the universe's first few seconds.)

Passionate opposition to scientific 'encroachment' into history exists, usually from a humanist perspective. The outline of these objections are alike: some feature of humanity is deemed essential to history: emotion, rationality, free choice, or cultural meaning. Yet that feature, it is argued, is in principle invisible to or inexplicable by to a scientific history. Behind these concerns often lies a more nebulous concern that an exclusive use of natural science in understanding the world will have deleterious effects on our understanding of ourselves, others and our relationships, and even on these things themselves. More specifically, the anti-naturalist typically disputes each of the distinctive scientific features already mentioned, viz:

- the commonality of scientific and historical evidence and our use thereof (as I've already suggested);
- the notion of objectivity implied by the idea that science is approaching the truth;
- that history (and the social sciences in general) are in the business of prediction and control;
- that there is a role for generalization and abstraction in history as well as science.

2. Abstraction and quantification

All successful sciences understand the world by *generalizing* and *abstracting*. Both designations are relative: 'Parisian merchant' is a more general property than 'Parisian grain trader', and 'French merchant' is a more general property than both. If we introduce more abstract terms – 'French bourgeoisie', or 'bourgeoisie' in general – we encounter terminology typically found in the social sciences. The natural sciences typically work at a high level of abstraction, notably so in the development of many of the most celebrated scientific achievements: a unified thermodynamics, the periodic table, sub-atomic physics and chaos theory. Consider the remarkable abstract property *energy*. A heated metal bar, a lit candle, a moving vehicle, a suspended block and a radio wave all exemplify this property; a set for which, without the abstraction, we would surely struggle to 'see' any similarity. Two things should be clear. Intuitive or observed similarity need not be the best way to judge the value of an abstraction.

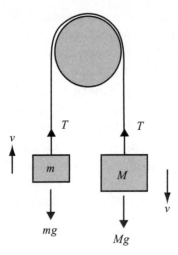

Figure 4.1 Diagram of a typical scenario covered by Newtonian mechanics

And no description of the world can 'escape' some level of generalization and abstraction: it is simply a matter of more or less.

Though generalization and abstraction are similar designations, I believe that it is important to emphasize the latter as well as the former. Abstraction[2] focuses our attention on scientific omission and creativity. Abstraction proceeds by omission: most of the real world is ignored as irrelevant, so as to better sharpen our understanding of what remains. The most dramatic examples of this omission are in physics, and in particular the physics of fundamental forces. An abstract physical representation of a system of forces is provided in Figure 4.1. There is no mention of most of the properties that would be necessary in a complete description of real world objects: colours, constitutive material, absolute spatial and temporal location, wind, air pressure, temperature ... Whether that level of omission should be accepted in history is a question that will be asked in the next two chapters. Abstraction requires construction, as well as pruning. A generalization covers all particular things of a certain type, but might remain rooted in everyday observation (for example, 'all people in this room have blonde hair'). But to emphasize abstraction is to emphasize the creative aspect of scientific theorizing.

The primary virtue of abstraction is scope: by abstracting we introduce new terminology that permits us to use relatively few statements to describe relatively many worldly features. And in describing aspects of the world with terms of wide scope, we are able to unify our understanding of those aspects of the world. The extent to which understanding has been unified can't usually be judged when considering concepts and properties one by one, but only as they are related with other concepts in a scientific theory. (I shall use the term 'scientific theory' as a general term to indicate any self-contained body of scientific knowledge.) Thus, we only see the epistemic power of the concept 'energy' when we appreciate its use in the principles of the conservation of energy, of the increase in entropy, and its relation to other abstract properties such as 'mass', 'velocity' and 'wave frequency'. And the introduction of the abstract terminology of social class permits an understanding of a wide range of historical phenomena. This is so only because of the relations that are drawn between the terminology of social class and those of economics: capitalism and feudalism, commerce and industry. Finally, a more prosaic example, inspired by Nancy Cartwright (1999: 40): today, I did the washing up, I looked after my baby boy, I replied to emails from a colleague about a chapter that we are preparing, and I continued to write this book. We can use the abstract notion 'work' to describe each of these activities; a description which is of value because (and only because) of the theoretical connections between 'work' and other abstract concepts, notably 'leisure' and 'value'. Through this abstract term, I can go on to describe my particular day in terms of the exchange value of the activities that I have been pursuing, perhaps gaining further insight by calculating the average and standard deviation of those figures.

Any term, more abstract concepts included, may be binary (all or nothing) or continuous (instantiated to a greater or lesser extent). 'Hydrogen' or 'feudal' are *prima facie* binary concepts; 'energy' or 'IQ' continuous. Where a property is continuous, one may gain precision by quantifying: numerically *measuring* the property. In addition, binary concepts may be instantiated in more than one case, which it may be useful to *count*.

As with all abstract properties, the introduction of number is justified by the new relations made possible: in this case, and at a minimum, relations of addition and subtraction. These relations are what make the approach quantitative, and where those relations are not available the approach is not genuinely quantitative. Roads, for example, are often identified by a number (in the UK, roads such as the M1 and M25); but no quantitative approach to the study of roads is thereby facilitated, since there are no arithmetic relations between those road numbers. Is there anything that can be said, in general, about what sort of cases are inappropriate for quantification? It is often maintained that quantification is a useful tool when studying human groups (sociology and economics), but not when studying individuals (much of political and intellectual history). That observation is on the right lines, though it only really accounts for quantification as counting, not quantification as measuring. We can therefore add that historians are able to quantify those continuous properties of individuals, and only those for which a suitably calibrated scale is empirically applicable.[3] Age can easily be measured in this way, goodness cannot. Intelligence is an example where the applicability of quantitative technique has been contested. The operationalization of 'intelligence' in terms of 'IQ' makes perfect sense in terms of ease of measurement: after all, we have very clear ways to measure the latter property, but the estimation of the former is a much more messy business. Nonetheless, given the strong evaluative overtones implied by describing someone as intelligent – or unintelligent – the fact that one may be of high intelligence and yet have a low IQ is a conclusion that is not simply a matter of arbitrary stipulation, but of profound ethical importance. I take up the question of 'value-laden' descriptions such as 'Mark is not intelligent' in Chapter 9.

Quantification in history can be treated as a special case of (sometimes second-order) abstraction in history, numerical properties being especially abstract in the sense that they are applicable to such a wide variety of worldly phenomena. In describing the world in terms of numerical relationships, we group together such highly divergent things as the growth of a human population, a company's income, an object's mass, the distance between two cities. And these abstract properties are especially powerful: describing historical phenomena numerically opens up a range of mathematical techniques that can lead us to new and sometimes surprising knowledge.

Counting is the most basic quantitative operation, and can be a vital instrument of historiographical *precision* (an observation that undermines any suspicion that an abstract approach need be imprecise). It might be sufficient to know that, during the 1942 battle for Stalingrad, many Russians ('Hiwis') fought on the German side. But replacing 'many' by a number provides more information, which may be useful depending on the wider historiographical aim. (The best guess is 50,000, or roughly 20 per cent of the German forces (Beevor 1999: 439).) Counting need not simply sharpen what we already know, or suspect, to be the case. Greer (1935: 97–8) counted victims of the French post-Revolutionary Terror according to their social class, finding that the aristocracy and clergy collectively accounted for only 30 per cent of those killed: a result that flies in the face of usual perceptions of the Terror. An example of quantitative measurement (rather than counting) is provided by Fogel, in his report of the labour-intensive study that he and Engerman undertook of the probate records of cotton estates (Fogel 1975: 337). On each female slave record, her age on the birth of her first surviving child had been recorded (measured). A simple arithmetic procedure permitted Fogel and Engerman to calculate the average of those ages; yet the high resulting average (over 20) challenged accepted preconceptions of slave culture.

Quantification is applicable not only to properties introduced by historians (age, social class, being a Hiwi), but to the relation between properties. Where we have evidence for the whole of a given population of interest, the calculation of those numerical relationships can be straightforward (Hiwis as a proportion of the German forces, aristocracy and clergy as a proportion of Terror victims). Where we have evidence for only a part of a population of interest, we can, with care, infer from the known part to the partially known whole. For example, given only share prices of the top 100 companies, it would be reasonable to infer the value of the stock market as a whole at those times. Indeed, if we had additional data concerning the relative value of the top 100 companies to the entire market at different times, we could even provide a realistic error margin to that estimate. Finally, quantification can be of use not only with regard to part-whole relations, but causal relations. Cuff (2005) examined the height records of 20,000 Pennsylvanian soldiers in the American Civil War, and correlated those heights to each soldier's region of origin. He found a correlation between being higher and originating from a region that was less developed economically, and less involved in market activity. Such a finding suggests connections, perhaps surprising, between economic development and health. (For a more detailed consideration of causation and correlation, see the following chapter. For now, I make the standard warning that correlation between two variables is not sufficient to draw any conclusions regarding the causal interaction between those variables.)

3. Positivism

I've emphasized that what is crucial about the abstract properties of science is their relation to other such properties. How should that relation be understood? One answer, once the received view, is that to be employed scientifically, properties should be related by *law*. Whether or not historiography, and in particular historical explanation, uses and requires law has dominated not only the naturalism debate, but (at least until the 1980s) the philosophy of history in general. Given that much historical explanation does not *seem* to invoke laws, then the appropriate naturalist strategy is to make explicit those laws that historians only imply. Conversely, if laws are essential to science then a possible anti-naturalist argument is:

(i)   Laws are essential to science;
(ii)   Laws require features A, B, C;
(iii) History does not possess one or more of A, B, C;
(iv)   Therefore history is not a science.

I will fill out this argument shortly, specifying what those essential features of laws might be. But first, we need to appreciate why it was thought that laws are necessary. Positivism, a term first introduced by Auguste Comte[4], reached its greatest sophistication and influence under the banner of twentieth-century logical positivism. Logical positivism was the dominant movement in the Anglo-American world from the 1920s to the 1940s, arguably maintaining hegemony until the 1960s or 1970s. The legacy of positivism still weighs heavily on philosophical discussion of the social sciences and of history. In what follows I present a simplified account of those aspects of positivism relevant to the concerns of this book.

Positivism is one variety of empiricism, the latter the demand that our senses provide the only fundamental justification of knowledge. The logical positivist (hereafter simply 'positivist') adds a distinctive concern with meaning. The meanings of *basic terms* are given in one of two ways. They should either directly refer to an observational property (as in the case of colour terms); or should be *defined* so as to refer to observational properties. In the latter case, the scientist 'operationalizes' their theoretical term, as in the case of 'temperature' in terms of 'converted heat'; and in the aforementioned operationalization of 'intelligence' in terms of 'IQ' (the latter itself understood as proportional to the propensity to score highly in tests of certain sorts).

A meaningful *statement* builds on the meanings of its constituent parts in one of three ways. The first possibility is that the statement's meaning is provided by the means of empirically confirming that statement. Thus, the meaning of 'the duration of Mercury's year is 88 Earth-days' is given by the astronomical observations that confirm that statement. In the same category, but more counter-intuitively: the meaning of statements concerning electrons is derived from one's observation of evidence gained by microscopes and such; and the meaning of statements involving Napoleon is derived from one's observation of present evidence concerning Napoleon's past existence. Second, the statement might be a tautology, true in terms of logic or in virtue only of the meanings of the component terms (as with 'all bachelors are unmarried males'). The final possibility is that the statement is meaningless. The austerity of the positivists' typology of meaning led to radical treatment of metaphysics and religion (both meaningless), ethics (mere expression of emotion, so not genuine statements) and mathematics (disguised tautology).

What is the meaning of explanatory statements in science and history? We would prefer them not to be regarded as meaningless, and neither are they logical or analytical truths. Thus, for the positivist, the challenge is to provide an analysis of explanatory statements such that they are empirically meaningful. This challenge is given bite by noting that the truth of an explanatory statement implies more than simply the truth of its parts. 'That DNA was discovered explains the fact that the Korean War began in 1950' is ludicrous, even though both elements are individually true. The additional, empirically respectable, property of explanatory statements was postulated to be *the generality of the connection between the explanatory terms*. In other words, a good explanation implies a general law.

Carl Hempel (Hempel 1942 Hempel and Oppenheim 1948) formalized these positivist demands in his – now notorious – Deductive-Nomological model of explanation ('nomological' being derived from the Greek for 'law'). From the start, it was Hempel's aim to argue that the Deductive-Nomological (henceforth abbreviated DN) model was just as adequate for historical practice as it was for (any other) scientific practice. This philosophical model provides an analysis of explanatory statements as deductive arguments. (A deductive argument is one in which the truth of the premises logically necessitate the truth of the conclusion.) Explanations are particular sorts of deductive argument: those whose premises include one or more true statements of law, and one or more true statements of particular fact, and whose conclusion is the particular fact to be explained. (In the jargon, what gets explained is the *explanandum*, what does the explaining the *explanans*.) This analysis, at least at first blush, fits standard scientific explanations well. A simple example might be the explanation for why this steel bar expands:

(i) 'The steel bar was heated'
(ii) 'Steel is a metal'
(iii) 'All metal expands upon heating'
(i)–(iii) *deductively imply*: 'The steel bar expanded'.

Moving closer to actual scientific practice; an explanation for why there is a force of 10 N acting on a particular mass could be as follows:

(i) 'The mass m_1 is 1 kg'
(ii) 'The mass m_1 is 1,000 m away from another mass, m_2, of 10 million kg'
(iii) 'Given two masses m_1 and m_2 at a distance r, the force F operating on those masses is always $G(m_1.m_2)/r^2$

(i)–(iii) *deductively imply*: 'there is a force of 10 N acting on m_1'.

The DN account provides us with an understanding of what an explanation adds to a knowledge of the particular facts: it adds the knowledge that the particular fact was determined, and in virtue of what law it was so determined. And, so long as scientific laws are simply what always happens – exceptionless regularities – then they are not empirically mysterious. Of course, these general statements are not conclusively verifiable: one could not literally observe every case of, say, gravitational attraction. But they are both inductively confirmable, and, further, capable of being empirically disproved by a single counter-example. In those ways, scientific explanations are appropriately sensitive to the evidence.

4. Laws

The journal *History and Theory* has been, since its inception in 1960, the primary venue for philosophical debate concerned with historical practice. In the opening paper of the very first issue, Isaiah Berlin rejected the application of the DN understanding of explanation to history on the basis that the explanations that historians offer need not and cannot be backed by suitable scientific laws (Berlin 1960). Statements that look a bit like the scientist's laws can be found – 'all power tends to corrupt', 'revolution is followed by reaction' – but closer inspection reveals that these supposed 'historical laws' do not meet necessary criteria for law-hood. These are general statements but not, according to Berlin, scientific laws, since they are 'tautologous, or vague, or inaccurate' (Berlin 1960: 11). But the historian should in no way be embarrassed about this conclusion: the explanations that they provide are usually quite satisfactory, and any explication of them as some 'historical law' adds nothing. Instead of finding laws, and theory-building in general, Berlin insisted that historical explanation proceeds and is justified by 'judgement' and 'common sense' (a plausible sounding, if vague, idea that I unpack in Chapter 6).

A scientific law can be regarded as a special sort of generalization. The paradigmatic form of a generalization is 'all Xs are F', though some laws are more naturally phrased 'no X is F', equivalent to 'all Xs are not-F'.[5] A generalization need not be universal: 'all Xs' can be replaced by 'most Xs', or a quantitative proportion ('40 per cent of Xs'). Generalizations that exemplify these different features include: 'everyone in this room has blonde hair', 'most British monarchs have been male' and 'no lump of gold weighs more than 1,000 tonnes'. Yet none of those are specifically scientific laws. Consideration of traditional desiderata of scientific laws – generality, universality, necessity – explains why that is.

Generality refers to the terms used in antecedent and consequent ('antecedent' covering those properties preceding the copula, 'consequent' the succeeding properties), and so recalls discussion, in section one, of abstract terms. With respect to the above examples, 'people in this room' and 'British monarchs' are properties that are intuitively ill suited for a role in scientific law, given their highly restricted range. Roughly, the terms in a scientific law will be of wide scope.[6] *Universality* is a feature of the connection between the antecedent and consequent of scientific law. A universal claim is exceptionless: it states a relationship that always holds.

We should take care to distinguish scientific laws from legal or ethical laws. Scientific laws (or 'laws of nature') – what we are interested in at this point – state how things are. Legal or ethical laws (and norms in general) state how things should be. 'Love is the only law'; but the sad fact is that it is a law more broken than followed. While that observation implies no criticism of the law of love, only of our behaviour, one cannot adopt such an attitude when faced with an exception to a scientific law. If one maintains the scientific law 'all swans are white' and is faced with a black swan, it is the law which must be criticized, not the swan. Historical generalizations often fail to be universal. The Marxist theory of socio-economic progression – a part of which is that all feudal societies are succeeded by capitalist societies[7] – is falsified by consideration of the Russian transition of 1917 and the Chinese transition of 1949. More prosaic generalizations tend, likewise, to fall short of universality. One can, without much difficulty, find exceptions to the following plausible social generalizations: 'deregulation leads to a reduction in price'; 'the more divided the political party, the less chance of it being elected'; 'the level of crime in a block of flats rises when the number of floors in that block is higher than

13'.[8] We can grant that universality is, at least, in short supply with regard to historical generalization.

Necessity can be seen to be required by considering the following standard philosophical example. 'No lump of gold weighs more than 1,000 tonnes' is a universally true generalization, containing suitably general properties. Yet it isn't a law, since it's only a matter of accident that the generalization is true; indeed no less accidentally true than the generalization 'everyone in this room has blonde hair'. But compare these examples to the necessarily true generalization – the law – 'no lump of uranium weighs more than 1,000 tonnes'. This is necessarily true because of the nature of uranium: lumps of uranium above a certain size are chemically unstable. There are various ways to metaphysically unpack this sort of necessity, but the clearest is in terms of counterfactuals. A genuine scientific law supports a corresponding counter-factual, an accidental generalization does not. Thus it is true that 'if anything were to be uranium, then it would weigh less than 1,000 tonnes', but not that 'if anything were to be gold, then it would weigh less than 1,000 tonnes', nor 'if anyone came into the room, then they would have blonde hair'. (Recall that counterfactuals of this sort provided the starting point, in Chapter 2, for my account of historical reasoning from evidence.)

Empirical precision provides the final desideratum for scientific laws. One (usually undesirable) way that the foregoing conditions, especially universality, can be met is by trading those desiderata for precision. Astrological generalizations and predictions routinely rely for any apparent success on that trade. 'A stroke of luck will benefit all Capricorns over the coming week' is sufficiently imprecise to fit almost any conceivable life, and thus to be almost universally true. One way to object to 'historical laws' is to maintain that these supposed 'laws' have, like the astrological example, no significant empirical content. At the limit, they might have no empirical content at all, being rather true analytically (in virtue solely of the meanings of the terms related).[9] This objection was implicit in Berlin's above-quoted charge that historical laws are 'tautologous', and is explicit in Geoffrey Elton's comments on historical law (Elton and Fogel 1983: 99). The charge sticks with regard to some examples better than it does with others. 'Nations which face more substantive geopolitical threats will suffer greater internal strain' one suspects to be largely analytic. Berlin's 'revolution tends to be followed by reaction' seems to exemplify the statistical phenomenon of 'regression to the mean', a logically necessary feature of any extended sequence of terms. But as a general criticism, the charge of analyticity is unconvincing, as any one of the other historical examples mentioned thus far illustrates.

What the charge of analyticity does help us to focus on is the fact that empirical precision is something which a generalization can have more or less of, as Popper's theory of falsification makes admirably clear (Popper 2004/1935: Chapter 1). Popper asked us to consider of a generalization what observation it would take for it to be falsified. Imprecise, and therefore less falsifiable generalizations might seem to be beneficial in being confirmed by so many observations. But Popper argued that the reverse is true: a generalization which can be falsified with difficulty is less valuable than one which is easily falsified. Worst of all are unfalsifiable generalizations, such as the astrological and – so Popper believed – the generalizations found in Hegel, Marx and Freud. Analytic statements are at the extreme limit of 'unfalsifiability': no empirical situation disconfirms them. This is, of course, no criticism of analytic statements per se; only of analytic, or near-analytic, statements *masquerading as* scientific laws.

5. Against universality

I will focus on the demand of universality, at the heart of the positivist insistence that explanation is a matter of citing exceptionless regularities that underpin explanations of particular facts. I have already hinted that such a demand sits awkwardly with historical practice, even where generalizations do occur in the course of that practice. I will first suggest substantive reasons why we are unlikely to find universal regularities in the domain that historians are interested in. Then, I will argue that this should not concern the naturalist, since universality is not in any case a requirement that one would expect all sciences to meet. The conclusion of that line of argument is that the naturalist should not adopt positivism.

In this section, I focus on an example of a 'historical theory': Randall Collins' theory of state collapse (summarized graphically in Figure 4.2; Collins 1995). I use the term 'historical theory' to mean a theory that is oriented towards particular events, processes and facts that are typically regarded as falling under the purview of historical understanding. The point that I want to make here is that the abstractions in Collins' theory are *comparative*, as is typical in historical theories. One positive variable for state collapse is being less resource rich

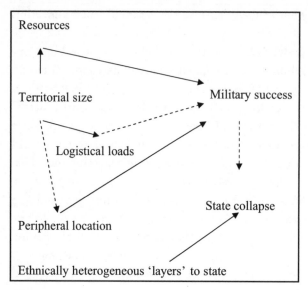

Figure 4.2 Collins' theory of state collapse (Collins 1995).
Solid arrows represent positive influence in the directon of the arrow.
Dotted arrows represent negative influence in the direction of the arrow.

than one's competitors: obviously a comparative property. A second positive variable is having a number of active borders (being at the centre of the states system), rather than being peripheral. This second property is also comparative, if less obviously so, since whether or not a border is 'active' depends on the nature of the bordering state (for that reason, Collins takes early twentieth-century Russia to be peripheral, but late twentieth-century Russia to be central).

What is instructive about the comparative terms in historical theories is that they have their roots in *mutual competition*. What happens to one historical object (a person, a group, a state or nation) is determined by the nature of a second – and vice versa. One side sets the second a *problem*, and in solving that problem, the second sets the first a different problem. The reciprocal sequence is without end.

The fact that historical theories focus on action – specifically, the reciprocal solution and setting of problems – provides us with a good reason to be suspicious of the possibility of universal historical laws. Many generalizations are possible in subjects whose focus is chains of problem-solution: 'all cheetahs are agile'; 'having money increases the chance of acquiring political power'. Yet, given the reciprocal nature of problem solving and setting, we should expect those generalizations to be broken as a result of a new design problem. If cheetahs become much more agile than their prey, that prey will have to adopt a different strategy in order to survive (perhaps moving to confined areas rather than plains), a strategy which sets the cheetah a new problem. The cheetah's response to that new problem, and the corresponding redundancy of the old problem, leads us to expect an increasing number of exceptions to the first generalization. A parallel argument is possible with regard to the second, social, generalization. While its basis may seem secure from the vantage-point of contemporary capitalism, it is no less mutable than the corresponding pre-Enlightenment generalization: 'having higher social class increases the chance of acquiring political power'.

Where the generalization concerns human action, then it is possible for it to be 'used'. Generalizations of body language – correlations of different bodily positions with one's inner feeling, or with the likely response of others present – can be taught and used in social situations. We can teach ourselves to respond differently independent of our feeling (perhaps maintaining an open pose despite feeling insecure) and upon our relationship with the other (perhaps mirroring gestures in order to manufacture a sympathy that is not initially present). In so doing, the 'laws' are broken. And given the competitive advantages to be gained in recognizing existing generalities in order to use them, we should expect these laws to be broken before too long. Not only are generalizations likely to be falsified over time as a result of reciprocal competition in the chain of problem and solution, but they may be altered as a result of more direct criticism. It may be that money increases the chances of political power; but realizing this can encourage attempts to change the system upon which that generalization depends.

We can conclude that universal law is not to be expected in history, a failure well explained by systemic features of historical processes. A historical science of action focuses on the solution to problems set by one's environment. Yet that environment is always changing, as a result not least of the solutions of other people and groups. Might it be possible to mitigate against this loss of universality by predicting *when* one generalization will subside, and another become manifest? In practice, neither an evolutionary biologist nor a historical theorist will be able to date at all precisely when such a shift is to be expected, at least beyond the next iteration of the reciprocal process. In Chapter 6, I offer other comments on why prediction is so hard for the historical process.

In any case, universality is not a demand that should be privileged, even with regard to explanations that are clearly scientific. A direct way to argue that universality need not be a scientific desideratum would be to cite examples of scientific laws which are not universal. Two sorts of suitable examples can be found. First, certain scientific laws are statistical, taking the form 'φ per cent of Xs are F'. In medicine, we find laws such as 'a smoker has a 40 per cent chance of contracting lung disease'. In quantum physics, we find laws such as 'a particle of type X has a 40 per cent chance of decaying in the first second after its formation'. The medical counter-example to universality is somewhat less convincing. It may be maintained that the probability in that case is an arte-fact of our own epistemic limitations, an imprecision that might be removed were we to replace the insufficiently abstract 'smoker' and 'lung disease' with more abstract and fundamental properties. Indeed, such an assumption under-pinned the positivist demand that everyday generalizations be *reduced* to more basic regularities. The quantum case, however, confirms that stochastic (prob-abilistic) laws are scientifically acceptable. (A claim which, given the recent development of quantum physics, has the interesting corollary that desiderata for scientific laws are not set as a timeless *a priori*, but themselves respond to scientific practice.) The probability cited there is irreducible; a result not of our epistemic limitations but of the world itself.[10]

A third example which *seems* universal is the Newtonian law of gravity, to this point my paradigm of scientific law. But – in practice – this law is not universal, for there are exceptions. Where there are other forces at work, the Newtonian law will not hold. The mass may be held by the tension of a cable or the friction of a surface, the gravitational force may be overridden by electromagnetic forces. Of course, my tongue is here planted firmly in cheek: we must surely recognize that this law, indeed any law, is true only 'other circumstances being equal', or *ceteris paribus*. Such a clause is intended to alert us to the need to discount the operation of other laws. Yet, consideration of *ceteris paribus* is useful in order to focus on the question: why does not such a clause render any law trivial? For, if used indiscriminately, one could hold a law true come what may, by holding that these seemingly disconfirming circumstances are ones where the *ceteris paribus* clause be activated. And if that is the case, then the Newtonian law is no better than the astrological.

Triviality is avoided in different ways in different sorts of sciences. In fully *abstract science* (such as – perhaps even only – fundamental physics), the *ce-teris paribus* clause can be explicitly and exhaustively filled out by specifying all of the other laws that must be taken into account, and how those laws interact. (It is currently thought that there are only four fundamental physical forces: gravity, electromagnetism, and the strong and weak nuclear forces. The effects of these forces can be simply numerically added: a point that I return to in Chapter 6.) Triviality is thereby avoided, since each apparent exception can be explained by the joint operation of the system of laws. This closed system of laws is, taken jointly (and excepting stochastic laws such as the quantum), universal. Yet this virtue is obtained at a heavy cost: while the system of laws applies transparently to the sort of abstracted systems indicated in Figure 4.1, applying it to the real world is far from straightforward. To adapt an example of Popper's (1957: 117), even a very simple real-world process such as a falling apple evades complete explanation by fundamental laws of physics:

> apart from gravity, we should have to consider the laws explaining wind pressure; the jerking movements of the branch; the tension in the apple's stalk the bruise suffered by the apple on impact; all of which is succeeded by chemical processes resulting from the bruise.

Those sciences that are not fully abstract, that deal with real-world complexity, I call the *causal sciences*. In those sciences – including medicine, dendrology and *perhaps* historical science – the *ceteris paribus* clauses indicate the fact that the theory uses causal powers, not exceptionless regularities. I expand upon this claim in the final section.

6. Rehabilitating causation

I suggest that naturalists wholeheartedly embrace the search for causal relations, and reject the search for exceptionless regularities. In the following chapter I positively (no pun intended) develop a causal approach, with reference to examples of historical theory. In this section, I summarize the reasons why causation should, *pace* positivism, be rehabilitated.

The positivist approach was distrustful of causation – unless it was taken to straightforwardly imply a corresponding exceptionless regularity – on the basis of the austere theory of meaning already outlined. That mistrust made it difficult to make room for the necessity of genuine laws, a demand previously noted. Logical necessity was admissible, natural or counterfactual necessity was not. The corollary was that accounting for the good scientific practice of *not* accepting any exceptionless regularity as a genuine law was awkward. That awkwardness is paralleled by the criticism of the DN model of explanation that focused on the possibility of constructing good DN arguments which were false or ridiculous explanations. Consider John, who takes birth control pills: should we explain the failure of John to become pregnant by the fact that John takes the pill, and the law that people who take the pill (usually) don't become pregnant?! Surely not – it's obvious why John isn't pregnant, and it isn't the pills. Yet the 'explanation' in the previous sentence seems to be a perfect DN argument. The obvious response to examples of this sort was to insist that the explanation had to be genuinely causal: exceptionless regularity is insufficient.

Causal applicability is required in order to rule out irrelevant antecedents. Natural scientists are wary not to be misled by confounds: 'silent partners' which tend to be associated with the genuinely causal variables, but are not causal themselves. Historians are wary not to be misled by empty 'rationalization': a way of making sense of an action which does not get at the genuine cause of that action (Davidson 2001/1963: 9–11). My reaching for a glass of water is not explained by my being thirsty, even if I really am thirsty, unless that thirst is a cause of my reaching for the glass. It need not be the cause in, say, a case in which my domineering boss ordered me to fetch him a glass of water.

I have already indicated that causation is a suitable replacement to exceptionless regularity with regard to concern over the operation of the *ceteris paribus* clause in sciences that are not fully abstract. In these sciences, the *ceteris paribus* clause is open ended (the apple will always fall to the ground, unless it is snagged on a branch, or it is caught by an animal, or it is destroyed by very strong winds . . .). The central claims should here be understood as locating causal powers, which, if successful, inform us about the *normal* operation of a type of cause. We should not expect that normal operation to be straightforwardly observable, since most real-world processes (the movement of bodies in the solar system being one of only a few exceptions) depend on the effect of the *combination* of many such causes. It is usually only where we are able to carefully design and implement experimental situations that individual causes are 'laid bare' to observation, and that causal generalizations can be directly confirmed. The skill, and difficulty, of scientific experimentation is well explained by the need to shield a real-world situation from many other causes that would usually interfere with the one of interest to hypothesis. And the importance of paradigm experiments in the pedagogy of science is thereby made apparent: those situations are some of the few real-world cases in which the relevant causal generalization can be directly observed and confirmed.[11] The *ceteris paribus* clauses would be trivial if we understood them as attempts to insulate a universal from empirical refutation. That triviality is avoided if we see these sciences as attempts to locate causal powers whose operation in the real world is usually modified by other types of cause.

That idea underpins a second pervasive criticism of the DN model of explanation. Not only was it found possible to construct DN arguments that weren't explanations; there were also clearly explanations that weren't DN arguments. The standard example in the literature concerned the rather unpleasant case of poor Jones and his acquisition of paresis. That Jones had syphilis explained why he suffered from paresis, given that paresis doesn't occur without syphilis. Yet, given that it is only a small minority of syphilis sufferers who go on to acquire paresis, there can be no law connecting syphilis and paresis, not even a 'probabilistic law' stating that 'syphilis is *usually* followed by paresis'. Again, one natural way to respond is to invoke causation: the normal effect of syphilis is to produce paresis, though that operation can be disturbed in many ways. Exceptionless regularity (or anything remotely like it) is unnecessary.

The rehabilitation of causation permits a useful re-evaluation of the desiderata of scientific theorizing presented when evaluating scientific laws. On *generalization*: scientists seek abstract properties with normal manifestations. On *universality*: scientists do seek connections between properties that go beyond the fleeting and temporary, since they seek to describe the normal operation of types of cause. Yet we should not demand nor expect exceptionless regularity, for reasons provided. On *necessity*: it is no surprise that observed regularity is insufficient for scientific theories, since scientists search for normal operation of types of cause, not the superficial manifestation of the combination of those causes. On *empirical precision*: the crucial demand is not that a cause is always manifest, but, as suggested by Popper's Falsificationism, that we can specify where it does not hold. Popper (1957: Part IV) pointed out that to locate a trend (say population growth, or average weight of a US citizen over time), and then to blindly project that trend into the future is a parody of scientific practice. Yet the above suggests that it would be a mistake to suppose that the scientific historian who examines past trends is limited to blind projection. Once we are able to provide conditions under which the trend will continue, and those under which it will not, we have accomplished something potentially impressive. Further, provision of *some* such conditions represents achievement in the direction of empirical precision, given that the open-ended nature of the *ceteris paribus* clause in general claims of mixed sciences preclude an exhaustive list of conditions.

There is both an analytical and methodological cost to adopting a causal philosophy of science. On the analytical side, it means that we have to attempt to make sense of the priority of causes over general regularities. In other words, we have to explain what regularities we do find in the world in terms of the interactions of underlying causal forces; not, as the positivists wanted to do, our talk of 'causes' in terms of regularities in the world. On the methodological side, the task of evidentially confirming theories has been made harder. The positivist could rely on enumerative induction: to confirm a law simply required finding lots of instances of that law. That's both non-necessary and insufficient for the causal theorist. The problem is particularly acute for non-experimental studies, history foremost among these. Both analytical and methodological issues will be taken up in the following chapter.

Further reading and study questions

Berlin, I. (1960) 'The concept of scientific history', in *History and Theory* 1, 1–31. A typical critique of the positivist approach to history.

Hempel, C. G. (1942) 'The function of general laws in history', in *Journal of Philosophy* 39, 35–47. A non-technical presentation of Hempel's approach to explanation.

Popper, K. (1957) *The Poverty of Historicism*. London: Routledge. Part IV is relevant to the material of this chapter.

(a) Choose a historical explanation that you think is a good one. Phrase that example in the form demanded by a Deductive Nomological understanding of historical explanation. What, if anything, does the law add to the understanding of why that explained took place?

(b) Taking the same example, make explicit any causal claims that it implies. What, if anything, do the causal claims add to the understanding of why that explained took place?

(c) What is positivism? Why is the positivist wary of causal explanation?

The causal sciences 5

1. Against causation in history

The philosophy of history has witnessed a good many attempts to claim that the category of causation is, in principle, ill-suited for historical scholarship. Given my emphasis on causal explanation in history, I want to begin the present chapter by refuting those critiques. Criticism tends to take one of two forms. First, it is claimed that cause implies some other notion that is clearly unsuitable to historical understanding. Second, it is claimed that there is in any case no need for cause, the 'imposition' of causal concepts rendered unnecessary by the historical understanding's possession of more suitable alternatives. Michael Oakeshott's critique of causation in history well illustrates the more general form. It will be noted that the following quoted paragraphs exemplify, in turn, the above two criticisms:

> What, I take it, is fundamental to [the causal] conception is that we should be able to separate the cause and its effect, and endow each with a certain degree of individuality; but it is just this which is impossible while we retain the postulates of historical experience. It cannot be achieved by selecting some single event and attributing to that any subsequent event of the whole

course of subsequent events. No single event in history is isolable in this manner, and if it were there would be no more reason to isolate *this* event rather than *that*. And abstractions like geographical or economic conditions cannot for one moment be considered to have the character of historical causes because these do not as such belong to history.

(Oakeshott 1933: 131–2)

Change in history carries with it its own explanation; the course of events is one, so far integrated, so far filled in and complete, that no external cause or reason is looked for or required in order to account for any particular event. The historian, in short, is like the novelist whose characters (for example) are presented in such detail and with such coherence that additional explanation of their actions is superfluous. This principle I will call the unity or continuity of history; and it is, I think, the only principle of explanation consonant with the other postulates of historical experience.

(Oakeshott 1933: 141)

The first paragraph sees Oakeshott argue against causation in history on the basis that it requires isolation of (at least two) events, to play the part of cause and effect. My reply is simply that causation is a broad church, going beyond the requirements assumed by Oakeshott. Processes are causal, as well as events: the steady rise in inflation over a decade has causes and itself leads to other events and processes. It would be a grave error to misunderstand historical explanation on the basis of an overly circumscribed understanding of cause, yet this is an error that has been made time and again. A second example, from the writing of historian Roger Chartier, illustrates the same error even though in its detail the criticism is quite different to Oakeshott's.

. . . under what conditions is it legitimate to set up a collection of scattered and disparate facts or ideas as 'causes' or 'origins' of an event? . . . When history succumbs to the 'chimera of origins', it burdens itself, perhaps unconsciously, with several presuppositions: that every historical moment is a homogenous totality endowed with an ideal and unique meaning present in each of the realities that make up and express the whole; that historical becoming is organized as an ineluctable continuity; that events are linked together, one engendering another in an uninterrupted flow of change . . .

(Chartier 1991: 4)

Chartier's comments are based on Foucault's (1977) 'Nietzsche, genealogy and history', itself an extension of Nietzsche's history of ideas. But without investigating that theoretical machinery, we are entitled to ask: why must the citation of causes imply the construction of a homogeneous totality? We are quite comfortable with the possibility of accidents, after all: events for which chains of causation converged that were heterogeneous and (prior to the accident) thought to be quite unconnected. As for the implication of continuity, we must distinguish between two uses of the notion. Given that the causal sequence itself is continuous, one could plausibly hold that a good causal explanation close any gaps between explanans and explanandum. Yet, that continuity need not rule out radical change. One may give a complete causal account of the story from mammalian rodents to *homo sapiens*, yet the outstanding feature of that account would be the lack of continuous identity (of species) from start to finish.

So much for the first sort of anti-causal argument. Let us return to the second sort, and to Oakeshott's second quoted paragraph. Oakeshott's competing proposal – that a description of historical change is quite sufficient for explanation – is ambiguous, and when the ambiguity is removed is either tacitly causal or erroneous. Changes of certain types (cellular aging, the apple blown in the wind, the radicalization of a revolution) are best regarded as causal processes. If those are the sorts of 'courses of events' that Oakeshott has in mind, then causality is presupposed. On the other hand, if we take the non-causal Oakeshott at face value (as suggested by such comments as that 'nothing in the world of history is negative or non-contributory. All relationship between historical events is positive' (Oakeshott 1933: 142)), then we must reject the principle as making a mockery of explanation. Not all events are causally linked; the fall of the Roman Empire in Europe and the rise of the Teotihuacán civilization in Mesoamerica are not causally connected, and hence nothing about the one explains anything about the other.

Other common proposals for notions to replace historical causation succumb to the same dilemma. Chartier (and Foucault) suggest that 'genealogy' should replace causation:

> Genealogy does not pretend to go back in time to restore an unbroken continuity that operates beyond the dispersion of forgotten things . . . it is to identify the accidents, the minute deviations – or conversely, the complete reversals – the errors, the faulty calculations that gave birth to those things that continue to exist and have value for us.
>
> (Foucault 1977: 146)

But to trace accidents, deviations and errors is to trace certain sorts of cause, not to abandon a causal approach altogether.

I do need to say more about what cause does imply, as well as what it does not. Further, anti-causal arguments of the sort considered can of course teach us about certain aspects of historical understanding, for the issue is not closed once we recognize the role of causation. Nonetheless, here I want to emphasize the fundamental and almost unavoidable place of causation in history. In everyday language, causal implication is hard to avoid; and history, as the ordinary-language discipline *par excellence*, is unsurprisingly steeped in it. Verbs are often implicitly causal.[1] Thus 'King John *signed* the Magna Carta' implies that King John caused words to be on the page by the action of his quill. And the description of properties often implies something about their history. Thus 'the soldiers suffered from heavy *scarring*' implies that the marks were caused by violent contact, with context carrying further implications about whether the instruments were blades, shrapnel, etc. We observe and describe the world in terms of causation, and (recall the final section of Chapter 4) its role in explanation accounts for the central demand that explanans be relevant to explanandum. It is a tool that historians should be perfectly comfortable with.

One final example of the claim that causation implies further, clearly disreputable, notions lies in the charge that to speak of 'cause' in the naturalist's sense brings back historical laws. I take up this specific issue in the following section.

2. Singular causation

To this point I have defended a naturalist understanding of historiography that focuses on causes, not laws. But the independence of cause and law should not be taken for granted, as Collingwood's concerns suggest:

> the historian need not and cannot (without ceasing to be an historian) emulate the scientist in searching for the causes or laws of events. For science, the event is discovered by perceiving it, and the further search for its cause is conducted by assigning it to its class and determining the relation between that class and others
>
> (1994/1946: 214)

The 'received view' of causation – David Hume's – would agree. How, Hume asked, do we know that there is a causal relation between two events? We perceive the first immediately followed by, and spatially contiguous with, the second. However, those observations aren't sufficient: for example, consider that the signing of the Magna Carta was preceded by a gust of wind upon the paper, though that wind was no cause of the signing. Hume, as a good empiricist, searched for something else available to the senses that enabled us to distinguish causal from non-causal relations. Despairing of finding anything in the particular connection between the two events – for we perceive simply one followed by the other – Hume turned instead to the general relation between events of the first type and events of the second.

> 'Tis therefore by EXPERIENCE only, that we can infer the existence of one object from that of another. The nature of experience is this. We remember to have had frequent instances of the existence of one species of objects; and also remember, that the individuals of another species of objects have always attended them, and have existed in a regular order of contiguity and succession with regard to them. Thus we remember, to have seen that species of object we call flame, and to have felt that species of sensation we call heat. We likewise call to mind their constant conjunction in all past instances. Without any farther ceremony, we call the one cause and the other effect, and infer the existence of the one from that of the other.
>
> (2003/1740: Book I, Part III, Section VI)

For Hume, to say that c caused e is to say that c and e were adjacent in space and time, and that things of type C are always followed by things of type E. If that analysis is correct, then any attempt to emphasize the role of causation in history will lead us right back to the question of historical laws. Arguing against Hume requires finding a place for causation in a singular, rather than nomic, sense.

John Stuart Mill was an intellectual descendent of David Hume, sharing the latter's fundamental commitment to empiricism. However, Mill's refinements of Hume's idea on causal discovery open up a possibility for the discovery of singular causation. Let us first note that Hume's criteria can be made to look too permissive (just as the closely allied DN model of explanation can be made to look foolish by examples like John and the birth control pills). Mill himself gives daytime as an invariable antecedent of night. Another common counter-example is the traffic-light: even if Amber is invariably followed by Green, the Amber light does not cause the Green light.

Mill agreed with Hume that cause was a matter of spatio-temporal contiguity, and invariable succession. But Mill regarded the true cause as *the whole* antecedent situation preceding the effect. Green might invariably follow Amber, but since the latter requires a further condition (an electrical switch must be triggered), we need not regard the former as cause. According to Mill, then, c causes e only if the whole antecedent situation of which c is a part is always followed by the whole consequent situation of which e is a part. Mill's proposal seems more secure than Hume's (indeed, is arguably presupposed by any deterministic understanding of causation), yet as it stands is spectacularly ineffective as a methodological device. In response, Mill bequeathed a number of fundamental methods of more practical use, foremost among these the Method of Difference:

> If an instance in which the phenomenon under investigation occurs, and an instance in which it does not occur, have every circumstance save one in common, that one occurring only in the former; the circumstance in which alone the two instances differ is the effect, or cause, or a necessary part of the cause, of the phenomenon.
>
> (Mill 1973/1843: 225)

While the Method of Difference is based upon the fundamental Humean proposal[2], it does permit an understanding of singular causation. In the happy circumstance that two cases differ only in effect and one other respect, we may infer that this other respect was the cause of the difference. In that circumstance, we would have inferred a cause without recourse to considerations of what type of thing follows another. I shall exploit the Method of Difference in understanding historical explanation in practice, later in this chapter.

Donald Davidson (2001/1963) has mounted a justly well-known defence of singular causation that depends on a simple and plausible claim. Causal statements, for Davidson, may describe cause and effect in any manner of different ways. Thus, the cause of Archduke Ferdinand's death may be called 'the shot that killed Archduke Ferdinand', 'the shot fired by Princip', 'the shot that started the First World War', 'the acceleration of mass M at velocity V'. Under certain descriptions (the last of these examples), cause and effect may be nomically related; under other descriptions (the first of the above) they may be analytically related; under others still there may be no significant relation. We can make sense of singular causation quite simply: although it may be the case that there is some way of describing cause and effect such that they exhibit a relation of law, there are many other ways of describing cause and effect such that no relation of law is implied.

Davidson's account of causal explanation fits well with the epistemic plurality that I urged in the first section. Cause and effect may, suitably described, take its place in a variety of epistemic approaches: those that emphasize continuity and those that emphasize discontinuity; those that emphasize rational action and those that emphasize natural regularity. I shall rely on this sort of catholic conception of causation in the discussion of interpretation and narrative, in later chapters. Here, we should note that Davidson's defence of singular causation is (deliberately) partial. Davidson still believes that the fundamental metaphysics of causation, what the causal relationship *is*, implies general laws. It is only in our *use* of causation, in description and explanation, that the requirement of law be dropped.

An epistemic defence of the appropriateness of singular causal statement and explanation can therefore be achieved by consideration of Mill and Davidson. To conclude this section, I want to briefly mention two more substantive (metaphysical) possibilities for disputing a Humean, or nonsic conception of causation. (I should, though, be clear that I do not think that the use of singular causal explanation by historians requires the successful defence of any such metaphysical proposal.) First, the implication of my talk of causal powers, at the end of the previous chapter, was intended to retain a role for general understanding, but without being committed to positivist exceptionless regularities. Taken literally, talk of causal powers implies a metaphysics at some remove from traditional empiricism, a metaphysics of tendencies or capacities (Cartwright 1989) that are not directly observable.

Second, one could attempt to understand causes in terms of counterfactuals. According to this proposal, to demonstrate that c caused e one must be able to argue that 'had c not happened, then e would not have happened'. And that latter statement requires a singular comparison, rather than the general comparison required by the Humean conception of causation. The relevant comparison, according to a counterfactual understanding, is that between the actual case and only a single other: that closest counterfactual situation where c did not take place. Counterfactuals are intimately tied to causation. One of the most natural ways to wonder whether some event or object was causal is to wonder what would have happened had that event or object not been there. If one decides that things would have turned out the same, then the event or object counterfactually removed by the imagination can not have been causal. To be causal, the event or object must have made a counterfactual difference. While the close connections between cause and counterfactual are undeniable, the direction of understanding can be disputed. I note here only that the proponent of an attempt to understand causes in terms of counterfactuals must be able to justify counterfactual claims without invoking causation. (This need not be decisive point, but the burden of proof is on the counterfactual analyst. David

Lewis (1973) notably defended a counterfactual analysis of causation with great ingenuity.)

3. Causation and contrasts

Contrast provides a useful tool with which to understand historical practice. And as I shall demonstrate, cause and contrast are epistemic tools that fit together well. Explanation is contrastive in so far as the aim is to answer a contrastive question (say, why there was revolution in France *rather than* in Prussia). It will often be the case that explanatory requests are implicitly contrastive: contrasts are implied by such conventions as verbal stress, or written italics: compare the effect of asking why the *French* Revolution happened in 1789, why the French *Revolution* happened in 1789, why the French Revolution happened in *1789*. Contrast is also understood (often in conjunction with these sorts of conventions) in virtue of the pragmatic circumstances in which the question is asked. If we had just been speaking of Prussia before you asked about the French Revolution, I would most probably understand your question as implying an implicit contrast between those two nations.

Contrastive questioning serves to focus inquiry on specific features of the target phenomenon: those by which target and contrast differ. What requires explanation (the explanandum) is some difference between target and contrast. What explains that difference (the explanans) is some difference between the histories of target and contrast. This insight can be credited to Peter Lipton's 'Difference Condition' for contrastive explanations:

> To explain why P rather than Q, we must cite a causal difference between P and not-Q, consisting of a cause of P, and the absence of a corresponding event in the history of not-Q.
>
> (Lipton 2004: 42)

Thus, in seeking to explain why there was a revolution in France, but not in Prussia, it will not help to cite the fact that France was a monarchical state, for there was a corresponding fact in the causal history of Prussia. Rather, we should focus on actual differences in history – perhaps (following Hegel) hypothesizing that the relevant difference is that Prussia went through the Reformation, while France did not. The first advantage of contrastive explanation is therefore its use in picking out a precisely defined explanandum.

With this in mind, we can understand why two historical explanations might seem to be competitors and yet, because their contrast cases differ, actually explain different facts. In such a case, historians 'speak past one another'. While the Prussian comparison directs attention to the lack of Reformation in the French case, a comparison with England will most likely direct attention to the lack of a genuine parliament in pre-Revolutionary France. It would be no good for proponents of these different explanations to thereby criticize the other, for they are explanations for different things.

A contrastive explanation need only cite differences between target and contrast; a set which, if the contrast is well chosen (as one presumes is the case with France/Prussia and France/England), is manageably small. That set is certainly smaller than the unrestricted list of causes for the target event. Contrastive explanation thereby whittles down the mass of potentially relevant causal information. For example, under *some* (perhaps unusual) perspectives, causal explanations for the French Revolution include that France was a monarchy; that there were disagreements of some sort; that there were people in France . . . Each of these was, after all, a part of the causal history of the Revolution. Yet each is irrelevant for any normal contrast (in particular, the contrast case of Prussia), since there will be a corresponding fact in the history of the contrast. The unmanageably broad scope of possible causal information has sometimes been thought to be problematic for historical practice, as the above-quoted passage from Oakeshott suggested. ('No single event in history is isolable in this manner, and if it were there would be no more reason to isolate *this* event rather than *that*.') A contrastive model deals with that breadth in a simple way: we select relevant elements of that causal history by choosing a certain contrast, a choice that need only answer to our interests. Our interests govern contrast, and hence what is explained and what element of the causal history is focused on. As the Difference Condition makes clear though, once that focus is set, it is an evidential and non-interest-relative matter as to what the correct answer is.

Explanations not only focus on different parts of the causal history of an event, but sometimes focus on the same part but at *different levels of detail*. This aspect is also well understood in terms of contrastive explanation. Alan Garfinkel (1981: 30) illustrated the application of contrast through the question 'Why did the car skid?' To explicitly complete the question by adding '. . . at that point, rather than 5 cm further on' would usually be inappropriate (subject, as ever, to the context of the questioner's interests). It might be that a difference of 5 cm is relevant due to the highly localized presence of oil on the road. But it may also be that the driver was tired, or drunk, and therefore that a contrastive focus on close patches of road is irrelevant. In that latter case, although it was part of the causal history of the crash that the skid took place at the precise point that it did, this part of the causal history is irrelevant for many of the most natural sorts of question that we might ask about the crash.

We can apply this account of contrastive explanation to more substantive naturalist debate. One common objection to historical theories at a level above that of individual people is that something vital is thereby overlooked by those theories. Consider figures 5.1 and 5.2, which summarize two historical theories which are resolutely supra-individual. Manicas criticizes Skocpol's sociological theory of social revolutions on the grounds that it gives

> exclusive attention to structures as causes . . . [and] leaves no room for history in one good clear sense of that word. That is, 'structural explanation' omits history in the sense that it omits an account which identifies, traces, and connects decisions, activities and events through time.
>
> (1981: 211)

Likewise, Tomlinson (1998), in a review of Diamond's environmentalist theory, states that

> Most important of all, human history requires history to be studied on a human scale, so that we can empathise with the past, and see it in the context of our present humanity.

The sociological or environmental approaches of the sort exemplified in the previous chapter ignore individual people and their personal relation, and therefore ignore individual choice, creativity and innovation. But without these, the phenomena that the sociological scientist wishes to explain would not be possible. Therefore the sociological scientific explanation is deficient.

The foregoing comment concerning contrast and level of detail can be readily applied in order to criticize this individualistic argument. More formally, that argument can be phrased as follows. The sociological scientist proposes an explanation for some important human fact, F. That fact could be why there was revolution in France in 1789, or in China in 1949 (Skocpol 1979; and see Figure 5.1); or why Western Europe industrialized and expanded faster than other parts of the world (Diamond 1998; and see Figure 5.2); or why the Russian Empire collapsed in 1989 (Collins 1995; and see Figure 4.2). The individualist critic of such explanations argues that:

(i) Historical science explains fact F without reference to individual attributes (choice, creativity, innovation).

(ii) A prominent part of the (causal) history of F concerns individual choice, creativity and innovation.

(iii) What is (prominent) in the causal history of F must feature in any explanation of F.

(iv) Therefore the explanation of sociological science should be rejected.

This argument looks valid, and premise (ii) is true by hypothesis. But a contrastive approach to explanation shows why we should reject premise (iii), and should amend premise (i). What the historical scientist seeks to explain is not F (say, the Industrial Revolution in Western Europe), but F rather than G (say, the Industrial Revolution in Western Europe, rather than on some other continent). As we have seen, such explanations need and should only cite those differences between the causal histories of the target-case and contrast-case. It may be that individual creativity and innovation were similar in the target and contrast cases. If that is so, then they can – indeed should – be ignored in answering the contrastive question.

Further, where the number of individual people is large, the assumption that individual creativity and innovation is constant across societies becomes plausible. Individual creativity and innovation have certainly been required to develop the astonishing achievements to be found in our shared history. Yet, clever and creative people are born in any human society. To explain why one society has progressed faster than another requires not that we cite individual creativity and innovation, since these are equally found in any contrasting society. Rather, supra-individual properties – societal or environmental – are required in any good explanation. Does this conjure the bogeymen of 'social determinism' or 'environmental determinism'? It need not, given that a contrastive explanation is partial (incomplete) in what it explains as much as in the causal history used to explain. Contrast is a tool with which to focus on an aspect of the event to be explained. So to accept an explanation based upon wholly social or environmental features is not thereby to accept that everything about the event of interest can be explained socially or environmentally.[3]

4. What is a historical theory?

In Figures 4.2, 5.1 and 5.2 I graphically summarize the three examples of historical theory that I will be focusing on in the remainder of this chapter

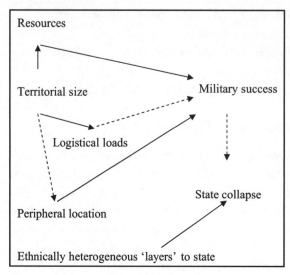

Figure 4.2 Collins' theory of state collapse (Collins 1995).
Solid arrows represent positive influence in the directon of the arrow.
Dotted arrows represent negative influence in the direction of the arrow.

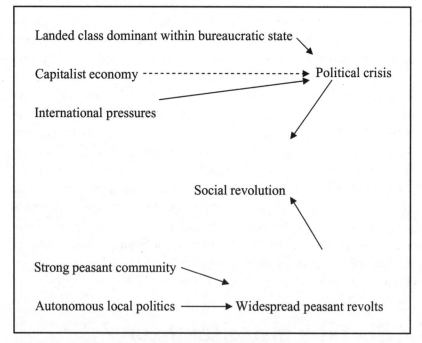

Figure 5.1 Skocpol's theory of social revolutions (Skocpol 1979).
Solid arrows represent positive influence in the direction of the arrow.
Dotted arrows represent negative influence in the direction of the arrow.

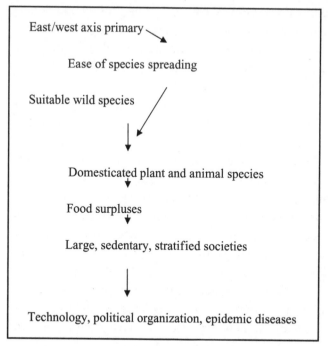

Figure 5.2 Diamond's theory of development (Diamond 1998: 87)
Solid arrows represent positive influence in the direction of the arrow.

and the next. I take these sorts of examples to be the most plausible current examples of historical theories: scientific theories that are oriented towards particular events, processes and facts typically regarded as falling under the purview of historical understanding. In this section I make three comments about these sorts of historical theory. First, they are to some extent functional theories. Second, they are at the social level, not that of individual people. Third, they are models.

The terms in historical theories tend to be functional.[4] Functional terms are those defined either by effect (output), or alternatively by cause and effect (input and output). A mathematical string (such as '+2') can be defined functionally, by listing the linked pairs of inputs and outputs (-1 and 1, 0 and 2, 1 and 3 ...). A biological term such as 'heart' is defined by its effects: pumping blood around the body. Likewise, a social term such as 'voting' is functional: it is the activity that has the effect of deciding the coming election. (Functional terms should be contrasted with structural terms; 'water', for instance, is defined not in terms of cause and effect, but according to its molecular structure.)

That named by the functional term (the heart, voting) can, in addition, be explained by its functions (pumping blood, deciding the coming election). Such *functional explanations* depend on the causal relations, though interestingly the explanatory relation runs opposite to the causal: things are explained in terms of the effect they have, not what brings them about.

Functional terms have a couple of interesting features. Two situations or objects may have the same intrinsic features, and yet one be a positive instantiation of the functional term, and one not. For example, someone may go through exactly the same motions (going into a booth; marking, folding and posting a piece of paper) in two different countries, but due to the political system one be voting where the other merely participates in a sham. Conversely, two situations or objects may have very different intrinsic features, and yet both be examples of the same functional term. Voting may be achieved by marking a paper, shouting out, typing on a computer, remaining silent: the list is potentially endless, since there are an indefinite number of ways to achieve the same effect. One functional state may, as the philosophical jargon goes, be 'multiply realized'. And, as the example of voting suggests, multiple realization is not only a possibility but to be expected when theorizing about social situations.

We can learn two things from multiple realization. First, the existence of functional terms provides another indicator of the focus of historical theory upon mutual competition (Chapter 4). This is because multiple realization is an indicator of there being a common design problem across different environments. We observe common functional solutions in animals with different evolutionary heritages: pterodactyl and archaeopteryx, goat and wallaby, lion and wolf. Similarly, human technological solutions tend to exhibit functional commonality. The missile weapon is a solution to the problem of how to kill at a distance, variously realized by slings, bows and arrows, rifles and more. The pyramid is a solution to the problem of how to build a large structure (in the absence of post-Classical engineering and construction skills), though built from different materials and to different specifications.

The second lesson from multiple realization is that we should not expect to be able to *reduce* the science that uses the functional term to a more fundamental science. This issue invites comparison between two visions of historical theory, or scientific history: reductive and individualistic, or non-reductive and social. The reductive vision has traditionally been favoured in philosophical and speculative attempts to found historical science, a classic example being John Stuart Mill:

> The laws of the phenomena of society are, and can be, nothing but the laws of the actions and passions of human beings united together in the social state. Men, however, in a state of society, are still men; their actions and passions are obedient to the laws of individual human nature.
>
> (1974: Book VI, Chapter 7)

According to this programme, history is reduced to its component parts: individual people. The more philosophically precise versions of the individualist vision have gone on to stress that 'reduced' should be taken to mean that the historical phenomena be explainable in terms of *laws* at the individual level. There are major difficulties with this programme, which explains why it has never been seriously carried out. Not only does one doubt the potential of psychology to deliver laws of the desired sort, but multiple realizability in any case renders a reductionism epistemically impotent. To see why, consider a putative law of historical science, each term of which is functional: 'All Fs are G'. To understand 'F' as multiply realizable is to commit to a claim of the form 'F is α, or β, or χ...', where the properties indicated by Greek letters are those of the more fundamental science. Thus, to reduce the initial law would lead to one being committed to a further law of which each term is disjunctive. What really counts against a reductive understanding of this sort is not so much the presence of disjunction, but the fact that those disjunctions are *open-ended*, given the unlimited number of ways that a functional term may be realized. In short: individualist *scientific* history is best left to science fiction.[5]

Historical theories describe models that contain related causal powers. Models provide more information than a simple list of generalizations (in which way positivism understood scientific theory). For example, the atomic model states not only that every atom has neutrons and electrons, but specifies the relation between atom, neutron and electron. Further, models have a structure that can be applied across different ontological domains. Classical mechanics could provide a description of electrical phenomena, even though electricity was never mentioned in the original formulation of that model (van Fraassen 1980: 66). Likewise, chaotic models can be applied to the weather, to biological populations, or to patterns of turbulence. Game-theoretic models can be applied to both superpower and evolutionary arms races.

The pressing questions for historical theories do not arise from *a priori* resistance, which I hope to have argued against thus far. Rather, the question is whether historical theories can be justified by the evidence; and if so, how? I have argued that it is not realistic to expect causal powers to be manifested universally because of the complex world that is the subject matter of the causal sciences. That makes the justification of general causal claims more difficult, though not impossible: as I now argue, theorists turn to suitable contrasts, quantitative techniques and mechanisms that explain how the suggested causal power operates.

5. Justifying historical theories: comparison and contrast

Jared Diamond provides an environmental explanation for the striking, disturbing, contemporary variation in 'development'[6], a variation most clearly seen in the relative wealth of nations (Figure 5.2). 'Proximate' causes of the variation are, Diamond claims, pretty easy to locate: the contemporary winners come from those areas of the world which first developed military technology (guns), which first colonized other continents (spreading germs), and which first industrialized (steel). Of more interest to Diamond are 'ultimate' environmental causes for the difference. The 'most important' of those environmental differences include differences in the stock of wild fauna and flora, relative continental area, degree of internal 'fragmentation' (provided by mountain ranges, for example), and direction of continental axis. Let's focus on the last point, which I will refer to as the 'axis claim'. Diamond's claim is that a nation's 'development' is causally dependent upon the nature of the axis of the continent from which that nation originated. Specifically, originating from a continent with an East–West axis, such as Eurasia, aids development, while originating from a continent with a North–South axis, such as the Americas, hinders development. How might Diamond seek to justify that causal generalization?

We might seek to justify a general claim by listing lots of particular cases where the general claim was realized, and finding no particular cases which contradicted that general claim. That would be to attempt justification by *enumerative induction*, one of the more intuitively obvious philosophical accounts of inference of generalizations. For example, 'all swans are white' would be justified so long as we had observed lots of white swans, and no swans of any other colour. Enumerative induction seems to be precluded in the case of the axis claim, given the small number of historical examples to call upon (presumably only Eurasia, the Americas, Africa and Australia). Yet we should not be too concerned on Diamond's behalf that the axis claim falls short by the standards of enumerative induction. The practice of scientists is a long way from amassing white swans. We can start to explain why that is by using the argument at the end of the previous chapter: the real world is a 'messy' amalgam of many causal forces, and in non-experimental settings we should not expect to observe the regular operation of a single causal force. Enumerative induction is a remnant of positivism. We should not expect or require it in scientific practice, and even if we were to find it we should – on pain of affirming 'accidental regularities' – demand additional justification.

Rather than looking for ways in which cases are alike, we would do better to look for ways in which they differ. The fact that historical theories are typically contrastive can aid us not only in understanding, as above, *explanatory focus*, but also *explanatory justification*. In the case of the axis claim, Diamond makes the contrasts quite explicit. The task is to explain why Eurasia was more developed than the Americas at the time of first cultural contact between the two. The explanation is in terms of a feature – having a predominantly East–West axis – that the former possesses, and the latter lacks.

We can rely on Mill's Method of Difference (detailed above) to see how a contrastive explanation of this sort can be justified. The Method of Difference permits us to infer a cause given two processes with contrasting end-points, so long as those processes differed in only a single earlier respect. That ideal explains the scientific practice of constructing a controlled experiment. In a controlled experiment, the scientist selects or produces two processes: the experimental process, containing the hypothesized cause, and the control process, differing from the former only in not containing the hypothesized cause. And, while historical theories must rely exclusively on non-experimental evidence, the Method of Difference also accounts for the social scientists' excitement with 'natural experiments': the non-experimental occurrence of cases approximating to the requirements of the Method of Difference. A natural experiment will be a pair of cases, one of which manifests the effect of interest and one of which does not, which otherwise are pretty much alike.

Diamond is quite aware of the potential of natural experiments. His clearest example (1988: Chapter 2) is of the conflict between Maori and Moriori peoples on the Moriori Chatham Islands, 500 miles east of New Zealand, in 1835. Both peoples were of Polynesian origins, diverging just 1,000 years earlier. Diamond claims that the differing environments of the Maori (New Zealand) and the Moriori (Chatham Islands) provide an excellent natural experiment by which to explain the Maori superiority, and (given that any result would locate a generally relevant causal feature) to suggest more general explanations of developmental difference between peoples. He finds that the key differences were in the land area of the island groups, the relative accessibility of other islands, and the environmental suitability of previously developed Polynesian agricultural techniques (Diamond 1998: 55–7). Skocpol also adopts a contrastive approach, concentrating not only on the similarities between the social revolutions that she examines – French, Russian and Chinese – but on the differences between these cases and those of nineteenth-century Prussia and Japan, and seventeenth-century England. Each of those cases is chosen in line with the requirements of the Method of Difference: they are, Skocpol argues, the non-revolutionary cases that bear most similarity to the nations which did experience social revolution.

Nonetheless, even the most aptly chosen natural experiment only approximates to the strict requirements of the Method of Difference. The contrast, if well chosen, will have been beneficial in winnowing down possible causes for the phenomenon in question, since we can exclude any historical feature which the contrast case shares. Nonetheless, there will always be a good many differences between target case and contrast case, any one of which could – according to a strict reading of the Method of Difference – provide the causal explanation. The 'axis claim', in particular, implies a contrast between historical properties of Eurasia and the Americas. Differences abound: from the intuitively more relevant (size, latitudes, native fauna) to the intuitively less relevant (precipitation levels, wind speeds, amount of underground oil). Many differences will be so manifestly irrelevant to the explanatory target as to be ignored by the historian: and rightly so, for one doubts whether it is even possible to list all differences, let alone investigate them in any useful manner. Further justification for one's theory of choice is therefore required. And, given our ease at discounting as 'obviously' irrelevant the vast majority of differences, it is clear that we do tend to find some other way to agree about what is causally relevant.[7]

Before examining what those other means might be, let us pause to ask how things change when the amount of data is large, in contrast to the case of the 'axis claim'. When the amount of data is large, a quantified approach is appropriate (Chapter 4). And though no amount of data alone justifies a causal claim, the potential pitfalls outlined in this section can be rendered less likely. Consider McCormick's investigation into the relation between economic status and political choice in the mid-nineteenth-century USA (McCormick 1959; used as an example in Aydelotte 1966). Where the evidence consists only of data about economic status and overall votes cast, the chance of justifying any hypothesis connecting the two is remote. But McCormick was fortunate, and clever, enough to find data derived from the voting patterns of a useful subsection of the electorate in North Carolina 1836–1856: only the rich (those owning more than 50 acres) voted for state senators, while all freemen voted for the governor. In this case, one can, according to the Method of Difference, compare any difference in voting patterns to the difference in economic status. And given the large data set, the possibility of confounding differences (analogous to precipitation, wind, oil mentioned in the previous example) is reduced. So long as the data is suitably spread: it would be no good, for example, if all senatorial voting occurred in one half of North Carolina, and all governorial voting occurred in the other half, because there would then be two obvious explanations of the ensuing difference in voting pattern. This requirement explains the standard practice in medicine and other applied sciences when using large data sets to test causal hypotheses, of assigning people to test-group and control-group by alphabetical order, or some other variable obviously irrelevant to the contrast to be explained.

6. Justifying historical theories: explaining how

Diamond's axis claim does not rest solely on a contrastive comparison between properties of the two continents. What makes the claim persuasive is that he provides a reason to think that primary continental axis is a causally efficacious variable. Diamond gives a mechanism connecting causal variable and differential outcome; a plausible story as to *how* the variable and outcome are connected. For the axis claim, the bones of Diamond's story are as follows. Transmission of technological innovation is vital for relative development, on the basis that a number of groups sharing technology will develop quicker than isolated groups forced to innovate all of that technology alone. Most technological innovations are environment specific, especially those which have made the most difference to civilizational development: agricultural innovations. A continent with an East–West axis has a more homogenous environment than one with a North–South axis, since the former spans fewer lines of latitude than the latter (latitude, but not longitude, correlates with features that make a significant environmental difference, especially mean temperature). Net result: predominant continental axis can be seen to affect development.

Given that outline, we can begin to appreciate the complexity of justificatory links, a complexity that was hidden when we first focused on the white swans. Diamond's justification by mechanism demonstrates that one does not simply find particular cases which tally with one's favoured hypothesis, or conflict with an opposing hypothesis. Additional claims are required, including of relative importance (consideration of which I shall postpone until the next chapter): 'agricultural innovations have had a greater impact on development than other innovations'. The justification also relies upon other general causal claims: 'latitude affects environment'; 'transmission occurs more quickly across more similar environments'. Given that each of these general claims can themselves be evidentially queried, we can see that the justification of a historical theory can be a complex endeavour.

Justification by mechanism are perhaps best seen not only as 'how' explanations, but as 'how possible' explanations (Dray 1957: 158–60). The 'how possible' explanation accounts for some puzzling feature of the world by suggesting a second feature that makes the first likely and, while not itself known to be true, does fit with our other knowledge. 'How possible' explanations are not determined by the evidence. That need not be a problem – they can be enlightening nonetheless – but we should be wary of the 'how possible' explanation that is nothing more than a neat and tidy story. Consider Kipling's *Just So Stories* (1902). The just so story 'explains' some animal's distinctive feature (the elephant's trunk or the leopard's spots) with a story that neatly fits that feature, yet for which there is no evidence. In fact, Kipling's stories are deliberately playful and ridiculous 'explanations' of the animal features. But it does not stretch Kipling's invention too far to use the term for any neat story that purports to explain how something happened, but for which there is no evidence. Does Diamond's justification deserve the title of a 'just so story'? A reason for thinking that it might stems from the possibility of formulating an equally plausible how-possible explanation for what did not happen. And if that is so, then *both* justifications should be regarded as just so stories. Imagine a close possible world in which we find an environmental historian arguing as follows:

'Why did China succeed in 'discovering' the rest of the world, developing superior military technology, and industrializing first? To answer that, one must compare the Chinese case with appropriate contrasts – particularly Europe – and explain the mechanism which ensured that China would emerge on top. It is not that European people lacked innovative skills, or the desire to explore and understand the world around them. No, it was geographical factors that counted against Europe, specifically the division of their lands by mountain ranges, major rivers, and an abundance of minor seas and inlets. For that reason, Europe could never become politically unified, no ruler ever being able to better in that respect the Roman Emperor Trajan. The Chinese could enjoy continued political unity, and hence a swifter route to development, while the European attempts were pitted against frequent wars with their consequential economic drain, and endemic suspicion that engendered a refusal to share technology across borders.'

If we want to be able to avoid just so stories in our justification of historical theories, we had better be able to properly ground the elements of any justification by mechanism that we provide. How can causal claims be justified in a way that does not simply assume other, equally problematic, causal claims? First, one could take the mechanistic analogy seriously, and refine one's theory by experimental manipulation in the way indicated in the previous section. Given the lack of possible experimental basis for historical theory, I won't fill out the detail of this approach here (instead, see Day and Botterill 2007). Second, one could take the story analogy seriously. This second approach would seek to justify general theories by working through particular narratives. That will be the topic of Chapter 6.

Further reading and study questions

Garfinkel A. (1981) *Forms of Explanation: Rethinking the Questions in Social Theory*. New Haven: Yale University Press. One of the pioneers (with van Fraassen 1980) of contrastive explanation, and with a specific focus on social topics. The introduction, and chapters 1 and 5 are particularly recommended.

Lipton, P. (2004) *Inference to the Best Explanation*. London: Routledge (originally 1991). Chapter 3 provides a detailed examination of the mutual relevance of causal and contrastive explanation.

Oakeshott, M. (1933) *Experience and its Modes*. Cambridge: Cambridge University Press. Pages 126–45 are a sustained critique of causal notions in history. This passage is reprinted in Dray, W. H. (ed.) (1966). *Philosophical Analysis and History*. New York: Harper and Row.

(a) What is singular causation, and why should the historian be inclined to think that it should be possible?

(b) Is all explanation contrastive?

(c) Is Diamond's 'axis claim' justified, given the evidence here provided? If not, could there be *any* evidence which could so justify it?

Theory and particular 6

Chapter Outline

1. The historian's role

Scientists aim to describe general relations, and to use the resulting general statements to understand what has happened, is happening, and will happen in *particular* cases. That claim was qualified in the previous chapter: the causal sciences do not seek perfectly universal regularities, since their focus is real-world complexity. But even here, understanding is provided by citing causal powers that produced the outcome, and these causal powers are general features of the world. If, for example, the claim is that it is Brown's smoking that has caused her cancer, then it is Brown's habit considered as instance of the general property 'smoking' that is explanatorily relevant. And if the claim is that the USSR's heavy logistical loads caused its collapse, then it is the general property 'having heavy logistical loads' that is explanatorily relevant. We have already challenged the supposed scientific ideal of universal regularity. In this chapter we take a further step in order to challenge the weaker scientific ideal of the prioritization of the general that is implied in these two examples.

If a scientific approach demands that we understand historical events and processes in terms of their general features, then one way of arguing for anti-naturalism is to argue that history is necessarily concerned with the particular alone. Historians, it is often said, deal with particular wars, elections, economic crashes, intellectual developments, and not with wars, elections, economics or thought in general. This objection to scientific history is not only popular among many working historians, but has a heavyweight philosophical heritage. Late nineteenth-century neo-Kantians, in particular Windelband (1980/1894), were keen to carve a unique epistemic role for the historical disciplines. Their proposal was that while the natural sciences are 'nomothetic', delivering understanding through theories composed of general laws, history is a necessarily particular, or 'idiographic' science.

Before expanding on this sort of 'particularist anti-naturalism', I want to clearly specify what the *naturalist* makes of the relation between particular and general in historical practice. We apply a theory to particular cases with a view to moving in one of two directions. Either the particular case is employed to test, confirm and modify the general theory. Or the theory is used to explain and understand the particular, and to infer backwards or forwards in time to generate further particular knowledge. The naturalist will *not* expect that all historians will become scientific theorists. No, the central focus of historical scholarship could remain the study of particular historical happenings, so long as those particular happenings were explained by general laws or powers, and so long as those particular happenings were used to confirm or disconfirm other general laws. The historian, according to this picture of the discipline, is rather like the experimentalist, though an experimentalist with the peculiar handicap of having to examine afresh old experiments, given their inability to implement new ones. (The institutional division that exists between mainstream history and the historical social sciences – political science, macrosociology and comparative sociology, economic history – is therefore rather to be expected according to this naturalist vision.)

Conversely, the anti-naturalist must emphasize that the historian's understanding of the particular can not be derived from general laws. I shall suggest some reasons why particular historical happenings fit awkwardly or not at all with general theories. That reasoning is either *a priori*, or *a posteriori*.

2. *A priori* argument from particularity

The first sort of argument that we shall consider is ambitious: from the premise that the historical past is a unique process, an unqualified anti-naturalist conclusion is drawn. This argument is *a priori* in the sense that we don't have to examine heterogeneous historical practice; the conclusion instead follows from undeniable features of the historical past itself. Karl Popper's *The Poverty of Historicism* (1957) well exemplifies arguments of this sort. Popper's main focus in that work was to criticize what he called 'historicism': to him, this was the doctrine that the historical past should be understood at a global level in terms of moving from one definite Period to another. (I warn the reader to consult my Chapter 9 for a more orthodox understanding of 'historicism'.) The movement of the Hegelian world-Spirit along the path to Absolute Knowledge (an approach explained in outline in my Chapter 1), and the transition of Marxist modes of production were among Popper's central targets. *Pro-naturalistic* historicism further explains this movement in terms of general laws, analogous to those of physics. Popper's arguments in his criticism of pro-naturalistic historicism can be used to elucidate the claim that we are at present interested in: that history's concern with the particular undermines naturalism.

The central thought is that *the past doesn't repeat* (Popper 1957: 108–9). Even as mundane an act as eating a meal is not repeated, in its every detail, by any other act of eating. Still more, then, should we say that each war differs from any preceding war, and that each intellectual breakthrough is correspondingly unique. From that premise, one can argue that naturalism is false, as follows:

(i) To confirm a law requires two or more instances of that law.
(ii) Multiple instantiation of a law requires repetition.
(iii) The subject matter of history doesn't repeat.
(iv) Therefore, there can be no confirmation of historical laws.
(v) Naturalism requires the existence of confirmed (justified) laws or causal generalizations.
(vi) Therefore, naturalism is false.

(The above argument is not diminished if we substitute 'causal generalization' for 'law')

Thus Popper argues:

> it is clear that any law ... must be *tested* by new instances before it can be taken seriously by science. But we cannot hope to test a universal hypothesis nor to find a natural law acceptable to science if we are for ever confined to the observation of one unique process. ... The most careful observation of *one* developing caterpillar will not help us to predict its transformation into a butterfly.
>
> (1957: 109)

If a process is unique, we can only observe what has so far happened; we have no handle on what will happen next. An example might be the quantitative series measuring *television money paid to Premiership football clubs*. As Popper notes, we may certainly *suggest* laws on the basis of such a unique process: we might hypothesize that all such series geometrically increase without temporal limit, or we might hypothesize that all such series reach a high point of 10 times its starting point, before then declining at the same rate. We might even – with luck – arrive at a *true* law given only a unique process. However, that law can not be *justified*, or confirmed, in the absence of multiple instances. Without repetition, we're condemned to blindly projecting existing trends, or to the guesswork of picking when those trends will cease or be reversed. (Recall the end of Chapter 4 for further discussion of trends and laws.)

Nonetheless, the argument can be challenged in two ways. Premise (i) is not nearly so secure as it might at first appear, given that the confirmation of general claims need *not* proceed by amassing instances (a claim examined in some detail in the previous chapter, and rather at odds with Popper's own comments on *falsification*, reported in Chapter 4). Premise (iii), while true for some sense of 'repeat' – the sense appealed to in the initial motivating examples of wars, intellectual breakthroughs and meals – need not be accepted by the naturalist. The naturalist may insist that history *does* repeat, when considered at a sufficiently abstract level: for example, at the level of the abstract concepts 'war', 'meal', 'intellectual breakthrough'. In Chapter 4 I pointed out that abstraction is a relative term: any language at all can be regarded as abstract to some extent. Thus history can be said to repeat, though that does not imply the obviously false idea that some later event is a minutely precise *replication* of an earlier event.

3. Applying general terms

I have suggested that there are two ways to investigate the relation between general theories and (historical) particulars: the latter confirming the former, and the former being used to explain or understand the latter. The issue of how particular observations confirm general theory has tended to hog the philosophical limelight. But the fact remains that, even according to the naturalist's picture of historical research, most historians will not be employed in the development and testing of general theories. Most will, rather, be concerned with applying general theories to particular events, processes and periods. That alone suggests that we pay more attention to the second disjunct, the use of general theory to illuminate particular goings-on. And we shall see that this use and application of general theory is by no means a straightforward business.

Let's first flesh out the naturalist understanding of the application of general to particular, by suggesting the following three principles. (These principles are intended to give a flavour of the relation between theory and particular envisaged by the naturalist. It may well be possible for one to remain a naturalist and yet deny elements of what follows.)

- General terms are applied to particular cases simply by observing whether or not the particular case exhibits a certain, measurable property. We generally have calibrated instruments to measure fundamental properties such as length or temperature. Even where there is no single calibrated instrument that can be used, the general term is sufficiently operationalized (Chapter 4) to permit unproblematic application to a particular case. To return to poor Brown and her cancer: the relevant observations to make might be technically difficult, but once those observations have been made the question of applying the term 'cancer' is definitively decided.

- Once we have understood the particular things as manifesting some abstract term, the application of the associated theory can be approached deductively. If the mass is x kg and the force upon it is y Newtons, then given that $F = ma$, we can deduce that the acceleration is y/x (metres per second per second). If Brown has cancer, and people with cancer have a 40 per cent chance of dying within the year, then we can deduce that Brown has a 40 per cent chance of dying within the year.

- If there is more than one applicable nomic relation, then one should understand their combination by numerical technique. Students of mechanics are trained to do this in a variety of fictional situations, in which forces of gravity, tension, friction, the centrifugal and centripetal are summed and so the resulting behaviour of the system deduced (see Figure 4.1).

We can make a case for the contravention of each of these three principles by historical application of theory. Let's begin with the ascription of abstract terms. We do find plenty of historiographical debate concerning the definition and scope of abstract terms. Consider *bourgeoisie*, as it has been applied to debate concerning pre-Revolutionary France. The traditional understanding of the term was derived from Marxist theory, and applied to the origin and development of the French Revolution by historians such as Georges Lefebvre (1947). The Marxist bourgeoisie were capitalists, industrialists and financiers. They were in the economic ascendancy. They were believers in Enlightenment ideals: unfettered commerce and trade, scientific advancement, the abolition of privilege of birth. Later revisionists, in particular Alfred Cobban (1964) and George Taylor (1967) turned this picture on its head. The bourgeoisie were, if anything, economic conservatives, not economic radicals. Although the revisionists were keen to emphasize the diversity of 'the bourgeoisie', they did believe that the majority made their living from the law, from crown bonds and offices, and they stood to lose much from the increase in unfettered capitalism. Indeed, it was those Marxist creatures of reaction – the nobility – who were more occupied with the accumulation of capital through commerce and industry.

What is interesting about this debate is that it concerns not only what should be ascribed to the bourgeoisie, but also how they should be identified; who they were, as well as what they did. Whether *bourgeoisie* is applicable, and how it should be applied, turns on two questions. First, on how homogeneous or heterogeneous those labelled 'bourgeois' in fact were. And second, on how wide or narrow the gap was between those labelled 'bourgeois' and others, notably the nobility. The abstract term is more appropriate to the extent that the former disjunct of each question is affirmed. Not only are these complicated empirical questions, but given that the questions permit answers on a continuous spectrum, some element of judgement is unavoidable in ascribing or withholding the abstract term.

Understanding of this sort of debate can be sharpened by considering a different example: Theda Skocpol's application of her own theory of social revolution to the Communist Revolution in China. Skocpol's general theory of social revolution states that two causes are sufficient for social revolution (1979: 154, and see my Figure 5.1):

(1) state organizations susceptible to administrative and military collapse when subjected to intensified pressures from more developed countries abroad;
(2) agrarian socio-political structures that facilitated widespread peasant revolts against landlords.

The problem with Skocpol's own discussion of the Chinese case is that the second condition does not appear to be met. The Chinese gentry were at the centre of rural life: organizing and co-opting peasants into militias, societies of various kinds, and poor relief. The local gentry thereby managed, in the main, to align 'their' peasants with themselves, and against agents of the central state. What 'peasant revolts' there were, therefore, were directed against the state, not against local landlords. It seems, then, that the second condition has not been met in the Chinese case, an inference which threatens Skocpol's general theory. But Skocpol's response is to re-interpret her second condition, such that it is exemplified in the Chinese case (1979: 151–4). Although the 'socio-political structures' did not facilitate solidarity of settled peasantry in opposition to landlords, they did have the effect of producing a marginalized peasant underclass, who strongly exacerbated any socio-political crisis. We could conclude from the example of Skocpol that historical theorists will go to a lot of trouble to save their theories from falsification. But I think that a rather kinder conclusion is more justified. In this not atypical case, the abstract term is *open ended*. There are different sorts of 'widespread peasant revolts against landlords', and different ways for structures to 'facilitate revolt'. The ways of exemplifying each of those terms can not be exhaustively specified, and certainly not in advance of carrying out detailed particular studies. For that reason, applying the term to the particular will be a matter of judgement, not deduction.

One final example is of a still more drastic modification of the general theory on the basis of a particular case (and, crucially, only for the service of that particular case). Ian Kershaw applies Max Weber's theory of charismatic leadership to Nazi Germany (Kershaw 1991). Weber (1964/1947) defines charismatic leadership as the prevalence of the personal, rather than the bureaucratic; and of emotive justification, rather than of 'rational' wealth creation and expenditure. Charismatic leadership flourishes in extraordinary situations, and in times of crisis such as war, or when society is faced with some important, unexplainable situation. The charismatic leaders 'turn away from the world' of routine organization and control (1964: 1113–14). To the extent that they attain power, they will find themselves subsumed by the bureaucratic and impersonal: 'the charismatic message inevitably becomes dogma, doctrine ... law or petrified tradition' (1964: 1125).

Kershaw explicitly, and without qualm, modifies central aspects of this theory to apply it to Nazi Germany. Most significantly, the Nazi state is understood by Kershaw as 'incessantly charismatic'; an observation which explains Germany's seemingly irrational need to keep expanding, to keep searching for new enemies, until the Charismatic state was eventually defeated. That inference runs exactly counter to Weber's insistence that the Charismatic leadership will become bureaucratized as it gains power. Naturalism would require Kershaw to adopt one of two routes. He should either refrain from applying the concept 'Charismatic rule' to the Nazi state, or in applying it he should conclude that Weber's theory is incorrect. Kershaw does neither: he modifies the theory for *this specific case*. That modification is justified by the degree to which the modified theory can illuminate the nature of the historical particular, in this case the Nazi state. And it seems to be able to do just that, demonstrating the connections between the importance of the prior collapse of the Weimar state; Hitler's obsession with prestige, theatrical effect and propaganda; the intensely personal nature of power from the Führer downwards; and the Nazi state's self-destructive (as well as other-destructive) tendencies. If we are to defend Kershaw's application, rather than criticize it as fragrantly unscientific, then the suspicion is that we must understand the application as one of 'shedding light', as an artistic style sheds light on a culture, or as an apt metaphor sheds light on a too-familiar activity.

4. The 'chemical' sciences

Let's turn from the application of abstract *terms* to particular cases, to the application of wider *theory* to particular cases. An interesting argument can be found in Collingwood's *Autobiography* (1970) for the conclusion that history is necessarily concerned with the particular, and that the discipline therefore requires an ineliminable judgement, or intuition, for particular cases. Even in a situation for which we have general laws, the interrelation of those laws requires assessment of the particular case. Collingwood's example raises the point in terms of moral rules, rather than scientific laws, but the argument can be adapted to the latter as much as the former.

> Thus everybody has certain rules according to which he acts in dealing with his tailor. These rules are, we will grant, soundly based on genuine experience; and by acting on them a man will deal fairly with his tailor and helps his tailor to deal fairly by him. But so far as he acts according to these rules, he is dealing with his tailor only in his capacity as a tailor, not as John Robinson, aged sixty, with a weak heart and a consumptive daughter, a passion for gardening and an overdraft at the bank. The rules for dealing with tailors no doubt enable you to cope with the tailor in John Robinson, but they prevent you from getting to grips with whatever else there may be in him. Of course, if you know that he has a weak heart, you will manage

your dealings with him by modifying the rules for tailor-situations in the light of the rules for situations involving people with weak hearts. But at this rate the modifications soon become so complicated that the rules are no longer of any practical use to you.

(1970: 104–5)

For each and every property of the given particular situation, we can grant that we possess a general rule for how to act when faced with a situation manifesting that property. Nonetheless, we can see that it is possible – even likely – that those rules will be unable to guide our action. And we can even go further than Collingwood's claim that the gap between general rules and particular judgement is due to the 'complication' of modified general rules. More fundamentally, it is not clear *how* to modify the rules for one situation (dealing with tailors) in the light of another (dealing with people with weak hearts). Certainly, the nature of the modification is not given in either the 'tailor-rule' or the 'weak heart-rule'. The combination of rules in a particular situation cannot be assessed by applying the individual rules.[1]

As I've said, we are not concerned so much with the use of rules (moral or otherwise) to guide our conduct, as with the application of general scientific theories in order to understand and explain a particular case. The latter can be illustrated by considering Skocpol's first necessary condition for social revolution: that societies are more prone to revolution when the state is subject to intensified pressure from more developed competitors abroad. That law will tell you what will happen in a case of intensified geopolitical competition. But what are we to conclude in a particular, real-world case, exhibiting not only intensified geopolitical competition, but also ruled by a shy and retiring though highly popular monarch, and experiencing a rise in wages? The assessment is just as difficult as Collingwood's ethical case. For rising prosperity is thought to decrease the chance of revolution, just as increased geopolitical competition increases that chance. (And the monarch might conceivably make a difference to the chance of revolution either way, or might make no difference at all.) How should this predicament be solved? Not, it seems, by appeal to general principles.

Consider how this predicament is solved in application of mainstream scientific theory. There are two possibilities, each rendering quite unnecessary any specific focus on the *particular* case at hand. First, the general claims might be situated within a relation of combined necessity and sufficiency, as in the case of Skocpol's two criteria. Each of Skocpol's criteria are individually necessary, such that if either wasn't present, then the effect (social revolution) would not occur. And they are jointly sufficient, such that whenever both are present, then the effect follows; a claim that renders the theory *as a whole* universally applicable. If a claim is genuinely universal then there will be no issue of how its effect must be modified by *other* general claims, because the universal by definition brooks no exceptions. This is all well and good if borne out, but, in Chapter 4, we found reason to doubt that causal theories of this sort would attain universality. The example of the previous paragraph compounds that doubt.

The second way to deal with the problem of combining theories is to ensure that the general claims are numerically additive. The case of applied mechanics, already alluded to, exemplifies that program. There is no difficulty in supposing that as many mechanical forces as you like are operative in a particular situation. For the strength of each force can be given a numerical value precisely comparable to values given to any other force. Further, the *tendency* of each force is the same, no matter what else is true of the particular situation. John Stuart Mill called sciences that exhibit this property of additivity the 'mechanical' sciences, against which he contrasted what he called the 'chemical' sciences: those in which the effect of combining properties is unpredictable and non-uniform. Though Mill recognized the distinction, he over-optimistically took the human sciences ('moral sciences', to use Mill's term) to be mechanical, not chemical:

> The laws of the phenomena of society are, and can be, nothing but the laws of the actions and passions of human beings united together in the social state. Men, however, in a state of society, are still men; their actions and passions are obedient to the laws of individual human nature. Men are not, when brought together, converted into another kind of substance, with different properties; as hydrogen and oxygen are different from water, or as hydrogen, oxygen, carbon, and azote are different from nerves, muscles, and tendons. Human beings in society have no properties but those which are derived from, and may be resolved into, the laws of the nature of individual man. In social phenomena the Composition of Causes is the universal law.
>
> (Mill 1974: Book 6, Chapter 7, Section 1)

Mill's confidence in the mechanistic nature of the historical sciences is related to his proposal that the historical sciences should be reducible to the laws of psychology. Precisely how general laws combine in particular historical cases is not a matter for philosophy, but for historical study itself. Nonetheless, regarding history as 'chemical' in this sense does account for some of the typical difficulty in historical theorizing and prediction. Identifying the causal elements that lay behind a given event or process with some degree of justi-fication is an achievable aim. But very rarely is it possible to be able to predict how those causal elements will combine. Writing in 2007, as the American-led war in Iraq drags on, one can identify what will be the major causal elements. But no one knows how they will combine in the particular potent stew that is post-Saddam Iraq. No one knows how the war will finish, though future historians will not have much difficulty in picking out causes of that ending.

5. Combining theories in practice

I don't mean to imply that all historical theories are *useless* when we are faced with a combination of causal properties; just that the application of a theory is a matter for particular judgement. Consider again Jared Diamond's expla-nation of European superiority in terms of environmental causes. I've already given some idea of the importance that Diamond places upon the continent-relative potential for diffusion of technology. But Diamond is sensitive to the potential for easy diffusion to hinder, as well as aid, development. Consider the case of early fifteenth-century China, a state significantly more technologi-cally advanced than its European contemporaries. Vast treasure fleets were sent across the Indian Ocean to Africa, and came close to rounding the Cape, open-ing the way to a Chinese 'discovery' of Europe. But these fleets were recalled; and within a century it was Mediterranean sailing vessels that came to China, rather than Chinese Junks to Europe. How should we account for the Chinese 'failure'? Diamond (1998: 412–16) points out that a political decision of this sort, resulting as it did from a highly specific local power struggle (in the Chinese case, between the Eunuch party and their opponents), could not have had the same sweeping effect in Europe. The reason was that Europe had long been politically fragmented, where China had been highly unified. And that dif-ference is explained by the greater ease of technological and cultural diffusion in China than in Europe.

To return to our central concern, should we regard Diamond's theory as being useless in application to the Chinese case? After all, he has given us two conflicting rules – that geographical ease of movement aids development, and that it hinders development. His (implied) answer must be that each rule holds under specific circumstances. Roughly, once political centralization reaches a certain point, the negative effects (towards economic and other development) of diffusion outweigh the positive. That answer is plausible, though it is notable that Diamond nowhere provides precise criteria for how the negative and positive effects of diffusion interact. And nor should he: historical theories, just as moral rules, are rules of thumb which must be applied sensitively, and with particular knowledge.

Gregory Hooks' study of US investment strategy in the Second World War provides another example of the task required to combine theories with regard to a particular case (Hooks 1993). Hooks explicitly privileges a scientific understanding, introducing three theoretical frameworks by which to comprehend the particular US case. Yet these three frameworks – State Autonomy, Business Dominance Theory (BDT) and Marxism – are incompatible. Roughly, the first says that investment policy is decided by the state (central government), in the interests of the state. The second says that investment policy is dictated by and is in the interests of big business. The third agrees that business is key to policy, but rejects the centrality of business self-interest for the claim that the central function of investment policy is the concentration and centralization of capital. But Hooks, in his discussion of US investment policy, refuses to champion one theory at the cost of the other two. Instead he, like Kershaw, adapts each theory to the particular case. And this adaptation is also justified by the fact that each theory 'sheds some light' on (different aspects of) the particular case (1993: 43). Hooks' adaptation is somewhat more conservative than Kershaw's, in so far as the application of each theory is *restricted* in the former, and *extended* in the latter. Hooks tightens the antecedent conditions of each theory. For example, he recommends restricting the application of BDT to government decisions where all of the following are met:

- Rules of governance are visible and openly debated.
- The decisions are salient to economic elites.
- State institutions are accessible to economic elites.

Hooks' antecedent restrictions allow him to keep the theoretical competition at bay. I have two concerns. The lesser concern is that there is a tendency for such conditions to drain empirical content from the theories. In particular, examine the third condition of applicability of BDT. State institutions are presumably taken to be 'accessible' to economic elites where those elites are able to influence those institutions. But if that is the case, then BDT becomes the claim that business shapes government policy only if business is able to influence government policy. (Hooks' explanation would then exemplify the charge made in Chapter 4, that historical generalization tends towards the analytic as it is universalized.) The more substantial concern is that the principle of no overlapping theory is surely incorrect. It is more likely that much of US investment policy manifested traces of state autocracy, business dominance and Marxist structure. Each theory will probably contribute something to explanation of the particular, but in ways and amounts that can only be decided by examining the particular process itself – not just the theories in the abstract.

Historians are always faced with this difficulty, and their practice shows awareness of that (perhaps none more so than the *Annales* historians who attempted to write 'total history'). Each process, or historical event, manifests causal elements derived from economic, intellectual, cultural, social and environmental theories. The mainstream historian attempts to overcome these difficulties by regarding the same historical phenomenon 'from different angles'. The presumption is that, since one can not say how general theories interact without examining the particular case, to be on the safe side one had better examine the particular using the tools of all available theories. Even in Collins' own explanation of Russian collapse (Figure 4.2), an explanation supposedly exemplifying his general theory, he sees it necessary to weave considerations of economics, armaments, ethnicity, intra-elite conflict, popular revolt, ideological resistance – and there is still a need to speak of 'accidents' (Collins 1995: 1587).

6. Narrative and theory

Collingwood drew the lesson that the historian's intuition for the particular required the 're-enactment' in the historian of the past actor's thoughts (to be discussed in Chapters 7 and 8). Here I want to emphasize how historians tackle the problems suggested in this chapter by turning to *narrative*. (Narrative will be further explored, though from a rather different perspective, in Chapter 10). Not all history is narrative: we also find quantitative surveys, extended descriptions of a single moment in time and discussion of general theory. Yet narrative is usually the form of writing that historians most comfortably reach for. As a philosopher, this reliance on narrative jumps out when I read a historian's treatment of what I would consider to be a philosophical or methodological question. In rebutting the (self-titled) 'holocaust revisionists', and assessing the plentiful evidence for the holocaust, Lipstadt (1993) structures her critique in the form of a narrative of holocaust denial. In describing the different historiographical approaches to the French Revolution, Tackett (1998: 193) provides us with an archetypal narrative for each. Even the paradigm works of scientific theorizing in history that have been my primary consideration – Skocpol, Collins, Diamond – contain far more narrative than they do explicit theorizing.

Focusing on narrative highlights four pertinent features of historical explanatory reasoning. Continuity: the explanation is justified by being situated in a narrative that bridges start and end without break. Detail: the explanation is justified by more closely examining it (rather than by situating within a more general theory). Causality assumed: in the process words that pepper the narrative. Importance: the saturation of narrative in explicit and implicit judgements of particular importance. The former two features provide an alternative way to understand justification by explaining *how*, considered in Chapter 5 with regard to Diamond's axis claim. To exemplify the latter two features, consider once more Collins' theory of state collapse.

Collins presents a narrative of Russian collapse in 1989, used to support the claims of his general theory (Figure 4.2). We are told in Collins' general theory that ethnic heterogeneity is a positive causal factor for state collapse, especially – as was the case for the 'Russian empire' – where there are two or more layers of ethnicity between the empire's centre and its periphery. (The pre-Second World War USSR already had one layer of heterogeneous ethnicity on its western border, in the Ukraine and Belarus. The second layer was formed by the incorporation of East Germany and other Eastern European states in 1945.) Collins' narrative explains how the general relationship between ethnic heterogeneity and state collapse manifested itself in this case. The era of openness (*Perestroika*) in 1980s Russia was a result of an intra-elite power struggle, the Gorbachev faction attempting to achieve public support at the expense of the military–industrial faction. *Perestroika* reacted combustively with the ethnic makeup of the Soviet Union. The liberalization 'let loose pressures for ethnic migrations all across the Soviet bloc' (Collins 1995: 1569). That causal claim is not explicitly justified, but is a sure bet *if* we are to grant the further fact that there was an underlying desire in many people to migrate for ethnic reasons. This agitation for ethnic movement, and the movement itself, is asserted by Collins to be a 'tipping point'. 'When Czechoslovakian borders, under pressure of mass movement agitation, were reopened on November 1, 1989, the flood of refugees turned into open regime opposition that mounted an attack on the symbolic border, the Berlin Wall' (1995: 1569). The particular causal processes are directly described, and so causal grounding is provided for the theory. Indeed, how could the situation that Collins here describes be written about *without* reference to causal processes?

One way of putting the problem of combining theories is to ask how one should *weight the importance* of those theories. I have argued that application of theory requires particular judgement. The same conclusion can be arrived at by considering the weighing of importance of causal elements. A given revolution will have many causes: how can we tell which are more important, and which less? If we mean which causes are *in general* more important for bringing about revolutions, then straightforward counting of the causes attaching to each revolution will probably suffice. If intra-elite conflict is a cause of four of five social revolutions, and inter-class conflict is a cause of two of five social revolutions, then intra-elite conflict is the more important cause of revolution in general. But if we mean which causes are more important in bringing about *this* revolution, then such frequency considerations will not decide the issue. Imagine a sixth revolution, accompanied both by intra-elite conflict and inter-class conflict. Given only the information presented above concerning frequency of causation, it is implausible to suppose that anything could be said about the relative importance of the causes of this sixth case. It is possible that inter-class conflict be more important in *this* case, despite being less frequently manifest in other revolutions.[2] (There is an interesting question lurking here that I shall bring out into the open in Chapter 9: to what extent are judgements of importance, and related judgements, the sort of judgements that can be *true*?)

In the previous section I used the 'chemical' nature of causal combination in historical subject matter to explain why one could explain an event in hindsight by identifying causes, but could not predict what would happen before the event. That point can also be put in terms of importance. There is so much potential causal information with regard to a particular event or process that one typically has a hard time identifying what *will* be most significant. With hindsight, a judgement of relative significance is much easier to make. Thomas Jefferson's much-quoted comment is apt: 'So inscrutable is the arrangement of causes and consequences in this world that a two-penny duty on tea, unjustly imposed in a sequestered part of it, changes the condition of all its inhabitants.'

Judgements of importance are implicit in all narratives, particularly the sort of complex narratives typical in history. In narrating historians select, arrange and establish significant themes, and connect causal processes. Judgements of importance are usually only implicitly justified – a fact which holds as much for the narratives occurring in the works of the 'historical theorists' as in more traditional historiography. Collins' talk of the 'tipping point' (quoted above) provides one example. Not only are judgements of importance typically present, but they seem necessary in order to apply historical theory to a particular case. Skocpol's criterion of intra-elite competition is often present to some degree, and yet plays no part in bringing about social revolution (consider the intense intra-elite competition engendered by the 2000 US Presidential election, which – of course – did not lead to social revolution). A judgement must be made as to whether the causal factor that is present is sufficiently important to satisfy the theory.

7. Is naturalism the best account of historical practice?

Let's take stock. Naturalism is the proposal that history is a science, not fundamentally different to other social and natural sciences. We have examined more specific forms of that proposal: that history is a completely abstract science like physics (Chapter 4), that history is a causally generalizing science like sociology (Chapter 5), and that history is the practice that applies and tests those causally generalizing sciences (Chapter 6).

One could, from a position of naturalism, regard the 'problems' identified in this chapter as an inevitable result of scientific theorizing in complex natural systems, and as challenges to develop better techniques of analysis and better application of results gained by scientific disciplines. Yet, these chapters have suggested other, anti-naturalistic explanations for historical practice, which will be pursued in the remainder of the book. We might regard history as:

- the application of contestable interpretations to the past, reliant not on scientific generalization but (poetic) analogy;
- the application of particular intuition or craft to the past, particularly in the form of narratives;
- the account of individual people in the past, tracing and assessing their motivations, beliefs and actions.

I pursue these suggestions in the remainder of the book.

Further reading and study questions

Tucker, A. (2004) *Our Knowledge of the Past: A Philosophy of Historiography*. Cambridge: Cambridge University Press. Chapter 4, 'Historiographic opinion', is noteworthy as being one of the few attempts to discuss the application of general theory to historical particulars, without collapsing that debate to that already covered in my Chapter 4.

(a) What, if anything, is problematic about applying general terms to particular historical cases? Can any general term be applied unproblematically?

(b) Given that the universe never repeats, how are natural scientists able to identify not only trends, but laws?

(c) To what extent do the problems raised in this chapter with regard to the application of theory apply to *any* real world science? (You might like to consider the science and prediction of flooding, volcanoes, buffalo populations in the Serengeti and atmospheric carbon levels.) To the extent that narrative is a plausible historical response to those problems, could one equally apply it to those examples?

Part III
HISTORY AS INTERPRETATION

Feeling and thought 7

1. Questions in the philosophy of interpretation

To interpret something is to make sense of it. We can make sense of speech and writing, actions, and works of art and literature, and so it is appropriate to speak of interpreting these things. Historians, in addition, provide interpretations of wider sections of the past (of periods and processes). Over the next two chapters I shall make use of cases of historical interpretation which exemplify this broad range. We shall examine interpretations of the *decisions* of the major European powers in July 1914; the *actions* of a group of eighteenth-century print workers in massacring cats; the *statements* made by a sixteenth-century miller to the Inquisition; and eighteenth-century English satirical *prints*. The interpretation of more extended periods and processes – the Renaissance, the process of German expansion in the 1930s, the French Revolution – will lead us into Part IV.

'Making sense' is perhaps too vague a notion. We can introduce more precision by connecting the task to the condition of achievement: one 'makes sense' in so far as one comes to understand the *meaning* of the object of interpretation. Meaning is obviously a property of speech and writing: without meaning we have only sounds and marks. Meaning is also a property of action; and a similar case can be made that without a suitable connection to meaning we have (mere) bodily behaviour, not action. So are works of art, historical periods, and historical processes meaningful; though whether in the same way that words and actions are is one question for the philosophy of interpretation. Finally, interpreting suggests some prior difficulty in finding meaning, or prior confusion of meaning that must be made clear and explicit. While to take part in conversation in one's native tongue requires one to understand meaning, it stretches normal usage to say that such conversation requires interpretation.

In approaching historical interpretation, I emphasize four issues: method, presupposition, evidence and naturalism. First, what is the methodology of historical interpretation; alternatively, how should historians interpret? Second, what does historical interpretation presuppose; in virtue of what is interpretation possible? It is important to see the difference between these first two questions. The target of the first is the explicit level of historical interpretation, the target of the second the implicit. The second has tended to be of greater philosophical interest. It is assumed that historians by and large know what they're doing when they interpret the past, and so don't need philosophers' methodological advice. On the other hand, to unearth the underlying presuppositions of interpretation requires digging of a distinctively philosophical sort. The philosophies of interpretation that will be surveyed privilege the second question in a similar way that Hempel privileged the implicit in his philosophy of explanation (Chapter 4). Hempel's central claim was that historical explanation presupposed general laws; without general laws there simply could not be an explanation. It was of secondary concern whether or not the historian's methodology counselled a search for such laws, and whether the explanations offered explicitly cited such laws.

Third, what relation does interpretation bear to the evidence? Does the evidence determine only one correct interpretation, or is correctness of interpretation underdetermined by the evidence? Fourth, does the fact that history is an interpretative discipline have consequences for the naturalism debate, begun in Part II? The last question will itself be largely a consequence of the first three, but it has often taken prominence in the philosophy of interpretation. It is usually supposed that those theorists who emphasize the interpretative nature of the historical activity are thereby arguing for anti-naturalism (in the sense defined in Chapter 4). But not only shall I challenge that inference in the next chapter, but there is in any case the danger that to place anti-naturalism at the heart of a philosophy of interpretation is to approach the issue of interpretation in a peculiarly negative way. Nonetheless, it is important to appreciate the putative connection between interpretation and anti-naturalism; to that end I offer the following brief history.

Giambattista Vico, writing in the late seventeenth and early eighteenth century, adopted the principle that the nature of the object of enquiry governs the nature of that enquiry (Vico 2002/1725). The key distinction in objects of knowledge was, for Vico, between those that the knower had created, and those which they had not: his *verum factum* principle. Where we have created something, we can know it more securely. Thus knowledge of history and the social world is more secure than knowledge of the natural world. Vico's insistence on such a fundamental divide between natural and historical (or social) knowledge was not echoed by mainstream Enlightenment thought; Vico was largely forgotten until the flowering of Romanticism in the early nineteenth century. (Indeed, it would not be too great a simplification to trace the genealogical tree of naturalism back to the Enlightenment, and that of anti-naturalism to Romanticism.)

Anti-naturalism, since at least the nineteenth century, has been an epistemic, not a metaphysical doctrine. Anti-naturalists do not commit themselves to the metaphysical distinction between mind and matter. In particular, they need not and typically do not affirm the dualism of substance that Descartes took to be a consequence of his foundational principle, 'I think, therefore I am'. Mind requires a different epistemology because it is free, because it judges and is judged, and because it is the locus of meaning. Thus, while natural scientists 'make sense' of the universe, their interpretative activities are quite different on account of the lack of meaning before they arrive on the scene. Newton found meaning and harmony in the universe, but before his description it was meaningless. Not so for the historian: the actions of print workers or diplomats are meaningful even before the historian arrives to interpret those actions. The historian is faced with a 'double hermeneutic': their object is already meaningful, the historians' meaning providing a secondary layer.[1] ('Hermeneutics' stems from the Greek word for the study of textual meaning.)

This line of thought has been pursued by German nineteenth-century Idealism, from Kant in the early nineteenth century, through Dilthey in the late nineteenth.[2] The epistemic consequences of the meaningfulness of mind have been emphasized in the twentieth century by French phenomenology, and by Anglo-American linguistic philosophy. Their conclusion has been that the apparatus of natural scientific understanding – laws, theories, causes, objectivity – is inappropriate for history (and social science). These tools can, to some extent, be applied to history, for it is undeniable that historians have used them, or at least believed that they were. But any such attempt creates a distorted understanding of history, which it is the task of the anti-naturalist philosopher to rectify.

2. Empathy

When I view a picture (perhaps *Quatre Bras* by Lady Butler), watch a film (perhaps *Downfall* (Der Untergang), Bernd Eichinger and Oliver Hirschbiege's magnificent recreation of Hitler's last days), or read a well-written historical description (as good an example as any other is Ginzburg's *Cheese and the Worms* (1992/1976), whose topic is Mennochio, the aforementioned sixteenth-century miller), then I feel that I am brought closer to the period. More than that: I am brought closer to those people of the past; to poor Mennochio, by some small degree to the unnamed British infantryman. (The sense to which one is brought 'closer' to those in the Führerbunker will of course require particularly careful specification, perhaps by carefully distinguishing empathy from sympathy.) We might, more precisely, regard this gain in understanding as a matter of my being able to empathize with those of the past.

Empathy is a good place to start our investigation of interpretation, not least because it has seemed to many to be at the centre of the historical activity. Johann Gottfried von Herder, one of the earlier Romantic anti-naturalists in the nineteenth century, was at the forefront of the 'Sturm und Drang' movement, an attempt to re-emphasize feeling and emotion following the neglect of Enlightenment thought. As such, the student of history should 'feel their way in' (*Einfühlung*) to that which they intend to interpret. The role of feeling in understanding the past is strongly emphasized in contemporary history teaching: see, for example, David Stockley's (1983) argument for the centrality of empathy for history teaching. Indeed, it might be doubted whether one can really avoid 'feeling himself into' the experiences of others. Only psychopaths can avoid observing another pain without feeling some echo of that pain. And recent research into mirror neurons suggest that the exact same part of the brain is activated when we observe an activity as when we perform that same activity.[3]

Any plausible account of the understanding of another in which empathy is to occupy a central role must, I think, refer to two steps. First: one must imaginatively adopt the experience of the other. For this, similarity of one's own prior experience can be valuable. If you have suffered a bereavement, then the fact that a good friend of mine died five years ago will help me to feel what you now do. More generally, we tend to accept that one who has had similar experiences can understand better. But similarity of experience is a help, not a requirement. What is crucial is use of the evidence to take an *imaginary* leap to what the other feels. While similarity of experience makes such a leap easier, it should be recognized that the importance of empathic understanding has been regarded in part precisely in terms of the test that it poses to our ability to imaginatively extend our own experience.

Second: the historian must not only feel what the other felt, but should then achieve self-knowledge of that feeling. To experience or feel something is not automatically to know that experience or feeling. True, self-knowledge often seems more direct than knowledge of what others are feeling, and it is on this presumption that empathic understanding is built: knowledge of another via knowledge of oneself. But we should not assume that self-knowledge is necessarily more direct, easy, or certain than is knowledge of others. The assumption that self-knowledge *is* necessarily different in these ways has been encouraged by the sort of foundationalist picture suggested by Descartes (see Chapter 11). In such a picture one's own mental 'objects' – thoughts and feelings – are known directly and with certainty, thereby providing a foundation for knowledge of the outside world, including other people. That philosophical picture will be challenged shortly; but really, we don't need a philosophical critique of Cartesianism in order to appreciate that self-knowledge can be less direct, easy, and certain than knowledge of others. One's partner, good friend, child and analyst often know us better than we know ourselves. (And we are quite familiar with the fictional plot featuring two people who outwardly detest each other and who are yet truly meant for each other; those two being the last to know.)

Let us return to the first step of empathic understanding, the imaginary adoption of another's experience. One might be sceptical of that possibility. How much of the others' experience must be reproduced? (Must one feel the infantryman's terror *and* excitement *and* concern for those back home (*etc.*) in order to have empathic understanding of any one of these feelings?) Can one adopt another's experience given that in our position of hindsight, we know how things turned out? (Does knowing that the British 28th Regiment in Butler's painting repulsed the French cavalry bar me from feeling the same desperate uncertainty of the British infantry?) Is it, in any case, ever possible to have two experiences that are exactly alike? (Perhaps the criteria of identity of feelings is like the infinitesimally detailed measurement of wavelength which defines colours, permitting similarity but never exact identity?) I won't dwell on these questions here, for two reasons. First, analogous questions can be more precisely posed and answered within the context of Collingwood's understanding of interpretation, to be considered next. Second, there is a more fundamental difficulty with empathic understanding.

How is one to arrive at the other's experience? By using the evidence. But it is crucial to be precise about exactly what the evidence is. The first possibility is that the evidence is a collection of descriptions of another's behaviour, descriptions which don't presume anything about the inner experience of that person. The second possibility is that the evidence is a collection of descriptions shot through with the language of inner experience. Both possibilities raise problems for the account of interpretation in terms of empathy. If the evidence is purely behavioural – the sudden movement of an arm, the fixed stare of the infantryman – then the well-known philosophical problem of other minds beckons. The suggestion would have to be that behavioural evidence combined with one's own experience is sufficient for knowledge of what the other experiences. That suggests an inductive argument: from the fact that I experience E when I do B, I conclude that you experience E when you do B. But this is a poor inductive argument, since conclusions are based on only a *single* case – one's own. All inductive arguments leave open the possibility that the conclusion does not follow from the premises (it is, after all, *possible* that the infantryman's fixed stare is a result of his happiness and relaxation); but such a poor inductive basis as this doesn't even justify the relative likelihood of one conclusion over another.

According to the second possibility, evidence for what another experiences is not itself divorced from the language of experience. And it seems clear that this second answer is closer to our actual practices, as can be appreciated both as a result of previous argument, and also by the extreme difficulty of describing another's behaviour in terms entirely shorn of the language of experience. (The relevance of the 'double hermeneutic', introduced above, is apparent in the recognition that what the historian studies is meaningful prior to that historical study.) But if evidence is provided in terms of inner experience, then in describing the other one *already* knows what they experience. Knowledge of another's experience can be quite direct, and does not require the intermediary movement through self-knowledge.[4]

I want to conclude this section by mitigating the critical tone adopted thus far. Nothing that I have said implies that empathy should have no part to play in history. For I have been concentrating on the question of presupposition, not methodology (in terms of the distinction made in the first section of this chapter). Empathy is no necessary presupposition of historical knowledge or understanding, though it can be one 'tool', one method, for historians among others. It is akin to the scientist's imagination; being one way to arrive at conclusions, though not the only way (compare others such as embarking in searching criticism of an opponent, conducting a series of experiments, following up what is implicit in another's idea), and never providing the justification of those conclusions.[5]

3. Collingwood and re-enactment

In philosophical discussion of history since the mid-twentieth century, no other work has been as influential as Roger Collingwood's. For that reason alone it is worth devoting space to the elucidation and criticism of his views, tasks which will occupy the remainder of this chapter and much of the next. Collingwood pursued an unusual double-track career, both Oxford-based philosopher, and practising archaeologist with a specialism in Roman Britain. Such 'hands-on' experience has no doubt augmented the reputation of Collingwood's more philosophical work among historians, thus ensuring Collingwood's influence beyond the small band of philosophers interested in history.

The major work of relevance to the philosophy of history is undoubtedly *The Idea of History*, published posthumously in 1946, and in particular the collection of essays published as an epilegomena to that volume. Collingwood's *Autobiography* (1939) is also a treasure trove of suggestive remarks on history, though by his own admission that work is more a popular presentation than a complete working through of his ideas. Indeed, I don't think it too unfair to remark that most of Collingwood's arguments tend to fall some distance from completeness; the reader must work hard to connect and project the significance of the claims that Collingwood makes. Given that claim, it is unsurprising that Collingwood's work has been the source of quite divergent interpretations, a divergence that I aim to do some justice to in what follows. My task will be to suggest three contexts within which to understand Collingwood's central claim about history: that the historian must re-enact past thoughts. Recalling Collingwood's dismissal of scissors-and-paste history, Collingwood reasons that:

> If then the historian has no direct or empirical knowledge of his facts, and no transmitted or testimoniary knowledge of them, what kind of knowledge has he: in other words, what must the historian do in order that he may know them? My historical review of the idea of history has resulted in the emergence of an answer to this question: namely, that the historian must re-enact the past in his own mind.
>
> (Collingwood 1994/1946: 282)

Before attempting to render Collingwood's thesis plausible in any detail, I want to make some clarificatory remarks about re-enactment. Collingwood's target is what is presupposed by historical knowledge, not what historians actually do (again, recall the relevance of the distinction drawn in the first section). Nonetheless, there will be methodological implications. The way to re-enact will not be through scientific laws or causes, the use of which by certain historians is explicitly condemned in *The Idea of History*:

> After the historian has ascertained the facts, there is no further process of inquiring into their causes. When he knows what happened, he already knows why it happened. This does not mean that words like 'cause' are necessarily out of place in reference to history; it only means that they are used there in a special sense. . . . The cause of the event, for [the historian], means the thought in the mind of the person by whose agency the event came about: and this is not something other than the event, it is the inside of the event itself.
>
> (Collingwood 1994/1946: 214–15)

Re-enactment bears some similarity to the empathetic approach, since in both the aim is to recover something 'inner' – thought, experience, feeling – and the means to do so is the reproduction of what is inner in another in the historian's own mind. But Collingwood is concerned to distinguish his own approach from appeals to empathy. Re-enactment is restricted to thought, which should be contrasted to a more general notion of inner experience that includes feeling and emotion. Thought, or cognition, is distinguished from feeling in two ways. Thoughts are fully expressed in language; in particular, propositions, such as 'Caesar crossed the Rubicon in 49 BC'. Feelings need not be fully expressible in language (even if we think that they are *describable* in language, and expressed in behaviour more generally). Second, while thoughts can be correct or incorrect, justified or unjustified, feelings simply are or are not.

It is high time for an example of re-enactment, and we may as well use one of Collingwood's own.

> The historian, investigating any event in the past, makes a distinction be-
> tween what may be called the outside and the inside of an event. By the out-
> side of the event I mean everything belonging to it which can be described
> in terms of bodies and movements: the passage of Caesar, accompanied
> by certain men, across a river called the Rubicon at one date, or the spilling
> of his blood on the floor of the senate-house at another. By the inside of
> the event I mean that in it which can only be described in terms of thought:
> Caesar's defiance of Republican law, or the clash of constitutional policy
> between himself and his assassins. . . . [The historian's] work may begin by
> discovering the outside of the event, but it can never end there; he must
> always remember that the event was an action, and that his main task is to
> think himself into this action, to discern the thought of its agent.
>
> (1994/1946: 213)

This passage illustrates the close relation in Collingwood's understanding between thought and action, close enough to permit the descriptions of his
position 're-enactment' and 're-thinking' to be usually interchangeable. The
thought is the inside of the action; it is thought that makes the action what
it is, not simply the external movements. Just as thought can be expressed in
language, so can it also be expressed in action. For example, in the right context
stepping forward may express the thought that one should volunteer, as much
as if one had expressed the thought in language. This tight relation between
thought and action can be exploited by the historian in either interpretative
direction: to infer thought from action, and to explain action by thought.

My final introductory comment concerns the relation between the historian's thought, and the thought of the historical actor. Collingwood is unequiv-
ocal: the thoughts are *the same*. They are not similar thoughts, nor are they
thoughts that fall under a common type (as 'Napoleon was short' and 'Goliath
was tall' both fall under the type 'thoughts about people's size'). The thoughts
are the very same. It might seem that this insistence places unbearable strain on
Collingwood's theory; but on the contrary, it provides the first way by which
one can argue for the necessity of re-enactment.

4. Living history

The first argument for re-enactment depends on the assertion that one cannot know what does not exist. In discussing Oakeshott's account of historical
knowledge, Collingwood finds the following dilemma. The historian would

like to think that they are investigating the past, but that cannot be correct because all their evidence is present. Yet to say that historians investigate the present leads to the collapse of history as a distinctive discipline. There are many things that one could say about this argument – and I shall say some of them in Chapter 11 – but at this point I want only to highlight Collingwood's resolution of the dilemma.

> Oakeshott supposes that there is no third alternative to the disjunction that the past is either a dead past or not past at all but simply present. The third alternative is that it should be a living past, a past which, because it was thought and not mere natural event, can be re-enacted in the present and in that re-enactment known as past.
>
> (Collingwood 1994/1946: 158)

Re-enactment thus provides a way to bridge the present and past; a way to understand the past as living in the present. (The use of 'living' and 'dead' is an interesting motif in Collingwood's writing, one that he shares with other philosophers of history (notably the earlier Benedetto Croce and the later Hayden White). Expanding on this suggestion, we might argue for the necessity of re-enactment as follows:

(i)   All knowledge must be of something 'living'.
(ii) The only way to bring history to life is to bring the past into the present.
(iii) The only way to bring the past into the present is to resurrect past thought.
(iv) The only way to resurrect past thought is to re-enact those thoughts.

The first premise is surely marred by an oversight of the possibility of knowing things that were, but are no longer. And it is not only history that deals with what was but is no longer: the physicist studies traces of distant and long-vanished quasars, stars and galaxies. At any rate, the first premise should not be conceded without further argument, which I shall return to in Chapter 11. That agnosticism notwithstanding, I suggest that it is useful to proceed hypothetically with this first premise, since in so doing we learn something important about Collingwood's understanding of thought.

How can a past thought be literally made present? If we regard thought as a happening in space and time – as an event like a solar eclipse, a feeling of happiness, or the firing of a group of neurons – then the demand is nonsensical.

However, as previously suggested, thoughts bear a close relation to language, in so far as the latter can fully express the former. To make sense of Collingwood's demand that the past thought be made present, we need to strengthen that relation: thought is not only expressed in language, but can be identified linguistically. To express the same proposition is to have the same thought. Thus if two people both think 'Napoleon is short', then they will have had the very same thought. And it is no more philosophically problematic to suppose that a present historian and a past actor think the very same thought than there is in attributing this identity to present thinkers.

In showing how a past thought may also be present, we also go some way to understanding why 'bringing history to life' requires re-enactment on the part of the historian. But the requirement is sharpened by comparing knowledge of past thought with knowledge of past feeling. I can assert that Caesar was fearful without myself feeling fearful. But to assert that Caesar thought 'crossing the Rubicon is necessary in order to defy the senate' requires me to think that crossing the Rubicon is necessary in order to defy the senate (Collingwood 1994/1946: 138, 288). True, I think the thought in English, while Caesar thought in Latin, but it is surely necessary to suppose that the same proposition may be expressed in different languages. And while a thought may be re-described in ways unrelated to its original thinking (Caesar's thought as 'his last before crossing the Rubicon', or 'the thought contemporaneous with Brutus' negotiations with Pompey'), one may agree with Collingwood that these re-descriptions *do not* bring the original thought back to life. Only genuine re-enactment does that.

If thought is not defined by its spatio-temporal location, but by its conceptual (linguistic) contents, it seems that we might have a powerful basis for regarding history (and any subject concerned with thought) as anti-natural. At any rate, Collingwood drew that conclusion, insisting that any genuine science of thought be founded upon the atemporal content of thought, not its place in the physical world of time, space and causality. For if thought is not spatio-temporal, then it cannot be causal, not least because causation implies change in time. We should not, says Collingwood, think of thought and action as being related as cause and effect, but related as inside and outside. To interpret is to re-describe, not provide a cause: 'when he knows what happened [under a certain description – MD], he already knows why it happened'.

Donald Davidson's reply to anti-causalism in the philosophy of action took much of the sting out of the distinction between thoughts that are atemporal, and material events located in space and time (Davidson 2001a/1963). As explained in Chapter 5, at the heart of Davidson's proposal, indeed of Davidson's philosophy of mind, is the very simple idea that the same event can be described in different ways. Some of those ways of describing fit the event into relations of scientific law. Other ways of describing may – if the event is an action of some kind – fit the event into relations of rationality, of reason and action. There will be many more descriptions under which the events may fall. But no matter how the event is described, its status as cause of some events and as effect of others is not disturbed. The very same event may be described as a thought, and as a material, spatiotemporal event. The event that is described as a thought *does* have causal relations, in virtue of its material properties.

Davidson's argument has brought clarity to the debate over action between naturalist and anti-naturalist. Yet it doesn't get to the heart of our issue. For even if the interpretation of action can be causal, and perhaps even must be causal (as suggested in Chapter 5), one need not suppose that it is the designation of causality that is interpretatively illuminating. While 'the cause of Archduke Ferdinand's death was the shot that killed Archduke Ferdinand' (Chapter 5) is quite true, and locates a causal relationship, it is spectacularly uninformative, and in particular moves us nowhere towards making sense of my actions and motives. Davidson did not claim that citing a cause is sufficient for interpretation: 'The most primitive explanations of an event gives its cause; more elaborate explanations may tell more of the story, or defend the singular causal claim by producing a relevant law ... ' (2001/1963: 17). A philosophy of interpretation is barely begun by noting that causal claims will be relevant to it, even though that note rebuts the anti-naturalism that Collingwood believed he had justified.

By considering Collingwood's argument from the need for 'living history', we have, I hope, got clearer about what thought is, and what re-enactment requires. Yet the arguments were not successful; neither for the necessity of re-enactment, nor that such a position implied anti-naturalism.

5. All history is the history of thought

A second argument begins with the assertion that all historical evidence derives from thought. But if that is so, then the use of that evidence must entail the re-enactment of that original thought. If those assertions can be accepted, then not only intellectual history, but 'all history is the history of thought' (Collingwood 1994/1946: 215). I shall defend the first assertion, but shall reject the suggested consequent.

It is clear that one's use of a piece of *written* evidence must involve the knowledge of the author's original thought (more on what 'involve' means in the next chapter). It is a little more instructive to be reminded that an analogous process takes place when the archaeologist approaches an *artefact*:

> The archaeologist's use of his stratified relics depends on his conceiving them as artifacts serving human purposes and thus expressing a particular way in which men have thought about their own life; and from his point of view the palaeontologist, arranging his fossils in a time-series, is not working as an historian, but only as a scientist thinking in a way which can at most be described as quasi-historical.
>
> (Collingwood 1994/1946: 212)

Evidence can be the result of thought, even though the production of that evidence was in no way an intention of the thinker. For example, the fact that soil in a particular area is deficient in nitrogen can be evidence for past farming practices in that area. Those past farmers did not intend to degrade future soil; nonetheless the evidence that we have is a result of some action that was intended, and hence was the expression of some thought. In general, if the historian's subject matter is human action, then it seems sensible to agree that all historical evidence derives from thought. The foregoing also suggests that, *in at least some cases*, re-enactment is required in order to use that evidence.

Roy Porter has written an interesting review article of a volume covering eighteenth-century English political prints (Porter 1988). Porter's central concern in that article is to determine the inferences that can, and those that cannot, be drawn from visual evidence such as these prints. It would, for example, be a blunder to think that one could infer that things were just as they were represented, not least because of the obviously satirical intention of the prints. Porter makes the sensible suggestion that one of the best ways to use these prints is to focus on their peripheral elements (their 'wallpaper'), those which the author would have been less likely to exaggerate or distort. In that vein, he notes that blacks are found in the background of these prints as servants, beggars, street musicians and sailors. Such depictions provide a sharp contrast with the earlier portrayal of the black as 'a figure of wonder, a monster or marvel'. Similarly, Porter notes that women are a topic

> on which our seven male authors are all but silent. Only about a third of the prints feature female characters at all . . . the female is most strikingly present aetherialized as emblem: Britannia, Virtue, Justice, Liberty (often as a French Revolutionary siren seductress). What is most striking of all is

how utterly 'sexualised' is the woman of the prints: courtesans, buxom
serving-wenches, the Whore of Babylon. . . . The 'collective unconscious' of
the prints tells us that because of their sexual nature, women can be fit only
for private life; the public business of politics must be left to men only.

(1988: 204–5).

In such a case, historians would seek to use evidence derived by thought,
in order to recover not the explicitly held thought but what was (most likely)
unrecognized by the author. One would need to expand upon what has already been said about re-enactment in order to cover such a case, but given
Collingwood's comments in his *The New Leviathan* (1942) it would appear that
he would be equipped to do so. In that work, Collingwood made it clear that
mind should be known by the expansion and clarification of the reflection that
we all, as thinking creatures, to some extent undertake (1942: 2/43). History can
teach us only what the thinker was *capable* of bringing to reflection, though not
only what *actually* was reflected upon. Collingwood is happy to admit, indeed
is at pains to emphasize, the active role of reconstruction of another's thoughts
in re-enactment.

Re-enactment can thereby cover a wide class of historical reasoning.
Nonetheless, we should reject any argument moving from the fact that all
evidence results from thought, to the conclusion that re-enactment is a requirement of using that evidence. The history of some piece of evidence will
contain thought, but that part of its history just might not be what the historian wishes to use. Cases where evidence is an unintended consequence make
this point. In inferring from the nitrogen-poor soil to past farming practices,
the historian does not re-enact the farmers' thoughts, even though thoughts
there were, and thoughts necessary to produce the evidence we now have.
The evidence that the historian possesses has a causal history, among which
is thought. But that evidence can be used to focus on any part of that causal
history, including that from which thought was absent. Likewise, the historian
uses an adorned body preserved in peat to infer technological development at
a certain time; or the height of Pennsylvanian infantrymen to infer the relationship between economy and physical health. Such inferences do not require
any knowledge of past thought.

Any further reply on behalf of Collingwood risks falling back on pure dogma:
that the evidence simply must be used in the context of re-enactment, or
one cannot be said to be properly practising history. Certain comments of
Collingwood's do indeed suggest simple prejudice in favour of the history of
thought. Thus:

> Military history . . . is not a description of weary marches in heat or cold, or the thrills and chills of battle or the long agony of wounded men. It is a description of plans and counter-plans: of thinking about strategy and thinking about tactics, and in the last resort of what the men in the ranks thought about the battle.
>
> (Collingwood 1970: 110)

I can only treat as purely dogmatic the implication that the following passage is not history:

> The lack of fuel in [the Sixth army's] retreat made the evacuation of the wounded more difficult than ever. Incapacitated patients who had been piled in trucks, which then ground to a halt, just froze to death in the open. . . . Lightly wounded soldiers and malingerers, appearing like a horde of beggars in rags, tried to rush the aircraft as they landed, in an attempt to board. Unloaded cargo was thrown aside or ransacked for food. The weakest in these hordes were trampled underfoot.
>
> (Beevor 1999: 357–8)

In the next chapter I focus on the third, and to my mind most promising, context within which to argue for re-enactment – the understanding of past actors' *rational actions*.

Further reading and study questions

Collingwood, R. G. (1994) J. Dussen (ed.), *The Idea of History*. Oxford: Oxford University Press (originally 1946). Two papers in the epilegomena are essential reading with regard to re-enactment: 'Human nature and human history' and 'History as re-enactment of past experience'.

Davidson, D. (2001) 'Actions, reasons and causes', in *Essays on Actions and Events*. Oxford: Oxford University Press (pp. 3–20) (paper originally 1963). The classic paper in the philosophy of action.

(a) On what basis is it possible to claim that the historian re-enacts the *very same* thought as the past actor who is studied?

(b) How can the historian know what a past actor thought?

(c) Is it plausible to suppose that interpretation is sometimes a matter of empathizing with those in the past, even if that does not exhaust the historian's interpretative activities?

8 Actions, reasons and norms

1. Rationality

The third way to approach Collingwood's insistence upon the necessity of re-enactment is to situate the idea within the context of rationality. The suggestion that drives this chapter is that history must do justice to the rationality of past thought and action. What is special about understanding in terms of rationality?

- Rationality connects thought and thought, and thought and action. Through these connections, thoughts and actions may be justified, motivated, praised and criticized.
- Rational connections, unlike connections of scientific law, are not uniformly coercive. Compare the scientific law that one cannot travel faster than light – a law which cannot be broken – with the rational requirement that one's thoughts should be consistent. This lack of universality should not be seen as a problem with regard to understanding ourselves and others. Rather, we presuppose that the rational actor has the possibility to not take the action, or to get the action wrong.
- In describing another in terms of rationality, we can perceive a fruitful way to develop the issue of the 'double hermeneutic' (stated at the start of

Chapter 7). By the end of the chapter, I will argue that the attribution of rationality must be anchored in the self-conception of the person or society being studied; yet the possibility of extending that self-conception exists in so far as the rationality is implicit or incomplete.

- Thought and action can be constituted (made what they are) by rational connection. To explain: one can regard the meaning of a word, and by extension a thought containing that word, as at least partly given by the inferential relations that it bears to other words. Thus, the meaning of 'red' is given by its relations with the other words 'colour', 'blue', 'scarlet' (and of course, many more). This holistic notion of meaning is at the heart of Ferdinand de Saussure's Structuralism (1998/1916), the influence of which will be exemplified later in this chapter. A similar theory can be found in the work of Robert Brandom (1994). Using Brandom's terminology, we can say that 'red' is inferentially related to the other words mentioned, though in distinctive ways: 'colour' is *entailed* by 'red', 'scarlet' is *permitted* by 'red', and 'blue' is *incompatible* with 'red'. The italicised words all imply connections of rational, inference.

We will embark on our investigation of rationality and historical understanding via the work of William Dray; work inspired by Collingwood's insistence on re-enactment. Dray's claim, in his 1957 *Laws and Explanation in History*, was that the most distinctive form of historical explanation was the explanation of past action by showing that action to have been rational. Dray's central example was Trevelyan's explanation of why Louis XIV withdrew military pressure from William of Orange's Holland in 1688, allowing William to invade England. This action Trevelyan regarded as the greatest mistake of Louis' life. Trevelyan's answer to why Louis acted as he did is that

> 'Louis calculated that, even if William landed in England there would be a civil war and long troubles, as always in that factious island. Meanwhile he could conquer Europe at leisure.' Furthermore, 'he was glad to have the Dutch out of the way (in England) while he dealt a blow at the Emperor Leopold (in Germany).' He thought 'it was impossible that the conflict between James [of England] and William should not yield him an opportunity.'
> (Dray 1991/1974: 69, quoting Trevelyan 1938)

Dray formulated this account at a time when the Deductive-Nomological model of explanation (see Chapter 4) was hegemonic. A preoccupation with this competing model of explanation dominates Dray's work. 'Rational explanation' was defended as a distinct form of explanation to explanation by scientific laws; one which did a better job of being necessary and sufficient for explanation of action. We can regard the issue as a matter of inference, as well as of explanation. We infer thought from action, just as we explain action by thought. Indeed, emphasizing inference rather than explanation brings Dray's ideas rather closer to Collingwood, and in particular to the latter's emphasis on 'question and answer'.[1]

In addition to the importance of the *historian's* questioning (the specifics of which are at least partly accounted for by the idea of contrastive explanation, presented in Chapter 5), historical understanding requires inquiry into the *past actor's* questioning. To understand a past action is to regard that action as the answer to a question. Two examples stand out in Collingwood's *Autobiography*. Collingwood passed Gilbert Scott's Albert memorial every day on his way to work. The question which he found himself asking was 'Why had Scott built the Albert memorial, a visibly mis-shapen, corrupt, crawling, venomous thing'? (1970: 29). Collingwood's question is to be answered by finding a second question: that asked by Scott that motivated the design of the memorial. The second example concerns Nelson's actions at the battle of Trafalgar in 1805, and specifically Nelson's statement concerning his medals: 'in honour I won them, in honour I will die with them' (1970: 112). Collingwood again asks: what is the question behind that statement?

There is a clear similarity between Dray's emphasis on rational explanation and Collingwood's on question and answer. Reasons – the beliefs and wants that motivated the action – stand to actions as questions stand to answers. How does the historian move from action to reason, or from answer to question? Collingwood makes it quite clear that the historian should seek, or at least prefer, a question which preserves the rationality of the answer. With regard to the Albert memorial, it is no good avoiding the question of Scott's rational motivation by presuming that he was simply a bad architect (Collingwood 1970: 29). A similar presumption is made in Dray's rational explanation. One could explain Louis' actions by referring to his poor judgement; but, while that is possible, an explanation which demonstrates the rationality of the action is preferable.

We can identify three possible responses to the question of *whether, and to what extent, rationality of action should be preferred in interpretation.* One may think that *no preference* should be assumed prior to examining the specific case: if the action is rational then it should be understood so, and if it is not rational then the interpreter has no business in pretending that it is. One may adopt a *weak preference*, in favour of an interpretation that demonstrates the rationality of the action, while accepting that there will be certain cases where rational interpretation fails. Both Collingwood and Dray (1957: 128–34) should be counted among this number. Finally, one may adopt the *strong preference* that all interpretation must make sense of the action in terms of its underlying rationality. Hempel's criticism of Dray stemmed from a belief that to accord any preference to rationality in explanation was mistaken, as I explain in an endnote.[2]

2. What is it to act rationally?

The first Part of this book contained an account of what it was for the historian to rationally base their beliefs upon the evidence. That sort of rationality – concerned with correctness of one's thoughts – is *theoretical* rationality. In this section I ask what it is to act rationally – *practical* rationality. The difference between the two can be dramatized by considering situations where believing something that is not theoretically, can help to achieve one's ends. For example, faced with an ambitious jump justified the daredevil biker, for whom confidence of approach is vital, must put out of their mind the fact that they have failed on a number of previous situations. In that case, adopting the belief is theoretically irrational, but practically rational.

As Dray insisted, assessing practical rationality is a matter of weighing things from the perspective of the actor, not from the perspective of the interpreter. Given the benefit of hindsight, we know that William did not get bogged down in England, instead succeeding in his military venture there. Louis believed that the reverse would happen. From the perspective of our beliefs, it was not rational for Louis to disengage from Holland. But from the perspective of Louis' beliefs, it was rational to so disengage. The perspective of Louis is the one that counts, so Trevelyan succeeded in showing Louis' action to be rational.

I want to expand upon this idea – that understanding rational action requires attending to the perspective of the actor – by considering a more extended example. James Joll offers a careful account of the decision making of the major European powers in the diplomatic crisis of July 1914 (1992/1984: for a useful summary, see pages 234–40). Let's focus on the three key players in that crisis: Russia, Austria-Hungary, and Germany. The crucial background to Joll's explanations of the action taken by those powers are the previous crises, particularly that of 1913. What is relevant here is that Serbia had done well out of the crisis, though with no thanks to their 'natural ally', Russia. Thus, in 1914,

Russia had the rather minimal aim of saving some credibility in the Balkans. The Russians believed that not supporting Serbia this time around would, given the events of 1913, lead to a total loss of credibility. Thus it was necessary for the Russians to act in support of Serbia. Austria-Hungary had the aim of avoiding internal turmoil. Given the failure to halt Serbian successes in 1913, it was felt that the only way to avoid internal turmoil was to use the assassination as a pretext for crushing the Serbian kingdom. Germany had the aim of retaining Austria-Hungary as an ally – 'at all costs' (1992: 234). Germany's aim was made more difficult by their weak support of Austria-Hungary in 1913, thus further compelling strong support in 1914.

As in Dray's example, the explanations provided for these three key actors is from their perspective, not ours. From our perspective, we can see that they had false beliefs; for example Austria-Hungary's belief that Russia would not mobilize so long as the former could count on the strong support of Germany (Joll 1992: 11). Their predictions were not always accurate; most tragically in the common notion that any war would be relatively short, and not overly costly or painful. Those inaccurate predictions affected both the prioritization of aims – that war was preferable to losing credibility, internal stability or an ally – and judgements of relative effectiveness (for example, the relative effectiveness of federalization as compared to ruthless suppression of nationalism as a means to the end of achieving internal stability in Austria-Hungary).

Perspectivalism is only a starting point. What I will do next is suggest two ways to develop that insight towards a philosophical account of practical rationality: answering how and when the historian moves from action to reasons. The first account of practical rationality – *instrumentalism* – is intuitively plausible, but nonetheless we shall find reason to reject it. The second account will bring us back towards Collingwood's re-enactment.

Stemming from Hume's claim that 'Reason is, and ought only to be the slave of the passions' (2003/1746: 236), an instrumental approach to practical reason would regard action simply as an instrument for achieving what one wants, one's 'passions'. Reason can guide one to the achievement of one's ends, but has nothing to say about the desirability of those ends. As Hume colourfully put it, 'Tis not contrary to reason to prefer the destruction of the whole world to the scratching of my finger' (2003: 236–7). Thus, to act in a certain way is rational just so long as it is necessary to achieve one of your ends, and we may regard another's action as rational just so long as they believed it to be necessary to achieve one of their ends.

A modification we might want to make to the Instrumentalist thesis stems from taking account of the fact that we want some things more than others.

Let's suppose that I want to go swimming on this hot day, but that I want more to continue writing this book. If we further suppose that the two activities can't both be pursued, then going swimming would not be practically rational, even though it is something that would satisfy one of my wants. The way to modify the bare instrumentalist account would be to treat a person's wants as a whole, rather than one by one, thereby permitting their relative strength to count in any assessment of rationality. We will end up with something like the following: 'rational agents act according to the relative product of the relative strength of their desires and the probability of satisfying those desires'. And that sort of principle is at the heart of an economic theory of rational choice. Joll's analysis, at least the part of it reported above, fits this economic theory well. He compares aims as more or less valuable to those who held them, as I have already illustrated with regard to Germany's valuation of retaining Austria-Hungary as an ally.

My criticism of Instrumentalism is that the position is unable to account for the knowledge that we have of another's motivation and beliefs. Joll notes that in at least many cases,

> Men are not motivated by a clear view of their own interests; their minds are filled with the cloudy residues of discarded beliefs; their motives are not always clear even to themselves. This makes the historian's task a difficult one.
>
> (1992: 239)

Motives are difficult to reconstruct, as are beliefs. One should not simply take what the agent themselves reports, as Collingwood notes (1970: 31). Not only may the actor be deceiving or self-deceived, but it is a common predicament for the historian to have no such direct reports at their disposal. The historian must use all available evidence, including but not exclusively the actor's direct reports of their own states, including but not exclusively the evidence provided by and the action itself.[3] That granted, can we say anything in general about how motives and beliefs are inferred?

One important *presupposition* of that sort of inference is that the actor being interpreted is, by and large, rational. To see why that presupposition is required, we can consider what parody of interpretation would result without it. Imagine an explanation of Austria-Hungary's actions consisting of citing the aim of avoiding internal turmoil, and the belief that holding the Emperor's birthday party later that month would be necessary for that. This is clearly ridiculous: the belief doesn't make any sense. But what stops us from attributing that belief to the Austro-Hungarians is not that there is no direct evidence that they thought any such thing, for 'direct evidence' of that sort is not a requirement for attributing belief. What halts the attribution of this belief (or, better, what explains why we never even consider such a ludicrous 'interpretation') is that it fails the presupposition of rationality.

Note that this belief–motive pair has been formulated so that it rationalizes the action according to instrumentalist criteria. So much the worse for instrumentalism. In its place, we should consider the second promised account of practical rationality, which returns us to Collingwood's re-enactment. The second proposal is that an attribution of practical rationality depends upon an understanding of *what the interpreter would do in that situation*. And to accept that claim is to insist on the necessity of re-enactment in understanding rational action.

The impetus to interpretation is puzzlement, and a more substantive interpretation tends to begin with deeper puzzlement. If Scott's memorial had been superb, we could still have asked what led him to build it in that way, but the question would have lost much of its interpretative bite. If I am puzzled by an action, then it is because, if I had been in the same context, I would not have done it. If I had wanted to assert superiority over Holland and England and had the means to do so, surely I would have acted as Louis did not and moved into Holland. Given that Louis did not do that, there is puzzlement. The attribution of the belief that William would get bogged down in England, a situation which would prove advantageous to France, removes that puzzlement. It removes it because I can agree that if I had that belief, then indeed I would have acted as Louis did, and refrained from pressuring Holland.[4]

If correct, this connects in a satisfying manner re-enactment, question and answer, and rationality. It also suggests why each of these notions will be central to much history (even if, remembering the arguments of the last chapter, not all history). The central and contentious move is that from the attribution of rationality to the question of what the interpreter would do in the same circumstances. That move seems unjustified in at least some cases. Isn't it possible to understand another's motivation, while holding that I would not behave in the same way? I can understand the motivation of an acquisitive dictator despite the fact that I am a rather polite and retiring person. Should the Collingwoodian response be that I must adopt the characteristics of the actor, in addition to their motives and beliefs? If so, then we are in danger of losing our grip on the idea of re-enactment. The same danger exists when considering an 'alien' practice. Mark Risjord (2000: 20) discusses the interpretation of *sati*: the ritual suicide of a newly widowed woman, traditional (though never the norm) in Hindu culture. Is it practically rational to commit *sati*? However one interprets this practice, the question 'if I had been in that culture, with those beliefs, what would I have done?' is – to me – unanswerable. In the remainder of this chapter, I focus on approaches to interpretation that depart from Collingwood's in foregrounding culturally alien practices of this sort.

3. Meaning and society

In this section I present arguments for the conclusion that any philosophy of interpretation that exclusively focuses on individual action and thought is deficient, on the grounds that meaning is not reducible to the individual. An alternative approach to interpretation privileges the society of which the interpreted individual is a part. Indeed, Joll's analysis is in terms not of individual people but individual states. Here, we might say, with Dray (1957: 141) that to talk of the reasons of some supra-personal entity is merely shorthand for those individuals 'appointed by' or 'typical of' that group. As we shall see, this reduction is less plausible in other cases.

The individualist would derive the interpretative meaning of the act from the individual's reasons for acting, of which the primary element is what they intended to achieve. Beardsley and Wimsatt, in their well-known paper 'The intentional fallacy' (1987/1946), put forward the suggestion that the meaning of a 'work' (artistic or literary) is irreducible to what the author intended. Beardsley (in a later restatement of that argument) imagines 'a large, twisted, cruller-shaped object of polished teak, mounted at an oblique angle to the floor'. The creator of the sculpture intends it to symbolize Human Destiny. We can't see any such meaning in it. 'Should we say that we have simply missed the symbolism, but that it must be there, since what a statue symbolizes is precisely what its maker makes it symbolize?' (Beardsley 1981/1958: 18–19).

There are a number of reasons to be wary of reducing meaning of an act or a work to authorial intention. One wonders whether the idea of being able to know another's intentions prior to knowing the meaning of their works and actions can make much sense. I return shortly to that suggestion. One might also consider that we tend to accept cases in which the language that we use has a meaning running contrary to our intentions. To use the word 'Boche' is to commit oneself to the idea that Germans are cruel, no matter what one intends to say about Germans. Ignorance is no excuse given that the word contains meaning as a result of its etymology and inferential connections. (An awareness of meaning running beyond intention' supports the now familiar demands of 'political correctness'.) One can also simply get meanings wrong, intending one thing while expressing another. I once thought that '*pace*' implied the approving reference to another's work, when it is actually a rather supercilious gesture. Meaning can diverge from authorial intention. (Although we didn't need Beardsley to tell us that. Gadamer quotes Chlademius, writing in 1742: 'since men cannot be aware of everything, their words, speech and writing can mean something that they themselves did not intend to say or write' (Gadamer 1989: 183).)

Beardsley suggests a stronger conclusion, that the intentions of the artist are neither 'available nor desirable' (Beardsley and Wimsatt 1987: 367). Not only should meaning not be reduced to authorial intention, but meaning has nothing to do with what the author intended. That stronger suggestion should be rejected. It seems that Beardsley bases his stronger claim on actual interpretations which divert from the author's stated intentions (for example, Beardsley 1981: 25–6). But to establish diversion from *stated* intentions is not yet to establish diversion from intentions. We have already seen that self-reporting is neither necessary nor sufficient for the recovery of intentions, a point which Cioffi (1964: in particular, 98–9) uses to criticize Beardsley's strong thesis. Wilson's interpretation of William James' *The Turn of the Screw* treated the text not as a straightforward ghost story, but as a tale of sexual repression in which the 'ghosts' were figments of the narrator's disturbed imagination. There is no reason to suppose that James thought of his book in the same way. Do we then have here an example which can support Beardsley? No, because Wilson *is* sensitive to the biographical evidence concerning James, claiming self-deception on the latter's part. Wilson treats the book as better evidence of the author's intention than the explicit self-reporting.

The conclusion is that meaning can go beyond authorial (or actor's) intention, but that it is a mistake to think that meaning has nothing to do with authorial (or actor's) intention. We can no more ascribe intention independently of meaning than we can ascribe meaning independently of intention. In interpreting action, language or artistic work, we assign meaning and intention together, so as to make sense of the product. This interdependence has been stressed by Donald Davidson, from whom we receive the following example:

> If you see a ketch sailing by and your companion says, 'Look at that handsome yawl', you may be faced with a problem of interpretation. One natural possibility is that your friend has mistaken a ketch for a yawl, and has formed

a false belief. But if his vision is good and his line of sight favourable it is even more plausible that he does not use the word 'yawl' quite as you do, and has made no mistake at all about the position of the jigger on the passing yacht.

(Davidson 2001c/1974: 196)

I return to the interdependence of meaning and intention at the end of this chapter.

A more fundamental critique of individualistic reduction of meaning is that the very possibility of meaning depends on society. Lewis Carroll, in *Alice Through the Looking Glass*, describes the following encounter between Humpty Dumpty and Alice: 'When I use a word,' Humpty Dumpty said, in a rather scornful tone, 'it means just what I choose it to mean, neither more nor less'. As Alice responds: how can that be? (For every word, rather than just selected ones?) Such behaviour would certainly make communication much harder. But there is a deeper concern: that without dependence on the agreement and sanction of others, meaning is not possible at all. Wittgenstein has been interpreted as offering an argument for the dependence of meaning upon social relations, most clearly so by Saul Kripke (1982). Wittgenstein/Kripke's argument, in outline, is as follows.

Meaning can be regarded in terms of rules; the word 'blue' in terms of the rule for blue things, the word 'wink' in terms of the rule for winking. A genuine rule requires the possibility that we can follow it correctly *and incorrectly*. A rule which permits any future action to count as 'applying' that rule is no rule at all (not everything should be counted as blue, not all actions are winks). The possibility of correctness and incorrectness requires social responses, in particular the possibility of one person sanctioning another's incorrect application of the rule. The key move is the last, and is highly controversial. Kripke argues for it by elimination, that (in)correctness cannot be made possible in any other way. In particular, Wittgenstein and Kripke point out that it is a mistake to think that one contains a rule 'in one's mind' that determines correct and incorrect application. It is only through society that correct application is possible.

4. Social norms

Peter Winch, in his *The Idea of a Social Science* (1958), developed an account of social scientific interpretation on the basis of Wittgenstein's comments on rules.

Winch's approach can be readily applied to historical interpretation which, if correct, would show historical interpretation to be more a matter of providing appropriate social context than of re-enacting thoughts. I shall first present the outline of Winch's argument, before extending it to history.

In social science – and history – we study action, considered to be behaviour which is meaningful; the 'inner side' to behaviour that Collingwood also insisted that the historian study. Meaningful behaviour is that which falls under a rule (where the rule is not explicit we might prefer to replace with 'norm'). Compare blinking and winking. There is – in our culture – no rule to blinking. It is 'mere' behaviour. But winking is something which – in our culture – can have meaning. Depending on the context, winking may express the rule of signalling complicity, reassuring one who is uncomfortable, or making apparent the attraction of winker to winkee. All actions fall under at least one rule, and rules are something that can be got right or wrong. The social scientist therefore studies behaviour for which normative assessment is essential. That doesn't mean that the social scientist focuses on whether someone was right or wrong to wink; rather that, the appropriate rule has been followed correctly, that a wink was successfully enacted.

This rule-centred conception of social science has at least four interesting consequences. First, at the heart of social science is description, not explanation. Indeed, in so far as describing in terms of rules is sufficient to make sense of the action, then explanation can be eschewed altogether in favour of progressively 'thicker description'. (The phrase is Clifford Geertz's (1973). An example of thick description will be provided in Robert Darnton's 'Great Cat Massacre', in the next section.)

Second, for the Wittgensteinian/Kripkean reasons suggested in the previous section, rules must be understood in the context of a society. Further, the rule must be understood in the context of *its own* society – not ours. If the anthropologist finds winking to be prevalent in a newly contacted tribe, then they had better understand that winking in terms of the tribe's rules, which need not correspond to our own. Winch pushed this claim far beyond rules such as those for winking. In a later essay (1964), he considered the possibility (and in some cases the likelihood) that the most fundamental rules differed between societies, including rules of rationality itself. I return to this issue shortly.

Third, Winch derives from his rule-centred conception of social science an anti-naturalist conclusion. Indeed, if one considers, as Winch did, that naturalism is committed to scientific laws, then this conclusion seems unimpeachable.

After all, it is in the very nature of rules that they be capable of being broken or mis-followed; just as Dray notes with regard to rationality of action, a rule provides 'the thing to do', not what is always done. More subtly, while a law relates its terms according to empirically discovered connections, a rule relates its terms analytically. The rule for voting, which we might express in terms of playing one's part in the democratic empowerment of a candidate, is analytically connected to, indeed constituted by, those concepts ('candidate', 'democracy'). If that is so, then it can hardly be a matter of the social scientist *discovering* connections between those terms in a scientific manner.

Finally, and as a consequence of the foregoing observations, to understand another's actions requires the use of *their* concepts. That consequence follows if we accept that to understand is to describe in terms of rules, that those rules must be the rules of those interpreted, and that the rules of those interpreted are constituted by their concepts. If the social scientist misses those concepts, then they will have missed the very thing that takes place. The claim is particularly clearly exemplified by interpreting a move in a game. The concept of 'knight' is essential to an action performed in the appropriate context; someone moving that piece without the concept 'knight' cannot really be said to be making a move in chess at all. In so far as we can appreciate that it is the concepts of those interpreted that must be used, then we can see an essential role for beginning with the other's *self-understanding*.

Those are the bones of Peter Winch's Wittgensteinian-inspired philosophy of social science. I will apply it to historical interpretation in the example to follow in this chapter, and in discussion of historicism in the next. At this point I focus on two criticisms of Winch's approach. First, it permits over-rationalization of the actions being studied. Second, it is overly restrictive with regard to the concepts available to the social scientist. The common concern that underlies both criticisms is that a Winchian social scientist would be too tightly tied to the self-understanding of those whom they study.

With regard to the three positions available concerning rationality and interpretation that I provided at the start of this chapter, Winch adopts a strong presumption: *all* interpretation should make clear the rationality of those interpreted. How strong that presumption is can be well demonstrated by the debate concerning rules of rationality for the Azande, a people in central Africa who have been well known to anthropologists and philosophers since Evans-Pritchard's study (1976/1937).[5] Evans-Pritchard found the daily lives of the Azande to be permeated by witchcraft. Witchcraft could cause illness and death, and only magical oracles could allow identification of the witch that was behind that harm. Winch argued against regarding witchcraft in terms of *our* scientific rules (a warning that he claimed Evans-Pritchard was oblivious to). Such an approach would lead to the mistaken interpretation that the witchcraft rituals were a scientific theory intended to explain (via the oracle) and permit production of (via witchcraft) certain phenomena. If we were to consider the Azande's practices in those lights, they would have to be regarded as not very successful. The alternative approach is perhaps to regard magic as having an expressive role in their culture, akin to ceremony in our own; according to their own lights, that practice is then understood as appropriate and successful.

More challengingly, Evans-Pritchard found that the Azande beliefs about witchcraft led to contradictions. One such contradiction stems from the belief in the heritability of witchcraft, from fathers to sons and from mothers to daughters. Whether someone is a witch is established by autopsy. There are many positive autopsies, enough to implicate every paternal and maternal line of descent. If every line of descent has one proven witch, then, due to the heritability constraint, all Azande are witches. But the Azande deny that they are all witches. In the face of such examples, Winch continued to insist that we regard the Azande as rational *according to their own rules*. Winch is rather unclear about how such an interpretation might be possible, but the approach was filled in more explicitly by David Cooper (1975), who insisted that we regard the Azande as possessing a three-valued logic. To our familiar two values, true and false, Cooper would regard the Azande as adding a third, 'indeterminate'.

I shall not follow the debate into the cogency of postulating different logical systems, but shall restrict myself to two general comments concerning the strong presumption of rationality in interpretation. That strong presumption seems highly unattractive. First, we are in danger of overlooking mistakes, particularly those that are systemic. Since Marx we have become familiar with the idea of 'false consciousness': that the real explanation for why a certain people are religious, or why hard work is held to be virtuous, is quite different to the self-understood explanation of those things. People don't always behave rationally; sometimes they are deceived, sometimes confused.

Second, not only is irrationality an experienced fact of life, but to postulate irrationality can make for an illuminating interpretation. Carlo Ginzburg (1992/1976) provides us with the moving portrait of Menocchio, a sixteenth-century Italian miller. Menocchio was uneducated, but was the possessor of wide-ranging and unorthodox beliefs, as we learn from the records of his trials by the Inquisition. Indeed, Menocchio was too outspoken, unable to resist discussing his heretical ideas with those in his village. His livelihood was ruined, much of his family deserted him, and his final punishment was death. What is relevant to our present consideration is the role of irrationality in Ginzburg's interpretation. Ginzburg speaks of the 'muddle' and 'contradiction' in Menocchio's beliefs (1992: 76). Contradiction is at the heart of irrationality (though we may think that there is more to irrationality than contradicting oneself, the latter is at least a sufficient condition of the former). Menocchio's irrationality is not 'explained away' as being merely apparent. Rather, the irrationality is permitted to lead to an interesting explanation of Menocchio's beliefs. Ginzburg argues that we should explain the irrationality inherent in Menocchio's thoughts by separating the content of those thoughts from their form (1992: 59). The content comes from oral, peasant traditions; the form, and what made it possible to express that content, was a result of written and high culture, most especially that which followed from the Reformation. In short, Menocchio is a man struggling – and often failing – to put his ideas in the language of his time.

The second concern with Winch's theory results from the requirement that the social scientist use the terms employed by the interpreted. Actually, Winch does not quite insist that the interpretation use the *very same* concepts as those interpreted. This is just as well, if we are to move beyond interpretation of the most banal sort. Just as I noted in the previous chapter that Collingwood permitted the re-enactor to focus on thought which was unconscious or implicit, so Winch allows the interpreter to use concepts which *could have been grasped* by they who are interpreted (1958: 46). Let us call this the *availability demand*: only use terms available to those interpreted. We should want to know what 'availability' amounts to, and why it is to be treated as an interpretative constraint. Any answer to that question must avoid twin dangers. Grant insufficient leeway to the interpreter, and perfectly good interpretations are ruled out. If, for example, one insists on a restriction based on the *actual comprehension* of the subject of interpretation, then good interpretations will be needlessly rejected. (There is nothing wrong with redescribing N's voting Labour as 'casting a vote for Industrial peace in election for the democratic second chamber in an additional member system method of proportional representation', whether or not N actually understands that redescription.) On the other hand, if we take 'availability' to stand for something more widely applicable, then the danger is that all interpretations are permitted, so the availability demand is doing no work. If, for example, one insists on a restriction based on the possibility of *translating* the interpretation into terms used by the subject of interpretation, then very little, if anything, will be ruled out.

I suggest that, while the terms of those interpreted must *play a part* in setting the starting point for an interpretation (a need reiterated in Chapter 9), the development from those terms should be regarded in terms of *explanation*. Despite the traditional antithesis between interpretation and explanation, I have refused to accept any such sharp distinction throughout this chapter and the last. So long as certain accounts of explanation are rejected, and most especially the DN account (Chapter 4), we are at liberty to regard interpretation as a certain type of explanation. I build on to this proposal in the remainder of this chapter.

5. The Great Cat Massacre

> The funniest thing that ever happened in the printing shop of Jacques Vincent, according to a worker who witnessed it, was a riotous massacre of cats. The worker, Nicolas Contat, told the story in an account of his apprenticeship in the shop, rue Satin-Severin, Paris, during the late 1730s.
> (Darnton 1991/1984: 79)

The 'Great Cat Massacre' took place on the orders of the print shop master, after one of the print workers, encouraged by the others, mimicked the sound of cats howling outside the master's bedroom night after night. The ensuing massacre involved the workers smashing all the cats they could find with broom handles and other tools of the printers' trade, collecting the half-dead cats in sacks, and staging a mock trial in the courtyard. The men were left 'delirious with joy, disorder, and laughter' (Darnton 1991: 81).

The starting point of the interpretation is puzzlement, arising from the obvious difference between the worker's attitude to this cat massacre, and our own. Further, there is a hope that this difference might lead to the appreciation of other differences between our culture and that of the workers of eighteenth-century France; that in locating this one difference we might be able to 'see where to grasp a foreign system of meaning in order to unravel it' (Darnton 1991: 82). In order to inquire in Darnton's interpretation of the massacre, I want to impose a framework of contrastive explanation. In so doing, we can locate various questions that the interpreter might ask about the massacre, and indeed that Darnton does ask, viz.:

(1) Why did the workers kill the cats, rather than leaving them alone?

Such a question is easy to answer, and not especially penetrating. The master treated the workers very badly, providing terrible accommodation, insufficient and unappetizing scraps of food, and demanding continuous hard work beginning at 4 or 5 in the morning. The poor treatment of the workers, and the master's love of cats, explains the workers' killing in virtue of an understandable desire to destroy something that the master loved.

(2) Why did the workers kill the cats by putting them on trial, rather than in some other way?

This question gets us somewhere more interesting. Darnton suggests that the workers regarded their trial as a metaphor for putting the bourgeoisie on trial (Darnton 1991: 97–8). If correct – and Darnton phrases his answer cautiously – it would have particular resonance considering the Terror that was to come later in the century.

(3) Why did the workers kill the cats, rather than something else (indeed, rather than venting their fury against the master in some other way)?

To this question, Darnton provides a more speculative, and more intriguing, answer. He notes that cats were widely used as symbols in a number of ways at that time and before (though such symbolic resonance has not entirely disappeared today). Cats were used in ceremonies, connoted sexuality (one is reminded of the English slang 'pussy'), were associated with witchcraft and magic, and were regarded as peculiarly near to humans as a result of the sound of their cry. There is some support for these connections provided by Contat's account. The sexuality of cats is suggested in connection with a reference to the master's wife's affair. Witchcraft is invoked by the mention of the 'bedevilled cats celebrating a witches' sabbath all night long'. And the connection between cats and humans is explicitly noted by placing the cats at the centre of the bourgeois household.

(4) Why did the workers find the massacre so funny (rather, perhaps, than reacting as we would)?

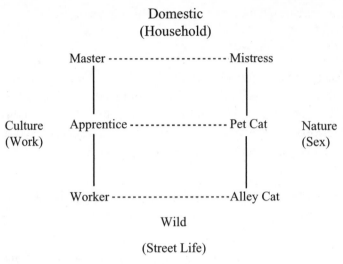

Figure 8.1 Reproduced from Darnton 1986: 233

In answer to this question, Darnton brings the whole interpretation together. In his original account, the explanation takes a 'how-possible' form (covered in my Chapter 5): 'Rabelasian' laughter and familiarity with Burlesque 'opens a space' for humour of this kind (1991: 100–1). But in his later commentary Darnton provides a bolder explanation:

> By bludgeoning her familiar, they accuse her of being a witch and then compound the insult by playing on the sexual connotations of pussy – a case of metonymic rape, the symbolic equivalent of murder, even though she cannot accuse them of anything more than horseplay because they have disguised their meaning in metaphor.
>
> (1986: 230)

The joke is explained by the virtuosity of 'playing' on these cultural themes: 'The symbols reverberated up and down a chain of associations – from the cats to the mistress, the master, and the whole system of law and order parodied by the trial' (1986: 230). This chain of associations Darnton represents structurally in Figure 8.1.

Darnton's interpretation provides a good idea of what a history that followed Peter Winch's demands would look like. A practice is understood in terms of rules. Some of those rules are commonplace, or 'thin' (mimicking, killing, laughing), but others make possible a thick description of the practice. The rules draw connections between concepts of the society in question. In some ways, Darnton's work embodies a more satisfactory account of interpretation than that explicit in Winch's work: by focusing on the *explanation* of behaviour in terms of postulated rules, Darnton avoids being tied too closely to the self-understanding of those involved. The influence of Structuralism on Darnton's interpretation must also be noted. Structuralism, originally a theory of language provided by de Saussure (and introduced above), was in the mid-twentieth century applied to action and practice, notably by the anthropologist Claude Lévi-Strauss. Darnton uses standard Structuralist notation in Figure 8.1, using horizontal lines to denote the identity of terms, and vertical lines to denote their opposition.

Darnton has been criticized, most stringently for the lack of evidential support for the rules that he postulates (Levi 1992: 109). Such challenges go with the territory, in so far as hypotheses concerning rules that are not directly mentioned in the evidence are more likely to be underdetermined by that evidence. I conclude by returning to the relation between evidence and interpretation.

6. Interim conclusion: interpretation and evidence

Quine famously imagined an anthropologist faced with the evidence that the natives cry 'gavagai' when confronted with a rabbit (1960: Chapter 2). The anthropologist's task is to interpret what 'gavagai' means. Of course, the foregoing description of the anthropologist's situation already implies one interpretation: that 'gavagai' means 'rabbit'. But Quine insisted that this was not the only possible interpretation. 'Gavagai' could (to give but one example) mean 'undetached rabbit part', given that the 'undetached rabbit part' and 'rabbit' could be appropriately uttered whenever 'gavagai' has been uttered. One might think that Quine could be criticized for ignoring the possibility of further questioning that could distinguish between whether the native meant 'rabbit' or 'undetached rabbit part'. But Quine stuck to his guns: while it might be possible to think of and put to the native such questions, that questioning would not be decisive. Either of the original translations could be retained so long as the anthropologist was prepared to make suitable adjustments to their interpretation of *other* of the native's words. Quine's conclusion was that meaning was not a real feature of our world, but (like possible worlds, or the perfect circle) merely a device that was sometimes convenient in understanding parts of the world.

Whatever the status of anti-realism about meaning, interpretations must be responsive to the evidence: not *any* interpretation is permitted. The possibility of arriving at different interpretations that account for the same evidence is a result of there being multiple criteria that an interpretation should meet. These criteria for interpretation permit underdetermination by the evidence because, first, *these criteria are interdependent* and, second, *the criteria are defeasible.*

The interdependence of interpretative criteria has already been suggested, by using Davidson's ketch/yawl example. In order to find out the beliefs of another, the interpreter had to assume that they already knew the meaning of the words used. In order to find out the meanings of their words, the interpreter had to assume that they knew their beliefs. How are those assumptions reached? Primarily, by reference to the position of the interpreter. To hold fixed another's meaning, we presume homophony – that they mean the same as us. To hold fixed another's beliefs, we presume truthfulness – that they believe the same as us. (After all, we believe what we take to be true.)[6] The third component to action, not mentioned in Davidson's example, is motivation. As with Davidson's example one may hold the other components fixed to enquire about motivation, or may hold motivation fixed to enquire about meaning and belief. To 'hold fixed' motivation requires undertaking the Collingwoodian exercise suggested previously, asking whether I would have acted in the same way. If one holds fixed the reasoning, one can vary belief (as in the case of Louis), or meaning.

In everyday life, we can presume homophony, and account for difference usually by ascribing different belief. In a more distantly removed society we would perhaps do better to be suspicious of homophony, and lean more on maximizing truthfulness. No hard and fast rules can be given by philosophy: it is sufficient to open up the space for possible interpretative strategies. And given that there are multiple strategies, evidential underdetermination will result. We can allocate values to the above three components differently, so long as the combination jointly does the job. (It is like asking for the factors of 10: 2 and 5 will do the job just as well as 1 and 10.)

The interdependence between motive, belief and meaning presupposes that the person interpreted is rational. The message of Davidson's Principle of Charity (2001b/1973: 136–7) is that the assumption that the person interpreted is by and large rational is not an assumption that is optional, for without it the evidence would imply *no* constraint on our interpretation of others. (Such a conclusion is echoed by the previous thought experiment concerning Austro-Hungarian motivation.) Nonetheless, the assumption of rationality is defeasible. On what basis do interpreters judge it best to count as irrational? A promising answer to that question would appeal to the overriding demand to produce consilient historiographies (Chapter 3). Consilience is a matter of accounting for a wide range of phenomena by postulating fewer hypotheses that explain that phenomena. One way to do that is to account for a practice in terms of its underlying rationality. That account will be consilient, and powerful, in so far as it enables the interpreter to explain a range of activity, and also to explain why other activity is refused. However, it is possible for the most consilient interpretation to postulate mistakes and systemic irrationality. Indeed, it is likely that mistakes of some kind will feature in most consilient interpretations; though whether that is indeed the case in any particular interpretation is not for philosophy to say.[7]

I began this chapter by applying Collingwood's notion of re-enactment to the interpretation of action, arguing that re-enactment is a necessary presupposition for understanding the action as rational. In that way the motivation of subject and object must come together. I then broadened Collingwood's exclusive focus on individuals by introducing Winch's philosophy of social science. The consequence of that position is that the concepts of subject and object – their meaning – must come together. Finally, through Davidson's principle of charity, we saw reason to suppose that the beliefs of subject and object must in great part co-incide. Each of these requirements holds by default, but one component may be dropped while still regarding the action as rational. (And further, rationality of the subject is an assumption that is itself defeasible.) The framework of subject and object that is here assumed receives further exploration in the following chapter.

Further reading and study questions

Collingwood, R. G. (1970) *An Autobiography*. Oxford: Oxford University Press (originally 1939). The relevant chapters are 'Question and answer' (V), 'The need for a philosophy of history' (VIII), 'The foundations of the future' (IX), and 'History as the self-knowledge of mind (X).

Dray, W. H. (1991) 'Historical explanation of actions reconsidered', in P. Gardiner (ed.) *The Philosophy of History*. Oxford: Oxford University Press (originally 1974). A short summary of Dray's position, contrasted to Hempel's scientific model of explanation.

Winch, P. (1958) *The Idea of a Social Science*. London: Routledge. The central chapter is 'The nature of meaningful behaviour'.

(a) What is instrumental rationality? Can that theory make sense of an action being irrational, or mistaken?

(b) In what ways is it necessary to assume that those we interpret are like us?

(c) Could one interpret the 'Great Cat Massacre' in the way that Dray would have us explain actions? Could one interpret it by using Collingwoodian re-enactment?

Part IV
FROM INTERPRETATION TO DISCOURSE

Subject and object 9

1. Historicism

In the history of ideas, we study such works as Thomas Hobbes' political philosophy, Plato's metaphysics, Aristotle's rhetorics and ethics, and the Jewish bible. How should we understand the ideas expressed therein? One answer – we can call it universalism[1] – would encourage us to treat past works as we do a contemporary work. We can learn from these ideas, since they can provide answers to (ethical, philosophical, scientific) problems that we have. Aristotle can teach us about rhetorics; Collingwood about the pitfalls of scissors-and-paste history. Not only do we learn from past authors, but we are at liberty to criticize those works, just as we should read contemporary works with a critical mind. The universalist position is that we do not read these books only for historical interest.

The opposing answer – historicism – would criticize universalism for giving insufficient weight to the distance between our intellectual culture and those of the works suggested. Herbert Butterfield's 1931 critique of 'Whig history' (exemplified in the writing of certain nineteenth-century political historians) has been the lighthouse warning four generations of historians from the rocks of Whiggishness. At the root of Butterfield's critique is a thorough-going historicism: an insistence that the historian must always be on their guard to avoid collapsing the difference between past and present. In four ways the Whig historian ignores this danger.[2]

First, they falsify the past by making it look more like the present. It is alleged that certain 'Whigs' claimed to find in the early Stuart House of Commons something very like a government and a unified opposition (Dray 1987: 137). This first mistake is obvious to spot (if one knows the period), and is obviously a mistake. Second, the Whigs distort the past by applying present terms that were unavailable to those whom they describe (Skinner 1969: 28). The result is anachronism. There is something unpalatable in, for example, the description of Oliver Cromwell as left wing in his politics, the interpretation of *Tristram Shandy* as a postmodern novel, and of Plato as the proponent of a Kantian divide between reality as it appears and reality as it is. In each case, the description is in terms that were not available to the thinker described. Third, the Whig historian illegitimately opens up a critical dimension by describing the past in terms of the present. It is only by describing Aristotelian physics as a failed version of Newtonian physics, or alchemy as a failed version of modern chemistry, that criticism of those practices is made possible. We would do better, the historicist claims, to treat these older practices in their own terms. Fourth, the Whig historian allows the present to set what is important in the past, and so worthy of study. The original 'Whig' historians assumed their own contemporary political and constitutional system as the central development in history, thereby ensuring that their history consisted of the constitutional changes (Magna Carta, the creation of the Church of England, the Glorious Revolution) leading to this present.

Historicism can be regarded as a general claim about the past, a claim which results in epistemic demands. All human ideas, ideals and norms are subject to change, and as a matter of fact do fundamentally change. As a result, the past must be understood on its own terms, according to its own ideas, ideals and norms. The historians should be ever alert to the danger of overlooking the fundamental difference between ourselves and the other person, period or culture. Historicism, as here understood, is the resolute working through of Ranke's demand to write about the past as it really was; unencumbered – the historicist adds – by the distortion of supposing that it shares the historian's own world-view.

One can perceive four stages of historicist development (a development, I hasten to add, put together for our understanding, rather than as an accurate reflection of the chronological development of the movement). While the notion of change is inherent in any historical study, the scope of change was widened with post-Enlightenment writers. In particular, Hegel's lasting legacy was the idea that the very structure of thought had changed over human history. Change went deeper than the rise and fall of dynasties and empires, even than the development of science and technology. In the *Phenomenology of Spirit* (1997/1807), Hegel told the story of change in what he regarded as the heart of human thinking, the idea of freedom. Still, considering the four-fold criticism of Whig history, we can appreciate that Hegel did not fully embrace (what we now regard as) historicism. Though thought has moved through different phases, Hegel saw the whole movement as a teleological unity which was resolved in Hegel's own time.

The second stage of historicism is exemplified in the revolution in biblical scholarship in the nineteenth century, most notably in the work of Friedrich Schleiermacher. The central methodological innovation was the critical inference from evidence, described in Chapter 3, and an influence on the historical community's own critical revolution. A consequence of that methodology was the insistence that to understand Scripture, one had to go back to the source. One should enquire into the *multiple* writers of scripture, and should not be misled by the subsequently accumulated layers of interpretative dogma. We should be reminded of Collingwood's insistence on finding the question to which the action (including linguistic action) was the answer. Interpretation is a matter of understanding authorial intention.

The third stage of historicism moves from authorial intention, to the society or culture of which the author is a part (a move that was mirrored in my discussion of the previous chapter). To emphasize original society more than original author is to take a step into so-called 'new historicism'. It is here that we can place the work of Michel Foucault, his reconstruction of past language (*The Order of Things* 2002/1966) and past practice (as his later work increasingly focused on) by unearthing the hidden discontinuities separating the present from the past. Here, also, we can find Thomas Kuhn's influential call for the history of science to precede the philosophy of science. The history of science should be no more Whiggish than the history of politics.

> Gradually, and often without entirely realising they are doing so, historians of science have begun to ask new sorts of question and to trace different, and often less than cumulative, developmental lines for the sciences. Rather than seeking the permanent contributions of an older science to our present vantage, they attempt to display the historical integrity of that science in its own time.
>
> (Kuhn 1992/1966: 3)

The fourth stage of historicism is to turn the doctrine inwards upon itself. If all past thinkers and actors worked in the context of their time, their culture, then so do contemporary thinkers and actors; and in particular, so do contemporary historians. This simple step – embraced by Nietzsche and Troeltsch towards the end of the nineteenth century (Iggers 1974: 457) – has momentous consequences. If the historian themselves should be regarded as a product of their time, then the history that they produce cannot be regarded as objective. That history will be the result of economic, political, cultural features of the historian's own time, rather than (only) resulting from the object of enquiry. There is a particular cost for the doctrine of historicism itself, since a contradiction is suggested. Historicism consists of the demand that the historian know their object as it is in itself; yet, when worked through, the historicist recognizes that no such knowledge will be possible because the historian cannot avoid regarding the past in any way but through the distorting lens of their own self or society.

In the remainder of this chapter, I explore two approaches to objectivity that can be regarded as diametrically opposed reactions to the historicist's dilemma. One could attempt to negate the supposed subjective or societal influence on one's historical work, thereby becoming more objective. I pursue the objectivist approach first. Or, one could embrace the subjective or societal influences, and show how, nonetheless, substantive history is quite possible. That embrace will lead us back to a *modified* universalism in the history of ideas.

2. Objectivity and evaluation

Objectivity has been one of the most disputed ideas in the philosophy of history, and unlike debate over explanation, it is a dispute in which historians have been as central as philosophers.[3] Ranke's *wie es eigentlich gewesen* has been for many a call for historical objectivity (though recall the warning of Chapter 1[4]), a demand echoed by Weber's insistence on value-freedom (1949). On the opposing side, objectivity has been taken to be meaningless, impossible, or undesirable; by Friedrich Nietzsche, in his broadside against disinterestedness in 'Uses and abuses of a history for life' (1873), by Charles Beard in 'That noble dream' (1935), and by Peter Novick in his lengthy reassertion of Beard's thesis in *That Noble Dream: The 'Objectivity Question' and the American Historical Profession* (1999/1988). The 'objectivity question' extends beyond the academy, debated in newspaper editorials, and the cause of political disagreement. In particular, I am reminded of the controversy that took place in the

UK in 2003, concerning the so-called dodgy dossier that was to be provide the justification for Britain's part in the invasion of Saddam Hussein's Iraq. 'The BBC must not be allowed to continue its hidden agenda' argued Alistair Campbell on behalf of the government (26 June 2003); the Board of Governors of the BBC replied that 'the Board reiterates that the BBC's overall coverage of the war, and the political issues surrounding it, has been entirely impartial' (7 July 2003).

Objectivity is an epistemic standard, that the subject's (the historian's) account result from the object of enquiry alone. Objectivity demands that features of the subject, or (recalling the third stage of historicism) features of the subject's society, not affect the resulting account. Subjective features that have typically been the focus of suspicion are

- interest: what the subject would like to be the case (in the sense that Bush and Blair had an interest in weapons of mass destruction being found in Iraq);
- interest: in the more anaemic sense of what the subject would like to study;
- concepts, or their mid-twentieth-century outgrowth, 'conceptual schemes' (see Chapter 12);
- theoretical or epistemic background: what the subject already knows, or believes;
- values and standards of the subject which permit evaluative judgements of another's morality, cultural norms, aesthetics and reasoning.

Responses will quite properly vary according to which of these features is the topic of discussion. Where interest, in the first sense, was to influence a historian's study, then the result would not be objective history but – on the contrary – biased history. The objective historian should disregard what they would like to be true, and report only what is. Interest in the second sense is on the contrary an unavoidable element of any study whatsoever; the supporter of objectivity would therefore do well to hope that interest in this sense need not upset an objective account. The role of the historian's concepts and theories will be the focus of Chapter 12. At this point, we shall focus on the role of evaluative judgement, and in so doing place Max Weber's call for value freedom in the social sciences at the heart of the debate.

> An empirical science cannot tell anyone what he *should* do – but rather what he *can* do – and under certain circumstances – what he wishes to do. It is true that in our sciences, personal value-judgments have tended to influence scientific arguments without being explicitly admitted. They have brought about continual confusion and have caused various interpretations

to be placed on scientific arguments even in the sphere of the determina-
tion of simple casual interconnections among facts according to whether
the results increased or decreased the chances of realizing one's personal
ideals . . .   (Weber 1949)

Weber did not deny that everyone, the social scientist and historian included, holds values. Further, it is to be expected that these values guide what the historian studies, and might even guide the uses to which the historical knowledge is put (as if one were to put to use the fact that no economic sanctions have ever brought a change in nation N's policy in order to decide to instead apply military pressure towards N). But the historian's values should play no part in the results obtained by historical study. Whether or not the historian is a communist should not affect their history of twentieth-century Russia; whether or not the historian of ideas is an Aristotelian in their ethics should not affect their history of the Athenian Academy. Fact and value must be sharply divided; once one adopts a certain topic, only the facts should shape the ensuing account. Historians should be, in this sense, *value-free* and in so far as they are can regard their work as objective.

There have been many criticisms of this idea of value-freedom, but at the core of most is the belief that what Weber demands is impossible. We are engaged in evaluating and judging the past, whether or not we are aware of so doing, and whether or not we would like to do so. And, the critic of Weber continues, it is highly beneficial to be aware that this is what we, as historians, are doing; since there are few more dangerous than the unreflective judge. We can start to substantiate this criticism of value-freedom by observing that historians do criticize and evaluate those in the past. Recall Ian Kershaw's history of Nazism, discussed in Chapter 6. There I noted that Kershaw criticized his object, Nazism, both in ethical terms, and on the basis that the Nazi ideology precluded the rational organization of administration and economy. But though suggestive, this example provides no argument against the demand of value-freedom. That is because one cannot establish that a normative demand is inappropriate on the grounds that someone, or even most people, have broken that demand (on pain of confusing the separate roles of facts and values!).

A more promising criticism of value-freedom is premised on the claim that historians evaluate in the course of any interpretative activity, and not only when formulating explicit criticisms. If that is correct, then it would imply that evaluation is both hard to avoid, and that it is fused with the factual in a way that undermines the demand of value freedom. One way that interpretation can be seen as implicitly value-laden items from a focus on reasons. A suggestion in Chapter 8 was that to locate another's reasons for acting and agree that the action was rational implied asking 'if I was in that mental and physical context, would I have done that?' That question is explicitly evaluative. A second suggestion focuses on the *terms* used in interpretation, noticing that these are often value-laden. If we, for example, interpret the Nazi regime's actions by postulating that they are, to paraphrase Kershaw, 'continually and aggressively expanding, at any cost', then negative evaluation is implied.

The defender of the demand of value-freedom need not be at a loss in reply. Weber was well aware that some language was both factual and evaluative, and consequently recommended that social scientists be wary of that portion of language. The ideal solution is to substitute value-free terms in place of the value-laden. As is standard practice in journalism, one can safely move from judgements ('Britain is a fractious island, hard to conquer') to reports on another's judgements ('Louis believed that Britain was a fractious island, hard to conquer'). The same applies to evaluations: the historian can report another's evaluation quite objectively, so long as they clearly distinguish that report from their own opinion. In other cases the more emotive language ('aggressive') can be replaced with the more sober, or simply discarded.

But value-freedom is more conclusively criticized in so far as we can point to terms which are undoubtedly value-laden, and which we could and would not want to do without. An excellent example is provided by Hans-Georg Gadamer: 'classical' (1989: 287–9). What we mean by referring to a period as 'classical', or to a work as a 'classic', is unavoidably evaluative. We do not simply locate that period or work at a certain date (a purely *factual* attribution), but also commit ourselves to a positive *evaluation*. In using 'classical', we imply that the period or work lies at some temporal remove to ourselves, but which nonetheless has enduring power to speak to us, and to remain a model for future activity. The programme of value-freedom is not decisively closed off until it is shown to be impossible; but examples such as Gadamer's build the case for thinking that value-freedom would be a revisionism too drastic to accept.

3. Selection and importance

As I have noted, Weber recognized the role of evaluation in the setting of research topics, in what is selected and what excluded. What has not been properly recognized until more recently is that selection and exclusion affects the objectivity of the account when *taken as a whole*. A simple fact, that Aristotle was born in 384 BC, or that Plato founded the Athenian Academy, remains so no matter why the historian chooses to include it in their account. Any evaluative reasons for that selection are irrelevant to the factual content. But that division does not carry over to the historian's whole account. On the contrary, by *selecting, excluding, privileging and suppressing*, the historian's evaluation makes itself apparent in the whole. One can appreciate this by considering historical accounts that contain nothing but truths, but which, because of the preceding operations, are biased and misleading. If we further grant that a biased and misleading account is for that reason not objective, then we can appreciate that the role of evaluation in setting the topic of research cannot be bracketed off from the assessment of an account's objectivity. Inspired by Jonathan Gorman's seminal treatment of historical objectivity (1974), consider the following proto-account of Hitler's life. It is in all parts true (or at least may plausibly be thought true), but I take it that it is nonetheless partisan and misleading.

'Adolf Hitler was an artist and a vegetarian. Following the imposition of the unfair terms of the Treaty of Versailles, Hitler's National Socialist Party began to gain the favour of the German people. After coming to power, an escalating arms race with Britain and France, and the support of the latter powers for Poland, led to war. Hitler's strategic thinking seemed amply confirmed with the rapid victories of the German forces. As the war progressed, traitorous elements within the German army plotted to kill Hitler, but failed. Hitler died in 1945.'

A second connection between exclusion and evaluation can be derived from the account of contrastive explanation, introduced in Chapter 5. The suggestion there was that the historical explanation concerns not so much 'why p?', as 'why p, rather than q?' As we saw, changing the contrast (q) served to change focus on what was explained, and consequently on the portion of the history of p that is relevant to the explanation. What is relevant at this point is that the selection of contrast also carries evaluative weight, and in so doing follow a line of argument found in Garfinkel (1981: Chapter 5). To select a contrast implies that one part of the causal history of p will be relevant, and not another. The point is brought out by one of Garfinkel's examples:

> A woman goes to a psychiatrist and says that she has been having fights with her husband. The psychiatrist says . . . 'let us see what you are doing that contributes to these fights. There must be *something*, for after all, it takes two to have a fight.' Obviously the burden of change has been placed

on the woman . . . Such a choice stands in need of justification, and we have
not so far been given one. Why has one causal factor been let off the hook?
(1981: 141)

So evaluation is implicit in both what is included, and in what is taken
to be explanatorily relevant. In these ways evaluation can be present in
an account which contains no explicit evaluation, and furthermore not
even value-laden terminology. I can see only one response available to
the defender of value-freedom: that selection, exclusion and importance can be
judged on objective grounds. If the choice of what to include (exclude, privilege
and suppress) is potentially an objective matter, then the above criticisms of
value-freedom will be vitiated.

This response is not, perhaps, as desperate as it might appear, since a possible
basis is to hand.[5] Recognizing that to provide an explanation of p requires citing
something that *made a difference* to p is to imply a counterfactual judgement
(Chapter 5). And it is no great leap from affirming that an unexplanatory event is
one that made no difference to that to be explained, to suggesting that an event is
more explanatory to the extent that it makes *more* of a difference. The suggestion
is that one should judge what would have happened had the event in question
not occurred, and should further judge how different that counterfactual result
is from the actual result. The more different those results, the more important
the cause. For example, one might reason that without the support of Britain
and France for Poland, war with Germany would nonetheless have broken out
as a result of some later Nazi expansion; but without Hitler, it is unlikely that
anything similar to the Second World War would have been expected. An event
which is more important, relative to what is being explained, is therefore more
worthy of inclusion in a historical account. Thus the selection and omission in
a historical account can be held to task, according to the requirement that it
should mention the important events, and omit the unimportant.[6]

Two large question marks hang over this proposed account of importance.
First, one might be sceptical of our ability to answer counterfactual questions
concerning what would have happened had such a causal factor not been
present. Such scepticism is no doubt sensible in a good many cases, though I
would want to remind the critic that counterfactual judgement is implied in
any explanatory claim whatsoever. To be generally sceptical about our ability
to make counterfactual judgements in history is therefore an unwise position
to take. Second, the counterfactual account requires judgements of similarity
and difference, between counterfactual results and actual results. I am inclined

to be more concerned about the second demand than the first. It is likely that evaluative judgement will enter into judgement of similarity, at least to the extent that one needs to have an intuitive sense of what is *relevant* in the similarity judgement.

To further enquire into the nature of similarity would take us too far afield; so we shall leave the defender of value neutrality at this point, and turn to that approach which would rather welcome the news that we relate to the past in ways other than critical knower to objective known. Yes, we know the past by reasoning from the evidence. But – as suggested in this section and the last – we also approach it evaluatively. In Chapter 3 I made a case for a further relation, the preservation of past knowledge. In the remainder of this chapter, I suggest that historians should be in a relation of dialogue with the past. The conclusion to be drawn is, I think, that the demand of objectivity misunderstands our rich relations with the past.

4. Dialogue

In the first section of this chapter, I presented the historicist dilemma. Historians should know the past objectively, as it is in itself; but this is impossible, given that historians themselves are historical products. In the second and third sections, I explored one important aspect of the attempt to meet the demand of objective knowledge, in the strict separation of subjective value from objective fact. We saw, in more detail, the extent to which the historian's viewpoint is so difficult to exclude from even seemingly straightforward historical claims. In short, the historian's evaluation is ineliminable from their description, selection and explanation. There are a variety of responses that tend to be made to arguments such as these. One might conclude that 'anything goes' (another memorable soundbite from the philosopher of science, Paul Feyerabend); that historians can say what they want about the past. (Keith Jenkins: 'to be in control of your own discourse means that you have power over what you want history to be' (2003: 85)) But we can do better than that. One can recognize the historian's *involvement* (in particular, though not exclusively, evaluative) with the past that they study, but not conclude that the historian may impose what they want on the past. In the remainder of this chapter I use the notion of dialogue to substantiate these claims.

A good dialogue depends on both interlocutors, and on the existence of a certain relation between them. The suggestion here is that interpretation is dialogic. If that is the case, then a good interpretation depends on both interpreter and interpreted, and on the existence of a certain relation between them. The approach has a certain intuitive plausibility; for just as good dialogue does not consist in one person talking at another, so good interpretation consists neither in what is interpreted simply speaking for itself (pure objectivity), nor in the interpreter saying whatever they want (pure subjectivity). But the major task for any appropriation of this idea in the philosophy of history is to specify what the dialogic relation amounts to in the context of *historical* interpretation.

The primary exponent of this approach is Gadamer, especially in his three-decade-spanning work, *Truth and Method* (1989/1960). At the heart of Gadamer's approach to dialogue is the relation of question and answer, which as we saw in the previous chapter was also a central element of Collingwood's philosophy of history. Gadamer inherits and extends Collingwood's tool. In dialogue, each interlocutor questions the other. Thus the interpreter comes to the evidence with questions. Using the idea that explanation is contrastive, I have stressed that the historian's question serves to focus upon aspects of the work or action being questioned. The contrast selected implies a focus on certain aspects of the history of that work, excludes other aspects, and in so doing can carry evaluative implication. The distinctive claim of Gadamer's dialogic approach to interpretation is that historians not only question the past, but *are themselves also questioned*. First, the historian is part of the interpretative dialogue that stems from the historical work in question, and so must respond to challenges raised by that tradition. As we saw in Chapter 2, it is commonplace for historians to recognize the necessity of 'engaging' with previous historiography focused on a similar topic to their own. If a prior historian has suggested an interpretation which disagrees with, or even stands in tension to, the historian's own interpretation, then it is not permitted simply to ignore that prior interpretation: the challenges that it implies must be answered.

Second, the historian can be questioned by the past work itself. This is easiest to appreciate in the case of intellectual history. As I have already suggested, interpretation begins with some kind of puzzlement, which we can loosely understand as a difference between what the interpreted did or said, and what the interpreter would have done or said. It is that difference that permits the past work to question the historian. In a genuine dialogue, one recognizes difference, and does not presume that one's own position will be correct prior to the dialogue itself. The same goes when engaging in historical interpretation. The certainty of one's own position is removed is put into question. To interpret Aristotelian ethics requires recognizing the fundamental differences between our (post-Enlightenment) ethical beliefs, and those expressed in the *Nicomachean Ethics*. Further, it requires holding open the possibility that Aristotle might be right, and that our own position might be wrong. Likewise, to interpret Contat's report about killing cats requires not closing off the possibility that there might be comedy in killing cats, thus putting into question a previously strongly held belief that there is no comedy in killing cats. Gadamer insists (with his stress on *Bildung*, 'edification') that such openness is an essential part of genuine education: the use of what, to us, is abnormal or strange in order to permit the possibility of remaking ourselves.

Charles Taylor introduces a useful idea (1999: 126–30) that permits us to apply Gadamerian dialogue more widely than its natural home in the history of ideas. Taylor recommends the use of the 'language of perspicuous contrast' in framing interpretations, a language which describes the practice of those interpreted not in their own terms, and not in ours either, but in a way that holds open the correctness of both. To see why this might be advisable, recall the question raised with regard to Winch's philosophy as to whether the concepts of those interpreted should set a limit on the interpretation (Chapter 8). We saw there reason to doubt the restriction to *their* terms. One could describe using *our* terms, but any understanding gained would risk being shallow, would indeed risk falling into all the traps of anti-historicism outlined at the start of this chapter. One could attempt to describe using *neutral* terminology, but it is to be doubted whether such terminology is available. (One way to appreciate that unavailability is by recalling the failure of the positivist project of linguistic reduction, mentioned in Chapter 4: the reduction of all terms to a neutral observation base.) The final option is to use terms which *contrast* our practice and theirs.

How would the 'language of perspicuous contrast' deal with an example already introduced: the magical practices of the Azande? One question we considered was whether to regard those magical practices as a sort of primitive technology (which would be to describe them in our terms), or as a form of expression. The second option comes closer to the self-understanding of the Azande, though still imposes our own rules upon them, since it implies a sharp distinction, alien to the Azande, between the technological and the expressive. Using the 'language of perspicuous contrast', one could describe the Azande's magical practice as *that which fuses the expressive and technological*. That is not to put things in their own terms, since they recognize no difference between the two realms. Neither is it to describe things as we understand them, since after all we do sharply distinguish the two practices. Rather, it is to describe the

Azande's practice in a way that challenges both us and them, holding open the possibility of which is right.

A dialogue is not usually resolved by coming to a knowledge *of* the other position, though that knowledge will usually be of help in the dialogue. (To know that you are an economic liberal will help me to conduct a sensitive dialogue with you about the state of the UK university system, but it is not the *point* of that dialogue.) Gadamer diagnoses the earlier attempts to base interpretative understanding on empathy, or re-enactment, as mistaken in so far as they see interpretation as a matter of knowing the other interlocutor. Thus:

> It is quite mistaken to base the possibility of understanding a text on the postulate of a 'con-geniality' that supposedly unites the creator and the interpreter of a work. If this were really the case, then the human sciences would be in a bad way. But the miracle of understanding consists in the fact that *no like mindedness* is necessary to recognise what is really significant and fundamentally meaningful in the tradition.
>
> (Gadamer 1989: 311)

It is not only that, in dialogue, we *can* do more than know the other person, but that, as a matter of ethics, we *should* do more than that. As I emphasized in Chapter 3, one can approach a text in two ways. One can treat it as an object, with a history, and thus as evidence from which inferences can be made. Or one can treat the text as something which refers, has an intentionality of itself, and which thus can speak to us about the world. To know one's interlocutor in the first way is to treat them as an object, and 'involves the fundamental suspension of his claim to truth' (Gadamer 1989: 309). Nor is a dialogue usually resolved by adopting one or another position. It is a matter of achieving, in Gadamer's language, a 'fusion of horizons'. Gadamer's phrase is metaphorical, or at least imprecise, but deliberately so. Gadamer is adamant that his hermeneutics offers no *methodology* of interpretation, only a set of presuppositions which underlie any successful interpretation. What 'fusing horizons' does remind us is that dialogue leaves both parties in a place removed from where they started. It reminds us that interpretation is a matter of bridging two fields of meaning; that the task of the historical interpreter is to permit the meaning *of the past* to speak *to us*.

One can certainly provide examples of good historical practice which do not seem to be well covered by the notion of dialogue. In critical historical reasoning, one should treat (some) texts (sometimes) as evidential objects. It is not appropriate to participate in dialogue with every text (for example, *Mein Kampf*); those should – ethically – be treated as objects, explained and not engaged. Finally, not all questioning can be live for us. A hot question was once why there were seven planets (in the solar system, we would now add). The accepted answer was that the number of planets was necessary, given the seven apertures in the head, the seven metals in nature, and other similarities 'which it were tedious to enumerate' (Francis Bacon, quoted by Garfinkel 1981: 7). Of course, there aren't seven planets, there are nine (or perhaps eight, if recent astronomical pronouncements gain authority). But the problem with this question is less the false explanandum, than the bizarre presupposition that anything like this *needs* explanation. Our reaction is not to engage with the question but to explain it, as a product of its (alchemical) times. To these 'counter-examples' I think that Gadamer would have been sanguine. Other relations to the past than dialogue are possible, though dialogue remains – for Gadamer – at the centre of understanding.[7]

Further reading and study questions

Gadamer, H. G. (1989) J. Weinsheimer and D. G. Marshal (trans.). *Truth and Method*. London: Sheed and Ward (originally 1960). As good a place to begin as any is Gadamer's discussion of question and answer, found at Part II, Chapter II, Section 3 (C) (ii).

Gorman, J. L. (1974) 'Objectivity and Truth in History', in *Inquiry* 17, 373–97. One of the many, though one of the best, articles on objectivity in history.

Taylor, C. (1999) *Philosophy and the Human Sciences: Philosophical Papers 2*, Cambridge: Cambridge University Press (originally 1985). 'Understanding and ethnocentricity', taken from a lecture given in 1981, covers both Winch's philosophy of social science and Gadamer's hermeneutics.

(a) Characterize in your own words what it is for a historical account to be objective.

(b) Even if a historical account can't be entirely objective, do you think that the historian should strive to be as objective as possible? Specifically, with regard to the debate of this chapter, is value-freedom an aim to strive for, even if perhaps not completely possible?

(c) What sense can be made of entering into a dialogue with those in the past, when those in the past are dead?

Narrative 10

1. What are narratives?

Narratives were invoked in Chapter 6, as the historian's preferred solution to the problem of integrating various elements into a single, coherent account. Temporal relations are an obvious, and fundamental, aspect of narratives, which provide a second motivation for turning to narrative as a way of making sense of history as the study of the past. And, as I will demonstrate, our understanding of action (discussed in Chapter 9) and narrative are closely linked. It is no surprise, therefore, that narrative should be a central topic for the philosophy of history. My delay in this book in foregrounding a substantive examination of narrative does not belie a belief in its lack of importance; rather, it reflects the rough narrative according to which I understand the recent development of the philosophy of history, in which the appeal to narrative followed the appeals to natural scientific and interpretative models.

Historical narrative was out of favour for much of the twentieth century, under suspicion from the twin forces of *Annales* history and of positivist-inspired history. In both cases, narrative was regarded as an inappropriately literary device for history, at least for history with serious epistemic pretensions. For all its variety of subject matter, the presupposition of the *Annales* school was that to concentrate on those topics that come most naturally to narratives of all kinds – personalities, actions, quests and struggles – was, for history, a grave mistake. Understanding was to be gained by digging down – to the economic and geographical structures underlying human activity – and by expanding one's vision to the very long term. Positivism (Chapter 4) was less explicitly opposed to historical narration, if only because its proponents took their foe to be the sort of idealist philosophy found in Collingwood's work. Historical narrative could be retained in positivist history, so long as we don't see it as any more than the stringing together of explanations secured by covering laws.

One could respond to these broadly anti-narrativist approaches in one of two ways. A deflationary response would seek to emphasize that narrative is a 'thin' notion. The thinnest understanding is that a narrative is any report of two or more events with some temporal ordering between them. According to this understanding, narratives are found in physics (concerning the development of the universe over the first minute), biology, geology, as well as in a variety of reports about human activity and behaviour. From this perspective, where the *Annales* criticism went wrong was in moving from a warning about a specific type of narrative – broadly, biographical – to an unjustified warning about narrative in general. Narrative is unavoidable in any subject that studies different events at different times. Yet nothing of substance, either critical or positive, follows from that observation. A thin concept of narrative, and the consequent demand that narrative be moved to the philosophical margins, is prominent in recent comments by philosophers of the analytic tradition (Lamarque 2004; Tucker 2004: 7–8).

The second sort of response is to insist that narrative is fundamental to history, and in a more substantive – thicker – sense than suggested in the previous paragraph. This claim has, since the late 1960s, been hugely influential for both the philosophy of history and historical practice. The 'revival of narrative' (Stone 1979) was encouraged by the work of Walter Gallie (1964), Roland Barthes (1981/1967), Louis Mink (1970), and Hayden White (1973). Practice was encouraged by theory; by 1979 Laurence Stone could argue that he could 'detect evidence of an undercurrent which is sucking many prominent "new historians" back again into some form of narrative' (1979: 3). So, what is typical of narrative, in addition to the thin relation of events as earlier or later?

(i) A narrative invites the reader to adopt the temporal perspective of that narrated. It invites the reader to enter into a different present to their own; in historical narrative a present located in the past and which moves towards the reader's present. Such a perspective accords genuine importance to the difference between *now, past and future*. In particular, the future is uncertain, changeable through action, thrilling or frightening. That is how we experience life, it is how past actors experienced their lives; and narratives encourage the reader to adopt that perspective of the narrated. Compare a history which proceeded entirely by assigning events to dates. In a non-narrative history of this sort, events would be temporally related by being simultaneous, earlier, or later. But there would be no sense in regarding any of those as 'present', nor future, nor past – excepting, of course, the obvious fact that from the reader's own perspective all the events are past. (A distinction between the series past/present/future and the series earlier/simultaneous/later was made by McTaggart (1908). It was an important part of his famous argument for the unreality of time that only the former series permitted a proper understanding of temporal change.)

(ii) The narrative implies the temporal perspective of narrator and audience, that may coincide or not with the temporal perspective of that narrated. The dissociation of these temporal perspectives permits the standard armoury of narrative devices, including:

- the premonition (prolepsis): the description or reference to an event that is in the future of the narrated ('Little was she to know that her decision would prove disastrous');
- the flashback (analepsis): the description or reference to an event that it is in the past of the narrated;
- 'saw-toothed history': a term of Roland Barthes (1981/1967), which he uses for the narrative technique of returning backwards to explain the origins of something (ancestors, where what is being introduced is a person), before continuing with the forward motion of the narrative;
- compression of the time of the narrated ('Years passed. The forest grew.');
- expansion of the time of the narrated, typically used to slow down the narrative when approaching, or during, an important event.

Premonition is the technique that most clearly demonstrates the difference between temporal perspective of narrator and narrated. The narrator must be situated later than the narrated, knowing, by virtue of hindsight, what those being narrated did not know. One might want to dispute the employment of hindsight, perhaps on the basis of the shared perspective insited by narratives, that was highlighted in point (i). It rather depends on what one thinks is the purpose of following a historical narrative. I still remember my disappointment when studying Valois France as part of my A-level history, in my teacher's insistence on first informing us of the end of the story, and only then filling in the steps to that end. Her argument was that we would better remember the facts; my feeling was that the excitement of the narrative was thereby vitiated. One could expand upon that feeling of disappointment, by claiming that what should be accomplished in a narrative is the appreciation of the past as the present that it then was, with the unpredictability, fear and hope that this perspective implies.

(iii) It is often suggested that the narrative implies authorial perspective in a wider sense of that phrase than simply the author's (narrator's) position in time. Yet it remains doubtful whether 'no narration without a narrator' is any less truistic than 'no description without a describer'. The most plausible way to substantiate the difference is to point out that, typically, narratives are told from a particular evaluative viewpoint; subtly justifying and criticizing by the tools of inclusion, suppression and highlighting. I return to this important issue later in the chapter.

(iv) Narratives typically respond to the audience's expectation for 'closure'. Here, as elsewhere in the theory of narrative, Aristotle's commentary provides an apt expression of this felt need (even if he does go on to *contrast* this requirement with 'historical compositions'). A narrative

> should have for its subject a single action, whole and complete, with a beginning, a middle, and an end. It will thus resemble a living organism in all its unity, and produce the pleasure proper to it.
>
> (Aristotle 1997/c. 303 BC: 48)

A starting point, often some challenge or break from ordinary routine, is developed, probably through further challenges and interventions, until some resolution is reached. We can point to narratives which frustrate this convention, from *Tristram Shandy* in the eighteenth century onwards, though it is significant that closed narratives remain the norm. The plot of the story will be dependent in great part on whether and how closure is found, and what sort of closure that is.

(v) Narratives contain one or more central 'characters'. Such characters may be individual people (Tolstoy's Napoleon), or may not (E. P. Thompson's English working class). These characters are entwined with the central theme or themes of the narrative (the hubris of the great, the response of the poor to challenging times), which indeed might perhaps best be regarded themselves as characters. One warning: we should be wary of presuming that narrative unity is dependent upon the unity of the central characters or themes. As we shall see, one can argue that the relation between character and narrative runs in the opposite direction.

With regard to the distinction between thin and thick narrative, I urge a twin caution. With those who emphasize the thinness of 'narrative', we should be wary of general philosophical arguments that draw conclusions about history as a whole on the basis of features that only certain narratives exhibit. In support of those who emphasize the theoretical weight of 'narrative', we should be wary of restricting our focus to features that are universally present, as if there could be no philosophical interest in anything but necessary presupposition.

2. Narrative and discourse

In previous chapters I have introduced scientific laws, causes, action and interpretation. Narrative is related in some ways to some of these concepts. In this section I trace those connections. The conclusion, however, will be that narrative is something that is over and above these already introduced ideas. That conclusion makes space for the idea that to understand narrative requires understanding the discourse used in narrative.

(1): *Laws* We do not permit just any development in a narrative; a coherent narrative cannot develop in just any way from a given point. As Aristotle pointed out, the elements of a plot must 'follow' in a special way; 'a well constructed plot, therefore, must neither begin nor end at haphazard', but must contain 'an orderly arrangement of parts' (Aristotle 1997/c. 303 BC: 14). Gallie made the contribution to the understanding of historical narrative with his claim that a coherent narrative is one which can be followed by the reader, who can perceive a directionality in the narrative. Yet, different outcomes are possible from the same starting point: there is no way that the narrative *has* to go. For that reason, one cannot regard the narrative as a matter of law, in which the outcome is guaranteed by the antecedent (a law of the form: in all cases of P, then Q). In a narrative of the French Revolution, the flight of the king and queen to Varennes is unexpected, yet fits into the narrative. We need, therefore, an account of that 'narrative following' or 'narrative development', and that will not be in terms of laws. (Whether or not there are laws that underpin the narrative development is not relevant to our understanding *of narrative*; any such reduction would require *replacing* the narrative with a nomic explanatory framework.)

(2): *Causes* The narrative is tacitly causal, as I pointed out in Chapter 5, in opposition to Oakeshott's anti-causalism. If the later part of the narrative develops from the earlier, then there will be a causal relationship between the earlier and the later. However, this does not tell us anything much about narrative development, or how narratives aid understanding. In addition to the permissive nature of causation (at least according to the account that I offered in Chapter 5), there is a more specific problem for any attempt to reduce narrative understanding to a matter of understanding cause and effect. That is that narrative understanding, unlike causal, moves in both temporal directions: the later is understood in terms of the earlier, but also the earlier is made comprehensible in the light of what comes after. Examples of this phenomenon will follow.

(3): *Action* W. H. Walsh (1970/1951: 24–5) (building on William Whewell's ideas of a century previously) introduced to the philosophy of history the useful notion of *colligation*. A colligatory concept is one that refers to a complex, and temporally extended, event or process in history: 'the Renaissance', 'the Cold War', 'the expansion of Nazi Germany'. Colligatory concepts are *complex particulars*, to be contrasted to general (scientific) concepts like 'mass', 'hydrogen', 'cancer' (that colligatory concepts can *contain* general concepts is of no consequence). Colligatory concepts are pretty clearly the stock in trade of most historians. Such concepts bear much similarity to historical narratives, indeed can fruitfully be regarded as proto-narratives themselves, a narrative development referred to by a single phrase. Examining how colligatory concepts bring historical understanding of the past can provide a first step to an examination of narrative understanding more generally. Walsh's primary example is 'the expansion of Nazi Germany'. That colligatory concept can be used to explain a more specific part of the overall colligated process: say, the invasion of the Rhineland. In that way, the specific can be explained not by a general concept, but by a wider particular within which the specific event is situated.

Yet we need to look closer at what colligatory understanding depends upon; and so doing we face the suspicion that we do not learn anything more by the introduction of 'colligatory concepts' than we have already obtained in a study of explanation of action (Chapter 8). The invasion of the Rhineland is indeed explained by being part of the expansion of Nazi Germany; but what is really doing the explaining here is the Nazi's *plan* to expand, which led to the invasion of the Rhineland, and which is manifested in what we call 'the expansion of Nazi

Germany'. Walsh's own development of colligation never really got beyond this point. Yet I suggest that 'colligation' remains useful, in so far as we recognize that colligated processes *do not have to be* planned or intended. The Cold War was the result of competing plans; the Renaissance planned by no one, and not even colligated as such until the nineteenth century. By this distinction we can raise what is perhaps the central question for any philosophical account of narrative understanding. *How is the earlier made comprehensible in the light of the later, where that comprehension goes beyond the teleology of planned action?*

(4): *Interpretation* Narrative can be regarded as a sort of interpretation. To ask questions of narrative understanding is to move in the same terrain as a philosophy of interpretation: what sort of meaning is there to be found, and how is it transformed in understanding? To what extent can the evidence determine one interpretation or narrative rather than another? Though narrative can be approached in such a way (which is roughly the way that Paul Ricoeur approaches narrative, as I shall explain), an influential approach has been to study narrative in terms of discourse. (Note that historians can approach the past through its discourse. Philosophers of history can then approach the historian through their discourse. It is the latter, potentially second-order, programme that will be our topic.)

Discourse is language considered as a whole (Barthes: 'sets of words beyond the level of the sentence' (1981: 7); recalling Chapter 8, we also see de Saussure's influence). A discourse has properties that are not apparent at the level of the statement: rules or archetypes which govern, for example, why one statement is said and not another, and how those statements are arranged, structured and privileged. A discursive approach will therefore insist that one must examine the whole in order to understand any one part. A second, related, feature of discursive approaches is the tendency to privilege the form of the discourse being examined over the truth or reference of that discourse. The aim is not to see what 'lies behind' the discourse, or what it 'points to', but simply what it is. Michel Foucault's programmatic statement of his 'archaeological' approach makes clear the difference between a discursive methodology, and that of the traditional interpretivist who was the subject of Chapters 7 through 9:

> Archaeology tries to define not the thoughts, representations, images, themes, preoccupations that are concealed or revealed in discourses; but those discourses themselves, those discourses as practices obeying certain rules. It does not treat discourse as a *document*, as a sign of something else, as an element that ought to be transparent, but whose unfortunate opacity

> must often be pierced if one is to reach at last the depth of the essential in the place in which it is held in reserve; it is concerned with discourse in its own volume, as a *monument*. It is not an interpretative discipline: it does not seek another, better-hidden discourse. It refuses to be 'allegorical'.
>
> (Foucault 2005/1969: 155)

There are of course many discourses that are not narrative. But narratives can be regarded as particularly suitable for discursive treatment, since one suspects that the importance of the narrative will largely result not from its individual components, but how they are related and the whole presented.[1] The account of narrative understanding presented by Louis Mink is a particularly clear carrying out of the discursive suggestion. Complete narrative understanding is achieved only by regarding each element in the light of *all* others. And that extreme integration is to be carried out purely through language, in a 'network of overlapping descriptions'. Mink's central example suggests how those overlapping descriptions are formed and used:

> We follow Oedipus on the road from Delphi to the crossroads where he is insulted by a stranger and in anger kills him. . . . the incident at the crossroads is *fully* describable only by a set of descriptions which jointly refer to all the rest of the story. The doomed man is a noble stranger to Oedipus, but he is also the king of Thebes, the father of Oedipus, the husband of Jocasta, the predecessor of Oedipus as husband of Jocasta, the man whose house is cursed, the man who sent Oedipus to be bound and exposed as an infant, the man whose wife is a suicide, the man whose son blinds himself, and above all the man whose identity is discovered after his death by his slayer. He is alive and he is dead, and he could not be elsewhere than at the crossroads in the sunshine.'
>
> (Mink 1970: 556)

3. Metahistory

A different sort of discursive approach to narrative understanding has been provided by Hayden White. White's guiding idea is that historiography is to be understood in terms of its rhetorical form. In *Metahistory* (1973), White conducted what was ostensibly an intellectual history of eight specific nineteenth-century historians.[2] In subsequent development of theses explicit in the introduction and conclusion to *Metahistory* (and embodied in the central chapters of that work), he made it clear that this was a philosophical approach that was intended to apply to any historiography whatsoever (1978). Historiography was to be regarded as narrative, even where that narrative was not made explicit. The specifics of that narrative were to be understood as the application of a set of rhetorical techniques. The historian could choose between a number of rhetorical techniques (in *Metahistory*, four), a choice that was not determined by their object of study. An important aim of White's analysis was to show that these rhetorics were *not* to be understood as the superstructure of historiography, imposed over the substance of the account merely in order to make *the substance* more readable or more persuasive. Rather, white insisted that the historian's rhetorics to a great extent constituted the substantive historical understanding, explanation and knowledge.

In the introduction to *Metahistory*, White traced the construction of the historical discourse from its starting point, the chronicle. The chronicle is a list of facts. One of White's favourite examples (White 1980) were the Annals of St Gall, part of which looks like this:

709	Hard winter. Duke Gottfried died
710	Hard year and deficient in crops
711	
712	Flood everywhere
713	
714	Pippin, mayor of the palace, died

The chronicle should not be regarded as history proper. It provides no understanding of the past, although it may provide the raw materials for such an understanding. The historian puts flesh on the skeleton by first turning the chronicle into story. Stories, as suggested in the first section, tie their elements together as beginning, middle and end.

But it is in moving beyond the level of story that White's account becomes distinctive. A story can be emplotted in a number of ways: in *Metahistory*, as suggested, there are four possibilities. The romantic emplotment regards the story as a triumph, the hero (which may be an individual, a class, a nation, or an idea) transcending the formidable difficulties that beset their path, transforming themselves and their world. The Christ story is an ancient example (a more contemporary one is *The Lord of the Rings*). The tragic emplotment similarly begins with division that must be overcome. Yet the ending is not a triumph, but disaster and, where appropriate, death. A tragic ending is not pointless, however; redemption of a different sort is purchased as a result, at least for those who observed the tragic drama (as, for example, in *Romeo and Juliet*). The comic emplotment begins with a division, but of a much less momentous sort. As in romance, division is healed, though in a superficial rather than transcendent fashion (in comedy, the world remains fundamentally the same). For example, people are separated from their natural partners, the narrative conclusion being reached in their (re)finding those unions (as in *A Midsummer Night's Dream*). Finally, the satirical emplotment likewise regards fundamental change as impossible, but here because the actors are prisoners of their circumstances. Despite believing that they can change and overcome, the reader is led to believe that such is mere vanity and hubris (as in Tolstoy's treatment of Napoleon in *War and Peace*).

It is important to reassert the thesis that these various emplotments are *imposed upon* stories, and thus that one story can support multiple emplotments. One way to appreciate this is to see that the characterization of the important points in each emplotment – in particular, the start and end – depends on one's evaluation, and often on ethical evaluation. To regard something as a tragedy requires taking the initial division to be *important* in a way that the comic author does not. To regard something as a romance rather than a tragedy requires identifying a hero. To regard as a satire involves assessing what counts as fundamental change. In all these matters and more, historians' evaluations lead to disagreement.

Over and above the understanding provided by story and plot, further explanatory value is provided by the 'mode of argument' of the narrative, that which provides an answer to 'what it all means'. In this rhetorical element we can find some of the philosophies of explanation examined earlier in this book, a fact which well illustrates White's desire to look at historiography *from above*, laying out all the options, but not arguing for the superiority of one over another. Mechanism is a type of explanation which provides underlying causes (as in Diamond's account considered in Chapter 5). Contextualism explains by situating the particular practice, action or event in some cultural or social context (as in Darnton's interpretation considered in Chapter 9). Organicism explains by situating the particular in a wider *temporal* context, exemplified by the cases of colligation considered previously in this chapter. Formism explains by locating what is unique about the particular item, contrasting that particular to others. White's own explanatory strategy is formist, in so far as he attempts to identify what is unique about each way of doing history.

Finally, White insists that the historian's discursive strategies go all the way down, constituting even the most basic elements of their historiographies and not just the big picture of emplotment. To substantiate this claim, he examines each historian's language, arguing that all use poetic 'tropes' to create their words and statements, the 'facts' that the explanation proceeds from. The historian does not use the technical language of the scientist, according to White, but uses instead: metaphors (which draw attention to similarity), metonymy and synecdoche (which draw attention to relations between part and whole), and irony (which draws attention to the tension between multiple meanings). In this way, the idea that the historian first finds the facts, and then weaves those into a narrative, is made impossible: for the very constitution of 'the facts' is tied to the rhetorical position as a whole. (This emphasis on the inevitability of poetic troping in historiography is what leads one to associate White with 'Linguistic Idealism', a position discussed in Chapter 12.) Over and above the creation of facts by poetic troping, operations central to historical understanding – inclusion, suppression, highlighting of events as important, drawing out of symbolic themes – are to be regarded as part and parcel of the rhetorical strategies adopted.

None of the elements of White's account are new; he is happy to credit the authors of the rhetorical tools with which his analyses proceed. And a rhetorical approach of this sort to historiography is strongly suggested by Structuralism in general, and in particular by Roland Barthes (1981/1967):

> historical discourse oscillates between two poles, according to whether it is indices or functions that predominate. When the indexical units predominate . . . [the historiography has] metaphorical form and borders upon the lyrical and symbolic . . . When, by contrast, it is the functional units which predominate, History takes on a metonymic form and becomes a close relation of the epic.

Nonetheless, the whole analysis that White has provided has enabled many to appreciate historiography, indeed historical understanding, in a new and fruitful way. From regarding history books as the gluing together of dates and facts by causal claims, we can appreciate the historical work as a whole, its most powerful effects a result of affinities and strategies embodied in its organization. His approach also holds out the attraction, as implied, of providing a 'view from above', promising the ability to fit together the differing positions in the philosophy of history according to White's master table (regarding in a new way old debates concerning universal and particular, naturalism and anti-naturalism, intention and structure).[3]

4. Narrative and truth

Two questions have dominated philosophical enquiry into historical narrative. The extent to which, and manner by which, narratives provide understanding of the past has been the topic of the first part of this chapter. The issue of narrative truth will be the topic for the remainder. The following two chapters will address the possibility and nature of truth in historical accounts. At this point, we focus on narrative truth specifically, by asking whether there is anything *peculiar to the narrative* that rules out the possibility of truth. To answer affirmatively, to agree that narrative does face a specific problem, it is not enough to note that narratives occur both in history and in fiction. For it is plausible (and certainly possible) to hold that a historical narrative shares the same form as a fictional narrative, but is distinguished from the latter precisely in being true.

Roland Barthes (1981) advanced the view that the historical narrative illicitly acquires a 'realism effect' in virtue of subtle rhetorical features. In common with the realist novels of the nineteenth century, historical narratives give the impression 'that the story is telling itself'. Most important is that no reference is made to the point of view of a narrator: the narrative is written staunchly in the third person, rather than the first person of the narrator. Second, the impression of truth is induced in the reader by the detail of the narrative, a detail that is even cleverly superfluous to the narrative's development. The truly Romantic narratives (exemplified in Chapter 1 using a passage from Thomas Carlyle's description of the death of Robespierre) clearly provided superfluous information of that sort; but the tendency for narrative to include detail that the narrator could not possibly have known is rarely avoided in extended historical narration. Finally, a continuity is constructed that further reinforces the implication that the narrator writes not from a partial and limited perspective, but with a 'view from nowhere'.

Peter Burke (1992) provides a historian's response to Barthes' charge that historical narration promotes an elicit 'realism effect'. Burke accepts the criticism, and takes the historical challenge to involve developing historical narratives that depart from the form derived from nineteenth-century realist novels. Indeed, he finds that certain historical narratives already do depart in significant ways from the model criticized by Barthes. Burke finds examples of narratives that use an unreliable narrator, and that use multiple narrators; that feature alternative endings (for example, a narrative of the First World War that terminates in 1919, and which then presents an alternative termination in 1939); and that 'narrate' events from later to earlier (for example, an account of Poland that moves backwards from the present). Most importantly, Burke accepts that the historian should clearly indicate their own point of view in their narrating, that they 'make themselves visible in their narrative ... as a warning to the reader that they are not omniscient or impartial and that other interpretations besides theirs are possible' (1992: 239).

I would not deny that these historiographical approaches are potentially exciting. But why should we think that they are *necessary*? We surely do *not* need to be reminded that the historian is not omniscient, and having followed the arguments of the last two chapters, neither should we think that only one interpretation is possible. More substantively, we should not conclude from the premise that certain devices *can* be used to illegitimately produce a 'realism effect' in the reader, to the conclusion that *any* use of those devices precludes truth. The best liars are able to add great detail to their stories, but that does not mean that adding great detail makes one a liar.[4] The most promising element of Barthes' critique is the insistence that narrative requires a narrator's point of view. To expand upon that element, we might insist that narratives are always constructed by somebody, and never found in the (past) world.

> Stories are not lived but told. Life has no beginnings, middles, or ends; there are meetings, but the start of an affair belongs to the story we tell ourselves later, and there are partings, but final partings only in the story.
>
> (Mink 1970: 557–8)

The distinction between life and story has been asserted on the basis that narratives are created, and therefore cannot have been discovered. But to assume a dichotomy between those terms would be unwise, since any account whatsoever is also created, but some of those creations will also count as discoveries. The distinction between non-narrative living and narrative telling has also been asserted on the basis that to suppose that narratives can exist without a narrator is to fall into a rather simple-minded mistake, perhaps even a mistake concerning the meaning of 'narrative'. There is some sense in which narratives require narrators, indeed the same sense in which statements require a stater and theories a theorizer; but that is hardly to preclude the question of whether something in the past might make those narratives true. The most persuasive argument against narratives lived is perhaps an 'argument from queerness' (to use the term that J. L. Mackie made famous in his critical assessment of what moral facts could be). Whatever the reality of the past is constituted by, it is outrageous to think that inherent in it are narratives waiting to be told; as if Simon Schama's (1989) satirical story of the French Revolution or Beevor's (1999) tragic tale of Stalingrad were already resident in the past itself.

How could the narrative realist point to real features of the past that have narrative form independent of a narrator? There is only one possible candidate: human action (Gallie 1964; MacIntyre 2003: 204–17; Ricoeur 1984). As noted at the start of this chapter, a 'thin' sense of narrative does not place any limits on the subject matter of narratives. But the 'thicker' sense of narrative usually presumed in debates in the philosophy of history does imply a focus on action. That focus does not seem to be coincidental, given that action and narrative are tightly related even before the historian arrives on the scene. The central claim of the realist is that there is an isomorphism, a structural correspondence, between planning, acting and remembering. To plan is to envisage a narrative that one wishes to take place, whether that concerns the activities of a weekend, or the development of one's life. One's plans are typically nested: writing a sentence is part of finishing an essay, itself a part of successfully completing a degree, which takes its part as the 'beginning of a great career as a historian' in the narrative plan for one's life. Actions are not performed at random, but are performed according to a narrative – sometimes in response to an explicitly made plan, sometimes in spontaneous development of an unfolding narrative. When one remembers correctly, then the same narrative is recalled – the very narrative that was planned and lived. Finally, if you can recall your own narrative truthfully, then why not another – the historian.[5]

Because of such considerations as these, I don't think that it is correct to rule out, *by fiat*, the possibility of narrative realism. Nonetheless, one might justifiably wonder what those considerations have to do with *historical narrative*, given that the above suggestions appear to be restricted to the narratives governing individuals. Certain types of microhistory, which we might term 'micronarratives', are indeed limited by individual narrative structures in the ways suggested.[6] The assertion that narrative guarantees a particular perspective is accepted. To the extent that more than one perspective is available and required, the account will allow the past to be known by combining different narratives. Thus, one might seek to know a particular battle through a narrative from the commander, a different narrative from a foot soldier in the thick of the action, another from a nurse, and yet another from a deserter. Yet these microhistories are the exception. A more familiar, and more ambitious, sort of historical narrative is not restricted to stories of individual lives as they were planned and experienced, nor to a collection of such. And as we have already noted in this chapter, it is not in general sufficient to understand narrative by appeal to action, and explanation of action. One source of the teleology inherent in historical narratives can be the teleology that is found in action and planning. But the teleology found in historical narratives goes well beyond what anyone plans and acts upon.

5. Collective narrative and metanarrative

What is the connection between the narratives inherent in individual action, and the historian's wider narrative? This is the central question posed in Paul Ricoeur's three volume *Time and Narrative* (1984–8). In that work, Ricoeur treats historical narration as that which takes action, 'prefigured' as it is the form of a proto-narrative, which creatively 'configures' that action, and which thereby provides material that is 'refigured' in the audience. In short, there is a connection between the final historical narrative and the raw material of human activity and experience, but it is not a connection that is straightforwardly isomorphic. Ricoeur's task is to substantiate that three-fold process. In what follows I present a simpler account that draws on Ricoeur's.

Consider first the idea of collective memory. Collective memory differs from memories that we hold in common (we might both remember the lead story in yesterday's *Times*, but that is not without further argument to be regarded as a *collective* memory). A collective memory is made so by relations between the individuals subsequent to the event remembered. Those relations are well illustrated by cases of reminiscence: if you and your partner reminisce about the day that you first met, that shared activity will be dependent your practical and dialogical relations subsequent to that day. You will, perhaps, have developed codes that refer to parts of the day that you both consider important (the 'dark-haired stranger', the fortuitous return to the pub). Those codes could be used to prompt laughter, embarrassment, joy, and could be employed more widely than in reminiscing over just that day. Most centrally, you will have – probably without intending to – integrated your memories into a shared account: a collective narrative. Individual memories are put to use in the creation of a collective memory, one filling the gaps left by another, one correcting the other.

A collective memory of a less happy event extends the notion of collective narrative. An argument between yourself and your partner will not be the subject of reminiscence, though may be collectively recalled. In recalling an argument, an important complication becomes apparent that was not present in the first example: the individual memories are likely to be to some extent opposed. Not only or even primarily are they opposed with regard to what did or did not happen. More significant is disagreement regarding the importance of things said, the use of explanation to implicitly absolve or place blame, and the location of the true beginning to the argument. While each individual might *explain* their own actions as being the result of the other's, and might *justify* those actions as a reaction to the other's (or is that just me?), a collective memory must resolve such incompatibilities.

In the previous section, I emphasized the correspondence between planning, acting and remembering. Just as there are collective memories, there are collective plans, in which the individual plans are incomprehensible apart from the whole. One cannot plan to have a party, or a game, or an election, apart from the planning of others. In the sort of adversarial situation envisaged in the last two examples, the individual plans can be opposed, neither likely to be fully realized, though nonetheless some common narrative is made possible. Feeding this notion of collective planning, action, memory and narrative into the question of narrative truth, we can conclude that the advocate of narrative truth need not be restricted to narratives that are purely individual. Indeed, in many cases the story lived cannot be made sense of without understanding that story as collective. (Ricoeur goes further: *all* action is also reaction to others' actions, in so far as actions are 'moments of responsiveness or failure to respond'.)

The historian continues the process of forming collective narratives, bringing together interlocutors that cannot meet as you and your partner can (because too widely separated, or simply because those individuals are no longer alive). Regarded in this way, it is the historian's task to mould fewer coherent narratives from many individual ones. Ricoeur would, additionally, demand of the narrative that it bring together action and structure, project and natural event: 'if description preserves the stratification of layers, it is up to the narrative to tie them together' (Ricoeur 2004: 246). For example, in narrative the historian brings together such heterogeneous elements as a long-term structure of domination together with a sudden battle. We find ourselves in a similar place to the suggestion at the end of Chapter 6: that the historian's narrative is above all a tool for bringing together the melange of elements by which we describe the past. Can we still talk of narrative truth, even where there is plainly no pattern of action, individual or collective, to which the narrative corresponds? I think that we can; but such an answer requires a closer look at truth, a task to be undertaken in the final two chapters.

A maximally collective narrative we might call a *metanarrative*. Jean-François Lyotard's *The Postmodern Condition* has exerted an immense influence over our self-image in the three decades since it was first published. 'Simplifying to the extreme, I define *postmodern* as incredulity toward metanarratives' (Lyotard 2001/1979: xxiv). (In Chapter 12 I suggest an alternative definition of postmodernism, in terms of choice.) A metanarrative provides a teleology within which one can make sense of the changes that have happened, and of our place within those changes. A metanarrative, as the name suggests, is not restricted to any one group or nation, but binds us all into the same story. To use a term introduced in Chapters 2 and 3, metanarratives are the most consilient ways to explain an extremely wide range of phenomena. Though, as Lyotard states, they are not (now) welcomed, but distrusted.

Hegel's narrative of the developing conceptions of freedom (outlined in Chapter 1) is one example of an influential metanarrative (not least upon Francis Fukuyama's well known 1992 thesis that, with the arrival of liberalism in politics and economics, we have reached 'the end of history'). Other metanarratives are perhaps more familiar to those outside academia. Marx, greatly indebted to Hegel, bequeathed the metanarrative of history as driven by changes in the means of production, leading to the succession of capitalism by feudalism, and to the eventual arrival of communism. Alternatively, the metanarrative of scientific progress would account for the increasingly radical change in our social world by reference to the scientific attainment of more accurate theories, the cumulative acquisition of more knowledge, and the cumulative achievement of technological innovation that is both based on theoretical knowledge and which hastens new discovery. Finally, the three great 'desert religions' – Judaism, Christianity and Islam – contain metanarratives which are at the heart of a believer's understanding of the world. God's will is to be seen at work in the world, stretched between the Fall and the final redemption.

Are metanarratives supposed by postmodernists to be impossible, undesirable, or both? I would take the message of the possibility of collective narrative to imply that there is no *metaphysical* reason to reject metanarrative, simply because collective narrative can follow collective planning and action. That does not – of course – mean that all metanarratives, or even any metanarrative, should be welcomed. Precisely because narrative, planning and action share a common form, the acceptance or otherwise of a narrative which encompasses our own activity is a choice that bears on the question of how we want to live our life, and how to organize our future. The question of metanarrative is, in other words, one of practicality, and often of political import. I return to and expand upon this point in Chapter 12.

Further reading and study questions

Carroll, N. (1990) 'Interpretation, History and Narrative', in *The Monist* 73. A sharp analysis of White's approach.

MacIntyre, A. (2003) *After Virtue*. London: Duckworth (originally 1981). Chapter 15, 'The virtues, the unity of a human life and the concept of a tradition' develops the suggestion that stories *are* lived.

Ricoeur, P. (1984) K. McLaughlin and D. Pellauer (trans.). *Time and Narrative*. Chicago: University of Chicago Press. Ricoeur provides an overview of his approach in Volume I, Part I, Chapter 3.

White, H. (1973) *Metahistory*. Baltimore: Johns Hopkins Press. The introduction and conclusion contain the explicit theory.

White, H. (1978) 'The historical text as literary artefact', in *Tropics of Discourse*. Baltimore: Johns Hopkins Press, 81–100. A readable introduction to White's discursive approach.

(a) According to White, how does the historian bring their audience to understand what happened?

(b) What is a metanarrative? How, if at all, does it differ from a collective narrative?

(c) Can stories be lived, as well as told?

Part V
TRUTH AND REALITY

The absent past 11

Does history generally provide the truth about the past? All agree that not all history is correct – historians aren't infallible. But reasons have been advanced which are intended to get us to think one of the following:

- that historians cannot find out the truth about the past (general scepticism);
- that finding out the truth about the past is unlikely (qualified scepticism);
- that there is no truth about the past to be had (anti-realism);
- that what historians call truth is of their own making (constructivism and idealism);
- that truth is relative to the historian or the historian's culture (relativism);
- that the historian can choose what is true (postmodernism).

To discuss these questions requires entering into the question of what *truth* is, and what *reality* is, and how our thoughts and language relate to it. Some of the arguments of the next two chapters are quite general, concerning any truth, any part of reality. Others will focus more specifically on the past, and on distinctively historical truths. We will have course to revisit historical reasoning, and so ideas developed in Chapters 2 and 3 will be deployed and extended. In the first two sections of this chapter, I introduce those positions, with regard to truth, knowledge and reality, that will then be argued for or criticized in the remainder of this chapter and the next. I am afraid that will necessitate the introduction of a variety of terminology that may appear a little overwhelming to the reader who is approaching these topics for the first time. My recommendation to such a reader is to regard the first two sections as reference material, to be re-checked as required by the substantive arguments that follow.

1. Overview: correspondence to reality

To begin, I introduce what may be the default position of most historians on these questions: that the past existed, our historical accounts are about that past, and those histories are true to the extent that they correspond to past facts. That package provides a first stab at making sense of the interconnected ideas of *truth*, *fact* and *past reality*, and their place in what historians attempt to do (or at least, what they should attempt to do). Whether or not most historians do hold such a position, it nonetheless provides a useful base against which to launch the sorts of criticism already suggested.

We can give the first words about truth to Aristotle: 'to say of what is that it is, or of what is not that it is not, is true' (*Metaphysics* Γ 7.27 1966/c. 300 BC). To some philosophers, those are also pretty much the last words on truth, a position which I hope that by the end of the next chapter I will persuade you is not without merit. To others, Aristotle's characterization is the prolegomenon to a correspondence theory of truth. A correspondence theorist insists that for a statement to be true is for it to correspond to the facts. (Alternative versions of the theory substitute propositions, or beliefs, for statements.) That idea certainly sits well with what historians are often inclined to say: that one's history should get the facts right, and should not make claims that are unsupported by the facts. How much is really being said in such phrases is, however, indeterminate until we know more about what work 'correspondence' and 'fact' are doing. For talk of 'correspondence to the facts' can be taken as no more than a rhetorical flourish. If we are to claim that the Bastille fell on 14 July 1789, and then to add that the foregoing statement corresponds to the facts, it might be best not to think that two assertions have been made, but that one assertion has been made in two different ways. If 'correspondence to the facts' is just a rhetorical flourish, then *any* theory of truth whatsoever could cheerfully agree to such talk.

A genuine correspondence theory of truth adds an account of the *structure* of statements, the structure of facts, and how those two match up. To an atomic statement, 'the Bastille was burnt', corresponds an atomic fact. The statement and fact correspond in virtue of their internal structure; specifically, 'the Bastille' names the Bastille, 'burnt' names the relevant property, and the Bastille satisfies that property. Not all statements are atomic. 'All buildings stormed in France in 1789 were burnt', if true, is not made true by a single fact, but by many facts. One of the more notable achievements of a correspondence theory is that we are told how precisely those many facts lead to the truth or falsity of the compound statement. The compound statement is 'truth functional': it is determined by the truth values of the relevant atomic facts. In the case of the current example, the compound statement is true if and only if, for each building stormed in France in 1789, that building was burnt.

A correspondence theory of truth has a certain affinity with *realism*. The debate between realists and anti-realists has traversed many domains: including moral values, numbers, atomic theory, universals, the past. Realism with regard to a certain domain of objects requires that those objects exist. Less obviously, realism also requires that those objects exist in a way that is not dependent on our thinking and talking about them. In what follows I also take the realist to be committed to a linguistic thesis; that the language in the domain in question is used to describe reality. In the following section, I start to sketch out ways that one or other of these realist claims are denied.

To think that historical accounts are made true in so far as they correspond to what really happened is to buy in to both a correspondence theory of truth and realism with regard to the past. A pairing of correspondence theory with anti-realism is possible, if unusual, on the basis that truth be a matter of corresponding to something constructed by or dependent on our thought about the past. More significantly, we should hold open the possibility of realism without a correspondence theory of truth. In particular, one might believe that historical truth is a matter of saying what really happened, without thinking that there is any more to be said about facts or correspondence. A *deflationary* position of this sort would refuse to say much about truth at all, on the grounds that Aristotle's platitudes are all that can be said.

There are challenges that any correspondence theory of truth must meet. Perhaps the hardest of those is to give an account of *facts* such that they are sufficiently similar to statements to permit correspondence, and yet sufficiently different so as not to be simply the projection of language onto the world. The danger of the second horn is that attributions of fact follow attributions of truth, rather than grounding them as the correspondence theory requires. We are back to the 'rhetorical flourish' objection: what does talk of a statement 'fitting the facts' add to the statement itself? Peter Strawson put the point nicely:

> what could fit more perfectly the fact that it is raining than the statement that it is raining? Of course, statements and facts fit. They were made for each other. If you prise the statements off the world you prise the facts off it too; but the world would be none the poorer.
>
> (Strawson 1999: 168)

I will say no more about general objections to correspondence, and shall instead focus on challenges to both a correspondence theory of truth, and to realism, that follow from specifically historical considerations. Before I consider those arguments, I present the second part of the initial overview.

2. Overview: anti-realism

In the previous section, I introduced one theory of historical truth – the correspondence theory – and one position with regard to past reality – realism. In this section, I introduce another three positions with regard to truth, and another three with regard to reality. Just as the correspondence theory and realism fit together comfortably, so we can pair off the other six positions, in a way summarized in Figure 11.1.[1] Note that one can quite legitimately take a different stance for different domains (such as moral values, numbers, atomic theory, universals, the past). One can also take a different stance for types of language within the same domain; as we shall see in the next section, a popular position is to claim that while the 'basic statements' of a historical account are made true in accordance with the real past, higher level claims of an interpretative or narrative sort should be regarded anti-realistically.

The first sort of anti-realism is quite straightforward: it is simply the assertion that nothing exists to ground talk in the target domain. How, then, are we to understand the claims made in that domain, those which *seemingly are* about something real? First, one could take all those claims to be false; though they purport to be about something real, there is nothing there, and the result is massive error. (J. L. Mackie adopted an *error-theory* of this sort with regard to moral statements, on the basis of the unreality of moral facts.) Second, one could adopt *non-cognitivism* with respect to some domain of language. A cognitivist about L takes L to be 'truth-apt': L is the kind of language that can be true or false. (Both standard realism, and error-theory, imply cognitivism.) Some language is non-cognitivist: one expresses emotion by screaming 'yuck!'; one issues an order by saying 'shut the door'. The way those statements are assessed is not in terms of their truth and falsity. It may be that certain kinds of statements have a surface form of cognitivism, but are nonetheless to be analysed in a non-cognitivist way. Once more, the position is a standard one in moral philosophy: the moral non-cognitivist would analyse moral claims as expressions of emotion or demand.

The second sort of anti-realism is less straightforward, not least because this anti-realist will *not* deny that there is something there to talk about. What is important to this brand of anti-realism is that what there is to talk about is *dependent upon our thinking or language*. Without us, the reality in question would not exist; just as dreams exist, but not without a dreamer. This second sort of anti-realism has gone under a variety of titles, but two that I shall be using are *constructivism* and *Idealism*. In order to explain the motivation of Idealism, we need to make a short detour into the metaphysics of Immanuel Kant.

Idealism is the thesis that reality itself is constructed by our thinking about it, a thesis that sounds *outré*, perhaps bizarre, but which has had an enormous impact upon contemporary thinking. Kant was not the first Idealist, but it is his version of that thesis which has been of enduring influence. One can trace the source of Kant's views to his concern with knowledge that is both *a priori* – not justified by any empirical investigation; and yet *substantive* – not simply a matter of defining words (Kant 1929/1781). It is usually supposed to be unproblematic to accept that we have knowledge that 'all bachelors are male', on the basis that we have defined the constituent terms such that the sentence is true as a matter of necessity. Metaphysical statements that are substantive, and yet known *a priori*, are usually regarded as more problematic: that all events have a cause (except perhaps the 'prime mover', God); that no object can be both red and green all over at the same time; that all coloured objects are extended; that the angles of a triangle add up to 180 degrees.

If one is to accept examples such as the above as genuine examples of knowl-edge, and further agree that they are true not simply as a matter of definition, then it is natural to wonder in virtue of what they can be known. Kant proposed an ingenious answer. They are not true because of the world in itself, for if they were then, given their lack of empirical basis, there would be no way of us coming to know them. Rather, they are true as a result of our mental construction of the world in itself. We organize the world in these ways – by imposing upon it cause and effect, space, time, colour, and other categories – and could not experience the world without those categories. If this is so, then we can deduce metaphysical truth: to experience requires that certain metaphysical facts be true; we do experience, therefore those metaphysical facts are true. This positive Kantian suggestion has, however, a critical corollary. Just as we can know the world as it is constructed by us (the phenomenal world, to use Kantian terminology) we cannot know the world as it is in itself (the noumenal world). Our categories, constructed by the mind, stand between us and the world as it really is. To use Bertrand Russell's analogy, it is as if we are all wearing blue-tinted glasses that cannot be removed.

As with realism, no specific theory of truth need be implied by Idealism. Yet a coherence theory of truth can be seen to fit well, given the Idealist notion that our statements are not made true or false by an independent reality. According to the coherence theory of truth, a statement is true in so far as it coheres with others, and false in so far as it does not cohere. To think that *justification* of belief is a matter of that belief cohering with others is quite a commonsense position to hold. The idea that truth itself is a matter of coherence takes a greater leap. But if reality is in some sense constructed by belief, it perhaps makes sense to think that the nature of truth be the same as the nature of justification.

The final pair is an attempt to sidestep the debates over the theory of truth, and those between the realist and anti-realist. *Anti-representationalism* is the thesis that statements should not be regarded in terms of representing the world or not. Thus, the realist is wrong because they think that true statements do represent the world; the anti-realist (including the Idealist) is wrong because they think that no statement (in that domain) can ever represent properly. I say no more about this position here, but shall return to it in Chapter 12. Anti-representationalism fits well with the deflationary theory of truth. To the deflationist, truth is not a substantive property – not correspondence to facts, nor coherence, nor any other of the properties picked out by the many theories of truth that have been offered. The deflationist agrees that the word 'true' can be useful – as a 'disquotational' device (as in 'everything that Bob said was

Table 11.1 Philosophical approaches to truth and reality

Theory of truth	Nature of reality
Correspondence	**Realism**
No truth: either error theory or non-cognitivism	Anti-realism: There's nothing there to ground statements.
Coherence	Anti-realism (Idealism): Reality is constructed by our thought or language.
Deflationism: there is no theory of truth, only platitudes about truth	Reject the distinction between realism and anti-realism.

true'), for praise, and for warning ('I know you've checked all the evidence, but it still might not be true'). But there is nothing that all truths have in common, nothing to ground a 'theory of truth'. 'Napoleon was short' is true if and only if Napoleon was short, 'the Nazis were evil' is true if and only if the Nazis were evil, 'the French Revolution was tragic' if and only if the French Revolution was tragic. There is nothing more to truth as a property than a platitudinous list of this sort. Thus, Aristotle has both the first and the last word on truth.

There ends the brief introduction to philosophies of truth and reality. To complete this section, I introduce two other terms necessary for understanding the arguments to follow. The justification of historical belief by the evidence was the subject of Part I, and Chapter 3 in particular. There I characterized that justification in two overlapping ways: through Bayesianism, and explanationism. The picture common to all accounts of evidential justification is of justification being transmitted, belief to belief. For example, the belief that witnesses were held together prior to testifying justifies the belief that the similarity in those testimonies is due to collusion. We could then ask what justified the belief that the witnesses *were* held together, finding a further belief to justify that one. One traditional question in epistemology is whether that chain of justification has an end-point, or whether every justified belief itself rests on a further belief. A different way of putting that same question is to ask about the *structure* of the historian's system of justification. If we imagine beliefs as nodes of a net, nodes connected by relations of justification, what structure will that net have?

The *foundationalist* expects the net to be grounded, either upon beliefs which justify themselves, or on non-beliefs. An example of a self-justifying belief is 'I exist'. That belief – so Descartes famously suggested – cannot but be true, since it is presupposed by even the most extreme doubt. (Descartes subsequently attempted to found the whole structure of belief upon that single, slender base; an attempt which philosophers, in a rare show of near unity, have regarded as a failure.) An example of the foundation of belief upon non-belief is foundationalist empiricism. According to that programme, of which positivism is an instance, basic beliefs are directly justified by perceptual experience, non-basic beliefs on a chain of beliefs passing through the basic.

The alternative position to foundationalism is coherentism. To the *coherentist*, the net of beliefs is unanchored. Justification points from one belief to the next, with no part of the net having the power to provide justification without also requiring justification. The foundationalist differs from the coherentist in two ways. First, the foundationalist, but not the coherentist, believes in the possibility of *certainty*; that some beliefs might be conclusively justified, and therefore unalterable. Second, the foundationalist, but not the coherentist, believes in the possibility of *directness* of justification; that some beliefs might be justified without relying on further beliefs. Directly justified beliefs might, in particular, simply rest on perceptual experience. One could argue that a 'moderate foundationalist' could buy into directness, and yet recognize that certainty is not to be had. (Robert Audi provides a useful introduction to and defence of moderate foundationalism (1998: 204–8).)

3. Beyond statement truth

The question of *historical* truth raises specific issues that are not relevant to the question of truth more generally. Two distinctive issues require attention. In the sections following this I consider the relevance of the truism that historical statements are about the past. It has been claimed that the past is not directly accessible to us, that the past is in some sense absent, and that such realizations make historical truth specifically problematic. A second distinctive issue for historical truth is perhaps less obvious, though has already been suggested in discussion of objectivity (Chapter 9) and narrative (Chapter 10). The historical account is a whole that is more than the sum of its parts. To recognize the holistic nature of a historical account is to raise the possibility that there can be historical truth that goes beyond the level of the statement. Standard philosophical debates about truth tend to ignore that possibility, in limiting the investigation to that in virtue of which statements (or propositions, or beliefs) are true.[2] The argument of this section is as follows. First, I draw on material already developed to substantiate the idea that a historical account is greater than the sum of its parts. Second, I explain why standard theories of truth might have difficulty with such a claim. Third, I examine whether holistic truth can be regarded in terms of implicature. Finally, I ask whether, as I will have implied to that point, the holistic nature of a historical account should be regarded as a matter of truth.

Why should we think that the historical account is greater than the sum of its parts? One reason was suggested in Chapter 9: that without a view of the whole one could not make sense of an account being objective (or not), and misleading (or not). The point was there exemplified by a proto-account of Hitler's life that contained only true statements, and yet which was the very model of bias. A second reason was suggested in Chapter 10, with regard to Mink's account of historical understanding. Mink's claim was that it is only by relating each part of the story to every other that full understanding was to be found. A third reason, also suggested in Chapter 10, results from White's *Metahistory*. The historian understands and brings understanding to their audience by rhetorical strategies that only make sense on the level of the whole account. The simplest case is the use of stories: the narrative connection between events that is vital to the understanding of those individual events. Another case is symbolism: the parts of the account are described using a particular poetic trope (metaphor, for example), which serves to provide a unified understanding of the whole. For example, the Romantic historian Jules Michelet, in his history of the French Revolution (1967/1853), symbolizes the French Revolution as a struggle for unity; manifest in the unity of the *cahiers* (the demands of the French people to the Estates General of 1789), of the elections, of the classes, and of the nation itself.

As I have mentioned, standard philosophical discussion of truth tends to overlook truth above the level of the statement. This omission is most clearly demonstrated with regard to the correspondence theory of truth. If the correspondence theorist does accept that historical accounts can be true or false in a way that goes beyond the truth or falsity of their individual components, the challenge is to find something in the real past to which that holistic truth can correspond. If we focus on narrative truth, we can see that something like this challenge was pursued in the latter part of Chapter 10. There I pressed the idea that narratives can be planned and lived, as well as remembered and told. Further, narratives can be planned and lived collectively, with the result that the correspondence theorist would not be restricted to individual action. Still, no matter how far one pushes this picture, it is implausible to restrict historical narrative to that which is collectively planned, and collectively acted upon. With Ricoeur, we can agree that while action and life itself is already narrative, the historian is not a mere copier, but a creator of new narrative from that raw material. If we wish to make sense of the truth of historical narrative, the idea of correspondence can only take us so far. (The only other resource available to the correspondence theorist is to argue that whole truth is a truth-functional result of truth of the parts. But narrative truth – if such there is – is clearly not truth functional. That can be appreciated by noting, with White, that account A and account B might truthfully mention the very same events, and yet exemplify different emplotments.)

'Holistic truth' might turn out to be an unnecessarily mysterious label, if we can make sense of the phenomena of objectivity and narrative by noting the presence of implicature. We imply much more than we explicitly state, and are able to recognize the implicature in others' statements. Because of this, a sentence can be explicitly acceptable, but implicitly misleading. A classic example is 'has Smith stopped beating his wife yet?' The implication is that Smith was beating his wife; if that is not true, then the question is misleading, and must be rejected, not answered. It is not unreasonable to think that biased accounts, such as that given concerning Hitler's life, are misleading in the same way. The implication of a set of statements concerning someone is that those statements are representative of them as a whole. Thus, if all those statements are critical, a negative overall conclusion is implied about that person. On the other hand, if all those statements exonerate the person, then a positive overall conclusion is implied. If the implication is false – if the person is worthy of criticism, when it is implied that they are not, or vice versa – then the account will be misleading without containing any explicit falsehoods.

If we can understand holistic truth in this way, then the issue appears less serious than I have suggested. That is because all truth *can* be truth of statements, but it's just that some statements are explicitly made, and others are only implied. However, I don't think that we can treat the holistic content of historical accounts as *only* a matter of implicature. That is because it is not always possible to make explicit the holistic content of a historical account, at least not completely. Consider, in particular, the import of a metaphor (such as Michelet's) which is made manifest in their account as a whole. Some metaphors (at least) are open-ended. A metaphor is a claim that A is like B; but that the ways that the one is similar to the other are open-ended.

> Thus when Romeo says Juliet is the Sun we can profit from the metaphor indefinitely: we can move among the respects in which someone's lover is like the Sun: warm, sustaining, comforting, perhaps awesome, something on which we are utterly dependent.... This process is quite open-ended.... The metaphor is in effect an invitation to explore comparisons.
>
> (Blackburn 1984: 174)

The exploration of a metaphor is a matter for interpretation. In the same way, the idea that a historical account takes a certain plot, or that it expresses a certain theory of human nature, will depend on interpretation (they may well not be the sorts of content that the original author *could have* made explicit). This doesn't count against the idea that this content is somehow implied by what is said explicitly. But it does count against the reduction of whole content to implicature of a straightforwardly sentential sort suggested by such examples as the implicit accusation of Smith.

My aim to this point has been to establish that there is content in the historical account as a whole that cannot be reduced to the truth of its parts. The final question to be considered in this section is whether that holistic content should be regarded as truth-apt, in other words, the kind of content that can be true or false. A popular claim is that atomic facts – in particular the mapping of events to dates upon which the historian builds their account – are truth-apt, but that the account as a whole is not. Keith Jenkins, for one, is happy to accept atomic facts, though not truth at the level of the whole interpretation or narrative:

> Are there 'past things' that seem to be factually correct? In one sense one can say yes. Thus we know that the so-called Great War/First World War happened between 1914 and 1918. We know that Margaret Thatcher came into power in 1979. If these are facts then we know facts. However, such facts, though important, are 'true' but trite within the larger issues historians consider.
>
> (2003/1991: 40)

One gets a similar impression from *some* things that Hayden White says (though not from others: the idea of poetic troping suggests that any lack of truth at the level of the whole account will trickle down to the level of the individual statement):

> If it were only a matter of realism in representation, one could make a pretty good case for both the annals and chronicle forms as paradigms of ways that reality offers itself to perception
>
> (1980: 27)

One could agree that there is *something* going on at the level of the whole historical account – that the whole is greater than the sum of its parts – and yet insist that what is going on is not to be understood in terms of truth. The most common way to fill out this suggestion is by adopting cognitivism at the level of the part, and non-cognitivism at the level of the whole. In the account as a whole, the historian expresses what they're interested in; what they consider to be right and wrong, praiseworthy and blameworthy; and what they consider to be aesthetically pleasing, not least in the construction of the past so as to form a pleasing unity. Just as the moral non-cognitivist understands moral statements as expressing some emotion or wish, so the historical holistic non-cognitivist understands historical accounts above the level of the atomic statement as expression of some value.

If one wants to defend the possibility that the whole historical account be true, I suggest that the best way is to show that the dichotomy between part and whole that is supposed is simply untenable. Part and whole are connected both *semantically*, and in *rational historical debate*; assertions which I now defend in turn. The non-cognitivist picture that is sometimes suggested is that historians are rather like competing chefs, each provided with the same ingredients, but who use those ingredients to make different meals. But that can't be right, because what makes the historian's 'ingredients' what they are is in part the whole account; whereas the chef's ingredients are, at least to begin with, quite independent. Mink's theory (Chapter 10) makes this dependence clear. The incident at the crossroads is a fact, part of that 'raw material' from which the narrative is built; but that fact – its being 'an incident', in particular – depends on its position in a narrative. Likewise, Napoleon's return from Elba, or the first battle of the Thirty Years War, or the epic battle of Stalingrad, turning point of the Second World War. (Given Mink's explicit defence of narrative imposition, the conclusion that *he* should draw from this collapse between part and whole is that *everything* about a historical account is imposed on the past.)

Over and above semantic connection, one finds that judgements of part and whole are entangled in rational historiographical debate. A very brief sketch of recent historiographical debate concerning the French Revolution follows (largely drawn from the essays in Kates (ed.) (1998)). The fundamental historiographical divide in contemporary debate tends to be found between the *neo-conservatives* and the *neo-liberals*. The neo-conservatives claim that the coming of the French Revolution was not inevitable, but, once begun, its progression to Terror was inevitable. The neo-liberals claim the opposite: the French Revolution was inevitable, but its progression to Terror was not.

Connected to these alternative accounts of development is the question of periodization. The neo-conservative, in closely connecting the inauguration of Revolution and its progression to Terror, will be less inclined to periodize the Revolution by sharply separating an 'earlier' and a 'later' phase. The neo-liberal, in contrast, is keen to use colligatory language so as to make clear that there were multiple revolutions (in particular, with a sharp divide the execution of Louis XVI at the start of 1793). Similar consequences are drawn with regard to whether the Revolution and adjacent periods be understood as a unity, or sharply separated. The neo-conservative emphasizes the similarity between ancien regime and post-revolution, the neo-liberal being more likely to emphasize the fundamental change brought by Revolution.

These commitments at the level of the whole account can be the basis of quite specific challenges to opposing historians; challenges which implicate the so-called 'basic facts'. The neo-conservative must provide an explanation for the financial crisis of 1787, without the neo-liberal notion that the increasing economic power of the bourgeoisie made such a crisis inevitable. The neo-conservative must also explain the seemingly radical nature of revolutionary discourse, given their commitment to a lack of fundamental change. The neo-liberal must explain the common tendency in both *Ancien Regime* and Revolutionary regimes to greater bureaucracy, greater centralization and greater administrative efficiency. The conclusion is that one should not be churlish in permitting cognitive commitment at the whole account level, so long as one is prepared to allow them at *any* level. To allow cognitive commitments is to rule out non-cognitivism, and to make a space for truth at the level of the whole.

4. Qualified historical scepticism

In this section, I examine the first challenge to historical knowledge resulting from that knowledge of the past. Unlike the arguments to come, it does not challenge the realist picture that there may be truth about a real past, independent of the historian's thoughts and language. It is not even a total historical scepticism, a view with the conclusion that all historical justification is moot. The scepticism is qualified: historical justification is not always impossible, but inevitably degrades over time. Given enough of a gap between the historian and the event that they study, knowledge will be impossible.

The children's game 'Chinese Whispers' ('Telephone' for Americans) has the players pass a whispered message one to the other, until the message reaches its way back to the originator. The hope is that on the way, the message has been distorted, with hilarious consequences. The concern that the transmission and inheritance of historical knowledge would ultimately suffer a similar fate was acute for eighteenth-century intellectuals. Pierre-Simon Laplace[3], in his *Philosophical Essay on Probabilities*, based on lectures given in 1795, invites us to

> suppose that a fact is transmitted to us by twenty witnesses, in a manner that the first has transmitted to the second, the second to the third, and thus in sequence; we suppose still that the probability of each testimony is equal to nine-tenths; that of the fact will be less than one eighth, that is to say that there will be more than seven to one odds against that it is false. We can better compare this diminution of the probability only to the extinction of the clarity of objects by the interposition of many pieces of glass, a thickness not that considerable sufficing to steal the view of an object which a single piece lets perceive in a distinct manner. The historians appear not to have paid enough attention to this degradation of the probability of the facts when they are seen to traverse a great number of successive generations; many historical events, reputed as certain, will be at least doubtful if we submitted them to this analysis.
>
> (1951/1814: 13)

John Craige (like Thomas Bayes, an eighteenth-century minister and mathematician) applied this idea to the claims of the biblical gospels. On the basis of similar concerns to Laplace's, Craige calculated that gospel reliability would be negligible by the year 3150. It is only our use of the written document to transmit knowledge of the past that has enabled us to stave off degradation for so long: had we been restricted to oral testimony, the chain would not have been preserved beyond the eighth century (see Nash (2002) and Coady (1992: 199–200)). There is something amusing about Craige's argument, yet perhaps that only derives from the precision of his dating rather than the general principles underlying it. Presumably those who transmit the messages from the past, in speech or in writing, are usually more conscientious than whispering children, and are much more so where the preservation and transmission of information from the past is a professional duty. Yet, everybody makes mistakes occasionally, and given only that admission it appears to be a matter of logical consequence that degradation of knowledge is simply a matter of time.

In Bayesian terms, the claim is that probability can never increase as a belief is transmitted from testifier to recipient. Further, as a matter of practicality,

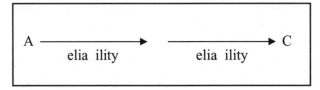

Figure 11.1 Arrows represent causal connections that carry information with a certain degree of reliability.
Reliability of the overall chain, from A to C, is 2/3 multiplied by 3/4 = 1/2.

decrease in probability will sometimes occur, at a rate governed by the proportion of cases in which what is reported is not what was received. The point is a quite general one about information chains. Consider Figure 11.1. The chain from source A to receptor B is only 2/3 reliable; one can think of this measure in terms of the proportion of cases in which what emerges at B is what entered at A. The chain from B, now considered as a secondary source, to receptor C, is 3/4 reliable. The reliability of the overall chain from A to C is found by multiplying the two parts: hence 1/2. It can readily be appreciated that, since the reliability of a chain can never exceed 1, reliability of information can only decrease as that chain is extended.

Yet this conclusion is at odds with successful historical reasoning. The way to avoid the discrepancy is to emphasize the use of *multiple* pieces of evidence by historians (and by detectives, journalists, private investigators, judge and jury). The need to use all evidence at one's disposal has been emphasized in the description of historical methodology in Chapter 2, and in the development of the accounts of historical reasoning in Chapter 3. The present challenge requires us to understand the use of multiple evidence more precisely, so to see how the inevitability of informational degradation can be resisted.

I suggest two sorts of ways that multiple evidence is employed. The first is a matter of applying supplementary evidence to develop *general principles* in order to make use of the central evidence. We have already come across some of these principles in Chapter 2, particularly those based on psychological evidence (of a loose and supposedly commonsense sort). We suppose, for example, that people tend to lie more if it is in their interests to do so, and that they tend to make themselves appear favourably in reporting some episode in which they were involved. Where the evidential basis is more rigorously acquired, we might (following Tucker 2004: 106–7, 124–34) call such general principles 'theories of fidelity'. Tucker (2004: 124) cites the example of vocabulary retention: the proportion of words retained in a given language over a given period of time. Such theories permit the estimation of the reliability of a given piece of evidence.

The second relationship is one of common cause: the multiple pieces of evidence have a common cause, which is either the event that the historian is interested in, or a later common cause (Tucker 2004: 102–24). For example, it is usually believed that, of the New Testament gospels, Matthew and Luke are dependent upon the lost gospel Q, but developed independently thereafter. An application more pertinent to our current discussion is corroborating testimonies. While one witness is unconvincing, corroborating testimony is powerful evidence. Let us imagine ourselves in the position of a detective questioning those present in a house where murder was committed. Witness A reports seeing a man in a passage, immediately prior to the murder committed in a room adjoined to that passage. So far we quite properly withhold judgement. But when a second witness, B, reports also seeing a man in the same passage at a very similar time, we should infer that there was a common cause of A's and B's testimonies. There are two alternative conclusions to the common cause hypothesis, neither convincing in this case. First, we could attempt to explain the similarity in testimony as that which we would have expected in the absence of any particular common cause; the example of Mesoamerican and Mediterranean pyramids in Chapter 3 showed how this could be plausible in certain cases. Second, we could claim that the similarity of reports was simply co-incidental. But the more detailed the similarity, the less likely the co-incidence, and we should remember that certainty should not be demanded: likelihood is sufficient for historical reasoning.

Similarity of testimony may point either to the nature of the event reported, or to a later common cause. An important case of the latter is witness collusion. The practical difficulty of judging whether collusion or corroboration should be inferred is noted by Marc Bloch: 'criticism [of testimony] oscillates between two extremes: the similarity which vindicates and that which discredits' (2004/1954: 115). (In the absence of more specific knowledge, a rule of thumb is to suppose that a certain degree of similarity between witnesses suggests independence later than the event reported, and hence – usually – suggests the truth of what they report; too much similarity suggests later dependence, and hence – usually – collusion.) Finally, where the historian can rule out later entanglement (collusion), they are usually entitled to assume the truth of what is reported. But not always; not where there is an alternative explanation of the way that the event produced similarity of testimony. A nice illustration of such an alternative explanation is provided by G. K. Chesterton's fictional detective Father Brown, in 'The man in the passage' (an example also used by Coady 1992: 148). The witnesses who reported seeing the man in the passage were wrong. Father Brown's alternative explanation was that there was a mirror in the corridor, and so each witness observed themselves. The murderer did not use the passage; a fact which altered suspicion in the case.

We can now return to the challenge posed by the argument that historical knowledge always degrades over time. From the first sort of relation, that concerning general principles, we can see that where the historian can call on supplementary evidence, then the history of the central evidence can itself be inferred. The historian is in that way not limited to knowledge of the most recent portion of the overall chain, but can use their knowledge of the reliability of portions of that chain. If the historian knows the differential rate of degradation, then they are able to discount certain evidence and rely on other evidence, and so acquire more accurate beliefs than one who is earlier in the chain, but is ignorant of such matters. Tucker extends his example of linguistic drift to remark that certain parts of language – the name of a deity, for example – remain unchanging over millennia, while other parts of language change comparatively rapidly.

From the second sort of relation, common cause of multiple evidence, we can see that where the historian can call on corroborating evidence, then they can make use of similarity relations between multiple later pieces of evidence. Those relations were overlooked in the above argument concerning the inevitable degradation of evidential chains. Recall figure 11.1. We can now argue that a historian at point C who had the benefit not only of testimony A but also corroborating (similar) testimony A* could be more sure of what happened than those at either A or B. That would be the case just so long as the historian could demonstrate the likelihood of a suitable common cause of A and A*, in the ways suggested above.

The later believer therefore *can* be more confident about what happened than those from whom they receive testimony. This has important consequences for our understanding of the predicament of the historian. Too often it is assumed that the witness always knows best. But far from being at the end of a chain of unreliable whispers, the historian can use the multiple evidence at their disposal to gain a more accurate idea of what happened than those temporally closer to the event, and even those who were witnesses of the event. Temporal remove from the past being studied need not be an epistemic impediment, so long as multiple evidence is available.

5. Construction of the past

In common with the previous criticism, one could be concerned on behalf of the cause of historical knowledge on the basis that the historian is not able to observe, or otherwise directly check, the past:

> [History is] an approximation, because it lies in the past and therefore cannot itself be brought before one's eyes.
>
> (Geoffrey Elton, in Elton and Fogel 1983: 101)

> As the past has gone, no account can ever be checked against it but only against other accounts.
>
> (Keith Jenkins 2003: 14)

> The historian is not an observer of the past that lies beyond his own time. He cannot see it *objectively* as the chemist sees his test tubes and compounds. The historian must 'see' the actuality of history through the medium of documentation. That is his sole recourse.
>
> (Charles Beard 1935: 82)

In this section, I develop such ideas not towards scepticism but towards a variety of anti-realism which claims that historians *construct* the reality which their accounts are about.[4] Historians' accounts are justified on the basis of present evidence. They cannot check what they say about the past by accessing the past itself. But if the past itself is never accessed, never checked, never observed, what sense can we make of the idea that historical truth is a matter of correspondence to past facts? The historian of the French Revolution can, in principle, carry out further checks in order to support their claims about the storming of the Bastille. But that is to be achieved by searching out ever more present evidence (newspaper reports, letters, rubble); it is never achieved by observing or otherwise directly accessing the past. There is no sense to demanding that a statement 'correspond to the past facts', over and above a straightforward justification of that statement. History is not made true by correspondence to past facts; indeed, it is not made true by the real past at all, but by present evidence. Rather than correspondence and realism, historical truth should be understood in an anti-realist manner as construction from present evidence. Or so 'constructivists' such as Michael Oakeshott and Leon Goldstein have insisted:

> If the historical past be knowable, it must belong to the present world of experience; if it be unknowable, history is worse than futile, it is impossible. The fact is, then, that the past in history varies with the present, rests upon the present, is the present. 'What really happened' (a fixed and finished course of events, immune from change) as the end in history must, if history is to be rescued from nonentity, be replaced by 'what the evidence obliges us to believe'.
>
> (Oakeshott 1933: 107)

> Where does this stage [correspondence to the past] of historical inquiry appear? . . . when we examine the practice of historical research itself we never discover a point at which we test the claims of a historian against the actuality of the past.
>
> (Goldstein 1976: 41)

A more precise version of the argument sketched in my previous paragraph follows. The conclusion to the argument is the adoption of a form of anti-realism: that the past, what makes historical claims true, is constructed. Unlike the sceptic, the constructivist agrees with the realist that historians know a lot about the past. The difference lies in what that knowledge consists of.

(i) If historical knowledge is to be possible, it can only be so on the basis of present evidence.

(ii) If historical knowledge is based purely on present evidence, then the real past plays no part in the justification of that knowledge.

(iii) If the real past plays no part in the justification of historical knowledge, then it plays no part in the truth value of that knowledge (i.e. the real past is no part of the truth conditions for historical knowledge).

(iv) If the real past does not provide the truth conditions for historical knowledge, then the best explanation is Idealist anti-realism: the historian's past is constructed by human thought, language and activity.

The constructivist argument can be plausibly challenged at every step; whether successfully challenged is harder to say. The claim, (i), that historians are restricted to present evidence is less secure than it might at first appear, and can be challenged by considering observation, memory and testimony. The past can be observed: the astronomer, for example, observes distant quasars as they were some 15 billion years ago, just as we observe on live television what happened on the other side of the world a few seconds ago. Such observation will count as *direct* knowledge of the past dependent on one's epistemology of perception. The foundationalist (both strong and moderate) takes perceptual belief to be directly justified by perceptual experience, an assertion which the coherentist will deny.

Arguments from Chapter 3 concerning testimony and (in passing) memory also bear on the constructivist premise (i). There I claimed that the historian had to uncritically accept a good deal of testimony, as do we all. That acceptance should be regarded as a matter of inheriting the justification that the testifier possessed; it cannot be a matter of treating the testimony as evidence that invites further reasoning. If that is correct, then if S tells you what they have seen and you believe them, then your belief is as directly justified by S's observation as S's belief is. This argument doesn't commit one to the obviously false claim that all testimony is justified; only that, where it is, the recipient's justification is the same as the testifier's. The argument is perhaps less contentious in the case of memory. To know the past by memory is not a matter of using some present evidence – a 'memory image' – to infer something about the past. Rather, it is to directly use justification acquired in the past.

Even if we grant that the distant past cannot be literally observed or otherwise directly accessed, one should not let constructivist premise (ii) pass without objection. Evidence can be present and yet still presuppose a good deal about the past. We observe items in the present in a way that presupposes something about their past. To observe a *relic* is to observe something that has survived from the distant past (Chapter 1). To observe something *as evidence* is already to suppose something about it; that it is, for example, a letter written in the past. Further reasoning then fills out the details of that history (Chapter 3). Finally, the observation of present objects often takes place in terms of categories that presuppose a causal history: scars, spillages, scorch-marks (Chapter 5). This objection to the constructivist premise (ii) does *not* claim that these presuppositions are necessarily correct. Rather, the claim is that in so far as we do use evidence to arrive at true belief about the past, that inference relies not only upon present-tense claims, but also upon past-tense claims.

To object to premise (iii), one might well complain that the philosophical question of whether the historian *describes the past*, or *constructs from present evidence*, is a false dilemma: they do both. The second accounts for their methodology of justification (excepting challenges already noted), but the first accounts for what makes those accounts true. This distinction raises a fundamental issue in debate between the realist and anti-realist: the extent to which justification-conditions and truth-conditions are separate. I limit myself to anti-realist comment that in our *use* of 'true', there is no radical separation. A historical claim is regarded as true in so far as its justification is unimpeachable, or at least sufficiently strong. If we insisted on a sharp separation of truth and justification conditions, such that the latter guided our activity while the former were unknowable, it is hard to see how the word 'truth' could ever be put to use. The constructivist refuses to divide justification and truth; a refusal squarely based in our usual practice.

6. Present truth and past truth

I suggested towards the end of Chapter 2 that the historian's reasoning presupposes a material connection between past and present. Its very status as evidence is a matter of its counterfactual dependence on the past, a dependence which the historian thinks they can make use of in their reasoning. This presupposition suggests a reason to be wary of the constructivist argument of the previous section. Without further defence, however, it can hardly count as a refutation of that position, on the grounds that it begs the question. We can never check whether the material relation really is holding between past and present, any more than we can check the past itself. But this attempt to connect past and present does point to a more promising reply to the constructivist.

The following argument is taken from Michael Dummett's paper 'The reality of the past' (1978/1969). Surely there is a relation between what *was* true and what *is now* true? Indeed there is, and it is semantically implied in our mastery of past-tense language. Dummett called the connection the 'truth-value link'. There is a relation between truth in the present time t, and what can truthfully be said about t by future historians:

> if it follows from the truth of the present-tense statement A [that Dummett is now in a particular place] that the past-tense statement B, if uttered in a year's time, will then be true, it seems thereby also to follow that the past-tense statement B will not then be true just in virtue of something which can then be recognised as justifying the assertion of B: indeed, it is entirely conceivable that no one, myself included, might remember where I was at that particular time, and no further evidence, direct or indirect, be available to settle the question, even though we could never be sure that no such evidence would ever turn up.
>
> (Dummett 1978: 368)

The constructivist claims that B is true only in so far as there is evidence available in the present. To accept the truth-value link makes that claim untenable. A present statement, such as A: 'Sheffield town centre is flooded', is made true by what is now the case. The right sort of past-tense statement uttered 100 years from now, B: 'Sheffield town centre was flooded 100 years ago', is true in so far as A was true, and false in so far as it was false. The evidence available at the time that B is uttered will determine any justification that B possesses, *but will not determine its truth value.* But if that is so, then we have found a way to specify truth conditions for history that is meaningful, and which does not collapse to the method of justification that historians use. We therefore have a good reason to deny the constructivist premise (iii).

How is the constructivist to reply? Dummett offers two responses. One might accept global anti-realism: the thesis that, for all statements, what makes that statement true is the evidence then available for that statement. In that case, the constructivist would not be impressed by the idea that past-tense statements are made true in the same way as present-tense statements. A second response is to retain the division between realism of present-tense statements and anti-realism of past-tense, while accepting the truth-value link. According to this second position,

> it is indeed correct to say that 'It was the case that Q' is true if and only if 'It is the case that Q' was true: but this is, however, that sense of 'true' in which it is used relative to a particular possible history.
> (Dummett 1978: 371)

The temporal anti-realist can accept the truth-value link between A and B, on the basis that truth of A commits one to truth of B, and falsity of A to falsity of B. But anti-realism is retained, since the past itself doesn't determine whether A is true or false. It might be that A is true in one possible history, and false in another. Dummett's conclusion is modest: 'an anti-realist view of statements about the past is at least not to be dismissed out of hand' (Dummett 1978: 374). We shall also leave this debate unresolved, though shall return to a more direct assessment of anti-realism in the next chapter.

Both the sceptical challenge, and the anti-realist challenge, have proceeded from a supposed difficulty that the historian has: that they cannot directly have access to (observe) the past, and must make do with second-hand evidence in the present. To conclude this chapter, it is of interest to mention Arthur

Danto's *narrative sentences*, since that notion is at the heart of Danto's attempt to turn the above complaint on its head. What is supposedly a problem for the historian – that they are not a direct witness of the events of which they write – is, Danto notes, what makes history possible. That is because historical knowledge is narrative knowledge, and narrative requires a position later than the event being described. The requirement of a later viewpoint is clearly brought out by narrative sentences:

> [The] most general characteristic [of narrative sentences] is that they refer to at least two time-separated events though they only *describe* (are only *about*) the earliest event to which they refer. . . . The fact that these sentences may constitute some measure a differentiating stylistic feature of narrative writing is of less interest to me than the fact that use of them suggests a differentiating feature of historical knowledge.
>
> (Danto 1968: 143)

A narrative sentence is, roughly, a narrative in a single sentence (and hence is not so different to the examples of colligatory concepts considered in Chapter 10). Danto's examples include 'The author of *Principia* was born at Woolethorpe [sic] on Christmas Day, 1642' (1968: 158) and 'The Thirty Years War began in 1618'. These statements could not have been justifiably uttered by observers to the event being described. If it is the case that they are paradigmatically historical claims, then not being in a position to have been there, and observed for oneself, is not a hindrance, but what makes historical knowledge possible. And if greater temporal distance permits richer narratives, which one supposes that it usually will, then temporal distance is to be welcomed by the historian, not lamented.

Further reading and study questions

Audi, R. (1998) *Epistemology: A Contemporary Introduction to the Theory of Knowledge*. London: Routledge. One of the many introductions to epistemology available, but one that focuses to a greater degree than most on epistemological issues of most relevance to historians. Chapters 2, 5, 6 and 7 are particularly pertinent to topics covered in this book.

Coady, C. A. J. (1992) *Testimony: A Philosophical Study*. Oxford: Clarendon Press. I repeat the recommendation made in Chapter 9.

Danto, A. C. (1968) *Analytical Philosophy of History*. Cambridge: Cambridge University Press (originally 1965). Chapter VIII: 'Narrative sentences'.

Goldstein, L. (1976) *Historical Knowing*. Austin: University of Texas Press. The chapter on 'historical facts' is of particular relevance.

(a) How is it possible that one can be a historical anti-realist, and yet believe that the past exists?

(b) What is non-cognitivism? What elements of a historical account, if any, are best regarded from a non-cognitivist perspective?

(c) Is it the case that all historical belief must be inferred from other belief? Can you give an example where that is not the case?

Underdetermination 12

1. Coherence and choice

Underdetermination has been of central importance to debates concerning truth and realism. Philosophers of science have questioned whether the evidence that scientists make use of underdetermines the theories that they produce, and if so, whether from that we can draw any conclusions about the truth of those theories and the reality which they purport to be about. Philosophers of language have questioned whether the evidence of what others do underdetermines what they mean. Underdetermination can likewise bring into focus a number of debates relevant to the philosophy of history. The central challenge running through each of the issues to be discussed in this chapter is that the historian's evidence underdetermines their conclusions. There is a gap between evidence and historical claim, a gap which can only be bridged by activity that does not result from knowledge of what really happened. The gap is bridged – according to different varieties of anti-realism – by societal pressure, by the deep structures of the historian's thought or language, or simply by the historian's free choice. (The insistence that one can choose what to believe is *one* of the messages from the diffuse movement called postmodernism.)

In the previous chapter we saw reason to believe that the structure of the historian's justificatory system was one of coherence; that there were, to use Collingwood's phrase, 'no fixed points'. An enduring worry about accepting that justification is a matter of coherence is that justification and truth become estranged. That is concerning not least because the sole point of epistemic justification is to ensure that belief thereby closer approaches truth. Is it not possible that a system of belief be as coherent as one requires, and yet have nothing to do with the real world, and therefore lack any truth? The estrangement between coherentist justification and truth can be clearly brought out by considering that there might be multiple systems of belief, each internally coherent, and yet which are mutually incoherent. Here I provide three examples of this phenomenon, reserving more peculiarly historical examples until later in the chapter.

We have already come across one famous example in Chapter 8, in Quine's anthropologist (Quine 1960: Chapter 2). The evidence provided by the native's behaviour underdetermined rival 'translation manuals' (to use Quine's term). The initial evidence was provided by the native's use of the word 'gavagai' in the presence of a rabbit. Rival translations included the (intuitively obvious) mapping of 'gavagai' to 'rabbit', and the (intuitively bizarre) mapping of 'gavagai' to 'undetached rabbit part'; there will be many other possible translations, perhaps uncountably many. Other evidence may become available, including the natives' responses to questions posed by the anthropologist, and yet, no matter what that evidence was, each rival translation manual could persist with the initial translation of 'gavagai' so long as the remainder of the translation manual was written or modified accordingly. Coherentism plays an essential role in Quine's account of the anthropologist. The possibility that any part of one's system of belief may be altered (according to Quine, this includes both beliefs about logic and analytic beliefs), makes it possible to retain some other part of the system of belief.

Jonathan Gorman (2007) illustrates the idea of underdetermination through the example of Willem de Vlamingh's observation of swans in Australia. De Vlamingh's previous belief was that all swans are white. Yet here is what seems to be a black swan: he is faced with a contradiction or, in Quine's terminology, a 'recalcitrant experience'. How is that recalcitrance to be overcome? One way is, of course, to reject the belief that all swans are white. But there is (at least) one other way: to reject the belief that what one experiences is a swan. It is, after all, a truism that things aren't always what they seem, that objects are not always classified by the most manifest properties. One has a choice, for which the evidence is no arbiter. Further, one can imagine two people who choose in different ways: one believes that all swans are white, and that this is not a swan; the other that this is a swan, and that not all swans are white. The belief systems of each are internally coherent, and yet are mutually incompatible, in those two ways.

A third example connects the topic with themes in the philosophy of science. Imre Lakatos (1978) criticized Karl Popper's falsificationist philosophy of science (outlined in Chapter 4) on the basis that decisive falsification is not to be found in science. Two nineteenth-century astronomers, Adams and Leverrier, calculated that the orbit of Uranus was contrary to Newtonian laws of gravity, but that the anomaly could be resolved if a seventh, as yet unobserved planet, could be assumed to exist. That planet – Neptune – was successfully observed, resulting in a dramatic confirmation of Newtonian mechanics. But, asks Lakatos, what should Adams and Leverrier have concluded had the planet not been found? They could have rejected Newtonian mechanics; but that would not have been the only option available to them. The planet could be hidden by an asteroid belt, or by a gaseous cloud; the telescope might be not be functioning correctly, perhaps as a result of interference with the earth's atmosphere; they might even have questioned the laws of optics upon which the telescope was built. The moral of this thought experiment chimes with the previous two cases. Though not any system of belief is permitted (the astronomers must, after all, come up with *some* explanation as to why the planet is not seen), the evidence permits a choice between multiple systems that do fit what has been observed.

What is one to conclude from these examples of internally coherent and yet mutually incompatible systems of belief? The least dramatic conclusion would be that disagreement is a result of insufficient evidence. Given that we never have all the evidence, there will be many occasions where two competing beliefs, or systems of beliefs, can each be retained, pending decisive evidence. But the above stories are intended to preclude this realist conclusion, on the basis that no possible evidence could force one or other belief system to be abandoned. If that is correct, then one might adopt the anti-realist conclusion that there is simply nothing there for the claims to be about: this was Quine's own conclusion to his argument for the indeterminacy of translation. Or, one might adopt the alternative anti-realist conclusion that what is there is constructed by the believer's own activity (Idealism). A third response to underdetermination is scepticism: there could be an independent reality, but we can never know what it is.

2. Bayesianism reconsidered

A second way to substantiate the claim that historical claims are underdetermined by the evidence is by critically re-examining Bayesianism, introduced and employed in Chapter 3. One concern is that the evidence never licenses a *conclusive* justification of one historical hypothesis over another. If that is the case, one might ask what the gap in probability should be in order to permit the claim that the more justified hypothesis should be believed, and the other rejected? If historians differed over the relative gap required, would it not be possible that one historian's historical fiction would be another's history? The Bayesian need not yet be unduly concerned. They might remark, first, that historians tend to be inferentially cautious, affirming one of a contrastive pair only when the probabilities are orders of magnitude different. And they might further point out that, while degree of justification is a matter for philosophical theory, whether one actually accepts and rejects a hypothesis is a matter of pragmatics; a matter of how much the hypothesis matters to the believer, what they intend to do with that hypothesis, and so on.

A more substantial concern for the Bayesian results from underdetermination of the values required for evidential justification (values in the equations B1 and B2, given in Chapter 3). Recall that, according to Bayesianism, the likelihood of any given historiographical hypothesis *posterior* to consideration of the evidence is to be regarded as being a product of two further values. First, the *prior* likelihood of the hypothesis, before considering the evidence. Second, the *likelihood* of the evidence, were the hypothesis to be true. Underdetermination of the posterior will result in so far as either the prior, or the likelihood, or both, are themselves underdetermined. And a good case can be made for regarding both of those values as not evidentially determined. (A third source of underdetermination results from the historian's *background* beliefs. To press the point that these backgrounds can legitimately differ on the basis of the same evidence would be to reprise the argument offered in the previous section.)

The subjective nature of the priors is accepted by most Bayesians, and was noted in Chapter 3. As pointed out there, the response of the Bayesian to the charge that priors are underdetermined will turn on regarding those priors as part of an extended process of reasoning. At this point I turn to the evidential likelihood term. In Chapter 3, I claimed that to successfully fill out this value required *explanatory* considerations. Roughly, evidential likelihood is rated highly in proportion to the degree that the hypothesis would provide a 'lovely' explanation of that evidence. Yet it does not seem that evidential likelihood is *determined* by explanatory considerations. This can be appreciated by considering how the historian's background must be applied, in order to assess any putative explanation. First, historical regularities are typically vague in application to particular cases ('people *tend* to make themselves appear favourably in reporting some episode in which they were involved'). Second, historical regularities can conflict with one another, a conflict which only particular judgement can resolve (S's memoirs might be self-serving, and yet S has been consistently shown to be truthful in similar past cases). Finally, there may be no regularities available in this case, and irreducibly particular judgement must suffice.

Two historians may therefore agree in all their background beliefs, including rules by which evidence is assessed. Nonetheless, as a result of the application of that background to the particular piece of evidence at hand, those historians might come to different and equally justified conclusions. Contrary to Tucker's version of Bayesianism (2004: 19), to understand historical reasoning in a Bayesian manner is not to preclude a role for 'historical intuition', that which cannot be exhaustively captured in explicit algorithm. One thinks of Raymond Martin's analogy: that 'there is no substitute for the brewmaster's nose, adapted to the art of producing historical brew' (Martin 1989: 105). (Similar points were made in Chapter 6, towards a conclusion that we might now state in terms of general theory underdetermining a particular historical explanation. If we accept that explanation has a central role in historical reasoning from the evidence, we should not be surprised that the same points reappear here.)

How far can this underdetermination be pushed? According to the historical sceptic, a very long way. The sceptic challenges our entitlement to claim that we have knowledge, or even well-justified belief, with regard to some domain. (Here we consider scepticism not of the qualified kind examined in the previous chapter, but of the more philosophically familiar kind which challenges entitlement to *all* knowledge of some domain.) One sceptical strategy is to claim that intuitively bizarre hypotheses are as justified by the evidence as are the hypotheses we usually take to be true. Descartes held that the hypothesis that an evil demon was consistently deceiving him was just as possible as the usual hypothesis that there was no such demon. The contemporary global sceptic tends to replace the demon with a scientist, challenging one to show that one is not a disembodied brain receiving sensory stimulation in a scientist's vat. A similarly bizarre hypothesis, though one specific to historical knowledge, was suggested by Bertrand Russell (Russell 2004: 160). One could logically maintain the hypothesis that the world *came into existence five minutes ago*, complete with 'fossils' under the ground, grey hairs on the 'aged,' and 'memories' seeming to point to the distant past.

Bayesianism seems to permit not only the conclusion that we cannot conclusively rule out the five-minute hypothesis, but the much more alarming conclusion that the five-minute hypothesis is just as likely as our usual hypotheses about the past. If the five-minute hypothesis were true, how likely would it be that the evidence that we have were true? The answer is that for any given piece of evidence, the five-minute hypothesis will make that evidence just as likely as our usual hypotheses. How likely would it be that there be a fossil that *seems* to be 30 million years old, if the five-minute hypothesis were true? Well, given the assumption that fossils popped into existence with the appearance of being 30 million years old, then the existence of such a fossil just five minutes later is very likely. What makes the difference is our relative estimation of priors, in particular that we rate the prior probability of the five-minute hypothesis extremely low. But, as already remarked, Bayesianism is not well equipped to argue that differences in priors can be justified by the evidence.

So much the worse for Bayesianism, we might say. Explanationism – the second theory of historical reasoning examined in Chapter 3 – may fare somewhat better in answering the historical sceptic. For while both the bizarre hypothesis and our usual hypotheses can offer some sort of an explanation for present evidence, there is reason to suppose that our usual hypotheses offer a *better* explanation. A better ('lovely') explanation is one which brings consilience or unification to what it explains, which is contrastively precise (in explaining why p, rather than q), and which is itself in a suitable network of explanation. The five-minute hypothesis is suitably consilient: it brings all present evidence under a single explanation. But it is drastically ad hoc, providing no explanation for why the evidence is as it is, rather than some other way. And it is itself unexplained: we have no reason to suppose that the five-minute hypothesis is true rather than any other arbitrarily chosen cut-off point. That is to say that the five-minute hypothesis is logically consistent with the evidence, but does not well explain that evidence. However, while the explanationist can account for our typical disregard of such bizarre hypotheses, they cannot close the issue of scepticism in particular and the issue of underdetermination more generally. For one might draw a sharp distinction between our methods for deciding what to believe on the one hand, and what the evidence requires and permits on the other. It might be that explanatory considerations of the sort sketched are part of what actually leads us to believe one historical claim or account over another, but that they are nonetheless no more philosophically relevant than a preference for shorter accounts over longer, or accounts phrased in verse rather than prose. This issue is continued in the following section, by focusing on historiographical disagreement.

3. Historiographical disagreement

Historiographical disagreement of *certain kinds* can be used to substantiate a claim of underdetermination. One can draw no philosophical conclusions from mere historiographical difference. It is no news to be told that historians study different things, nor even to be told that historians study the same things in different ways (*pace* Jenkins 2003/1991: 5). Neither is it enough to show that new historical approaches, theories and concepts emerge over time. It is sometimes thought that the ever-increasing multiplicity of historiographical sub-fields and foci is problematic for the idea that history can be true (Novick (1999/1988) often raises precisely this worry; Martin (1998) disagrees). But without further argument, why should we not accept the new ways of describing the past as at least potentially true? After all, 'quasar' and 'quark', both arising from recent scientific theories, were necessary before the physicist could truly describe certain parts of the real world.

For there to be underdetermination, historiographies must disagree, not just differ. We can tentatively characterize genuine disagreement as being that according to which the two positions are *incompatible*. Further, that incompatibility should be irresolvable, or at least persistent. It should not, for example, be the result of mistake or error on the part of one of the historians. Given this situation, an argument for underdetermination could run as follows:

(i)   Historiography A and historiography B disagree (they are, or appear to be, incompatible).

(ii) The disagreement cannot be resolved by the current evidence, nor conceivably by any future evidence.

(iii) Therefore: the evidence underdetermines the issue over which A and B disagree.

What sorts of historiographical issues are taken to be underdetermined by the evidence? Sometimes, as in Russell's five-minute hypothesis, an attempt is made to demonstrate a gap between the evidence and *any* claim about the past (well, the past more distant than five minutes ago). More usually, banal historiographical claims are admitted on the basis that historians do tend to agree about the 'basic facts' of history. Underdetermination is, rather, reserved for the result of disagreement over *narrative, interpretation, meaning* and *explanation*. It is not always obvious whether the disagreement is genuine, whether the two accounts A and B are really incompatible. One way to resolve the apparent disagreement is to claim that A and B are incomplete; once properly completed, the disagreement vanishes. In Chapter 5 I pointed out that explanation is typically incomplete until a contrast class is specified. FR: 'France being a non-Reformation country explains the Revolution' and the negation of FR may be compatible, if we can understand FR as explaining why the Revolution happened in France rather than Germany, while the negation of FR explains why the Revolution happened in France rather than Spain. A similar strategy would be to claim that T: 'the execution of Louis XVI was a tragedy' and C: 'the execution of Louis XVI was a comedy', can be compatible on the basis that it is only sets of events not just a single execution, that can be emplotted. Even if we take tragedy and comedy to be incompatible, the same event can feature in both, in virtue of the other events in each plot. Those who draw substantive conclusions from underdetermination make bolder claims: in particular, that the very same contrast can be explained in incompatible ways, and that the very same set of events can be emplotted in different ways.

As suggested in the previous section, one conclusion to draw from underdetermination is the sceptical one that there is something to be right and wrong about, but that we have no way of knowing which. A more commonly made move is from historiographical disagreement, through underdetermination, to anti-realism. Such arguments, often with reference to specific historiographical debate, can be found in the literature:

> [my model allows me to explain that] although nineteenth-century historical thinkers studied carefully and completely, within the limits of their several competences, the same 'data' in the historical record, they came to such different and seemingly mutually exclusive conclusions about the meaning and significance of those 'data' for their own times. By constituting the historical field in alternative ways, they implicitly committed themselves to different strategies of explanation

> (White 1973: 431)

There are many disagreements as to Hitler's intentions after gaining power, and the causes of the Second World War. One such famous long-running disagreement has been between AJP Taylor and H Trevor-Roper. This disagreement was not based on their merits as historians; both are experienced, both have 'skills', both can read documents and in this case they often read the same ones, yet still they disagreed. Thus whilst the sources may prevent just anything at all from being said, nevertheless the same events/sources do not entail that one and only one reading has to follow.

(Jenkins 2003/1991: 13)

For each [Sahlins and Obeyeskere, in their debate over how the Hawaiian natives thought of Captain Cook], substantive assumptions about the basic nature of human cognition must first be made, and these assumptions drive subsequent interpretations of the evidence. The different assumptions result in logically incompatible but empirically equivalent judgments regarding what or how natives think. It is not just that claims to understanding are underdetermined by the available evidence. ... *There is no distinguishing here between imputing our standards to others and 'discovering' that, after all, they share that standard.* Either philosophical assumption – we've made them into us, or we've discovered that they are, in essentials like us – accommodates the possible outcomes. No *evidence* could *possibly* decide between 'how natives think' in this regard.

(Roth 2003: 317–18)

White and Jenkins do not (in the quoted passages) advance the argument beyond a demonstration of underdetermination, though it is obvious from their other writings that anti-realism of some sort will be the eventual conclusion (at least, anti-realism for all bar the most 'basic' historical facts: see Chapter 11). The anti-realist conclusion is made explicit in Roth's argument. Roth makes the move from underdetermination to anti-realism very quickly, but one could plausibly reason as follows: if no *evidence* could determine which historiography is correct, then the *past itself* cannot determine which historiography is correct. Anything may be said with regard to x, since there is no x to constrain such talk.

Let us return to the key claim that the evidence underdetermines which historiography is correct. To recap, the underdeterminationist needs to claim two things. First, the evidence favours neither historiography over the other. In that sense, the two historiographies are 'empirically equivalent'. Second, the historiographies should be not only empirically equivalent with regard to the present evidence, but also to all future evidence. Without this second claim, any 'underdetermination' may be trivial, a result of the contingent processes that lead us to possess some evidence and not other. It is possible to query each of these requirements.

It might well be questioned as to whether the fit between evidence and historiography should be regarded in as permissive a way as the underdeterminationist presumes. The underdetermination argument relies on the idea that any account that is consistent with the evidence is permitted by the evidence. Consistency is a very minimal demand, and we might seek to strengthen it (with, for example, explanatory demands, as suggested in the previous section with regard to the five-minute hypothesis). How minimal a demand consistency is can be seen by realizing that a refusal to face the evidence, burying one's head in the sand, and being as vague as possible, are all strategies that can be logically consistent with any evidence. Yet these are paradigmatically poor epistemic strategies. We can also be concerned about the projection to future evidence: after all, who is to say what we might be able to achieve with future evidence? Here, though, I think that the underdeterminationist can be defended. The argument does not require the underdeterminationist to justify the claim that no future evidence will be available to decide between the incompatible accounts. Rather, the argument is best regarded as one of best explanation: underdetermination is the best explanation for the lack of decisive evidence and our current inability to conceive of there ever being any such decisive evidence.

4. Social Construction

Social Construction is a strategy of explanation and critique that is deployed widely, not just with regard to history, but also to scientific knowledge, mathematics, economics. The more we would usually regard a practice as a matter of acquiring truth, enquiring into reality, the bigger news it will be to be told that in fact that the practice is socially constructed. (It would be no news to be told, for example, that humour was socially constructed.) The Social Constructivist claims that historiography is produced by the same social pressures as any other activity (business, politics, leisure time). It is those social pressures that explain historiography – not 'the past' or 'the truth'. (The exclusion of the latter from a Social Constructivist explanation of practice is made explicit in Barnes and Bloor (1982)). Further, showing the activity to be the result of contingent social pressures shows the activity itself to be contingent – the practice need not have ended up in the way that it has, indeed it might have been very different, if it is based on social forces that are themselves highly contingent. That result could appear alarming with respect to those activities that are usually regarded as objective; we might be told, for example, that under different social circumstances we might have constructed a gene-less biology.

A more ambitious form of Social Construction does not just explain the social background to some practice, but does so in order to 'unmask' the relations of power behind some practice. Such relations are usually unconscious, hence the need for unmasking. For example, Foucault talks of the nineteenth-century medicalization of both madness, and sexual perversion. Medicalization permitted control, hence power, though that increase in power was no part of anyone's explicit plans. Of course, not all practices are based on unjust or unethical relations, but it is fair to say that those are the type that most social constructivists revel in unearthing. Should the revelation that some practice depends upon and promotes relations of power lead us to be concerned about the *objectivity* of that practice? Quite possibly, as suggested in Chapter 9. What about historical *truth* about the real past? Not necessarily; objectivity, as suggested in Chapter 9, can be seen as a tougher demand than truth (I argued there that an account can be entirely true, and yet profoundly biased). My claim in Chapter 1 was that we should not presume that why x is done has any affect on x's truth (I may work on a maths problem out of boredom, because I have been told to, because I am fascinated by maths, or because it will help me make lots of money; but whichever of these is the case will not affect in the least the correctness of the answer that I produce). In the language familiar to philosophers of science, we should not confuse the context of discovery and the context of justification.

A still more ambitious form of Social Construction will not rest with an explanation of why a certain practice is carried out, but will seek to draw conclusions about reality. One might be a little suspicious about many of the new psychological syndromes that are 'named' with increasing frequency, one such being 'Intermittent Explosive Disorder'. That disorder has causes such as conflict with spouse or significant other, abuse of alcohol/drugs, being of lower socio-economic order, and is treatable with medication or psychological counselling. An understandable reaction to hearing of this 'discovery' is to remark, first, that there's no such thing as IED; and, second, to explain its invention in terms of money and power. Drugs and counselling cost money, and prestige is gained within a discipline when it is buttressed by technical and exclusive terminology. Further, the second reaction buttresses the first, in so far as we thereby acquire an explanation for the creation of IED that does not require any corresponding worldly property.[1]

There are two different ways that the Social Constructivist promise that is latent in the above example might be achieved, which by this point in the chapter should be sounding familiar. First, one could take the anti-realist message that there's simply nothing there that would ground any statements about IED at all. Second, one could take the Idealist message that reality is constructed. In the following section, I examine the sort of Idealism that has proven popular over the last three decades to some philosophers of history, and even to some historians.

5. Linguistic Idealism

Kant's account of Idealism provides an excellent starting point by which to understand influential contemporary Idealist accounts. Kantian Idealism was motivated and introduced in the previous chapter. Two alterations to that picture have typically since been made. First, beginning with Kant's great critic, Hegel, we have come to accept that the categories imposed on the world can change over time. (One example might be the post-Kantian rejection of Euclidean geometry in scientific theory.) Instead of Kant's unchangeable, transcendent *a priori*, we have become accustomed to the *historical a priori*: categories at the foundation of our thought, not according to the Idealist a reflection of the reality of the world, and yet categories which can and do change. There may, therefore, be different and incompatible categories, each of which is true relative to a given culture, or way of thinking; and each of which constructs a different reality.

The notion of truth relative to a way of thinking requires substantiation (one of the few to make a concerted attempt to do just that has been Nelson Goodman, in his *Ways of Worldmaking* (1978)). If the ways of thinking are simply different, then the realist can accept them all as true, and drop the implication that truth is relative. One could follow the suggestion of the argument from historiographical disagreement in the previous section, and insist that the different truths be incompatible. But that pushes at the limits of sense, given that 'x and y are incompatible' means that it is not possible for both x and y to be true. An alternative proposal is to suppose that the ways of thinking, and the consequent different realities, are *incommensurable* (Kuhn 1996/1962). Incommensurable theories or realities cannot be compared, for they have nothing in common. For example, Kuhn argued that no neutral considerations could permit us to decide whether to adopt Newtonian or Einsteinian physics; each was preferable, according to its own lights. One important reason for this incommensurability is that they simply divide up the world in different ways. Though they appear to share the same concepts – for example, 'mass' – on closer inspection that is not the case, since those concepts are individuated by the overall theory. 'Mass' for Newton meant something different to 'mass' for Einstein. There is, therefore, no theory-neutral item for which it can be asked which theory provides the best account. I return to incommensurability shortly.

The second alteration to Kantian Idealism has been the emphasis not so much on the relation between mind and world, but on that between language and world. Such a move is one way of adopting the 'linguistic turn', the privileging of language over epistemology, that provides the underlying theme behind so many twentieth-century philosophical and theoretical programmes. The result of regarding Kantian Idealism in this way we can call 'Linguistic Idealism'. In a passage specifically concerned with historical discourse, Barthes claims that

> The fact can only have a linguistic existence, as a term in a discourse, and yet it is exactly as if this existence were merely the 'copy', purely and simply, of another existence situated in the extra structural domain of the 'real'.
>
> (Barthes 1981/1967)

Russell's metaphor of the blue-tinted glasses (Chapter 11) is insufficiently strong to carry the weight required of it by Linguistic Idealism. Such a metaphor holds out the possibility of knowing how the distorting mechanism works, and therefore being able to correct it to achieve knowledge of what is real. Just as the historian can use biased evidence without producing biased history so long as they are aware of the bias in the evidence, the distorting glass can be used without producing distorted knowledge so long as we are aware of the distortion. The Linguistic Idealist claims that such 'correction' is never possible, in principle, since the relation between the phenomenal and noumenal is no more available than the latter alone. Such claims as that one is 'in the prison house of language' (Nietzsche), or that one is 'a prisoner of one's conceptual scheme' are characteristic of Linguistic Idealism.

We are not at a loss for ways to reply to the counsel of despair that the Linguistic Idealist offers. First, one could emphasize that language and world do meet directly, by the first *referring* to the second. What is important about reference is that a referring term – a name – need not be tied to a conceptual scheme. As such, reference need not be caught up in the prison house of language. In particular, the 'causal theory of reference', developed by Saul Kripke

(1980), has been taken by many philosophers to have demonstrated that Kuhn's notion of incommensurability is founded on a faulty theory of meaning. Kuhn's treatment of 'mass' required that each term find its meaning only in the theory of which that term is a part. Kripke, however, insisted that continuity of reference is ensured in the transmission of that term from user to user via an appropriate causal chain. The understanding of a term like 'mass' can vary greatly from user to user, and yet as result of continuity of use still refer to the very same property in the world.

A second reply to Linguistic Idealism is suggested by Donald Davidson: 'Conceptual relativism is a heady and exotic doctrine, or would be if we could make good sense of it' (2001c: 183). Why can't we make sense of conceptual relativism? The Linguistic Idealist, as we have seen, supposes that there are, at least potentially and probably actually, different conceptual schemes. Indeed, more than different, but unbridgeably different, or incommensurable. Incommensurable schemes 'fit' or 'organize' the world, though of course in different ways. Thus the Linguistic Idealist presupposes a 'dualism of scheme and content, of organizing system and something waiting to be organized' (Davidson 2001c: 189). Davidson's central claim is that to understand two 'schemes' as both organizing the same thing requires some common understanding between those schemes. And that common understanding is sufficient to rebut the presumption that those schemes are incommensurable. Of course, languages can differ greatly, but 'what enables us to make this point in particular cases is an ontology common to the two languages, with concepts that individuate the same objects' (2001c: 192).

If the picture of incommensurable schemes is untenable, should we retain Idealism, even though the multiplicity of schemes goes by the board? Davidson suggests not:

> It would be ... wrong to announce the glorious news that all mankind – all speakers of language, at least – share a common scheme and ontology. For if we cannot intelligibly say that schemes are different, neither can we intelligibly say that they are one.
>
> (2001c: 198)

What follows is my gloss on Davidson's argument. The Linguistic Idealist supposes there to be content in the world, and content in our linguistic schemes, and an unbreachable barrier between the two. One could, in response, either claim that there is no barrier, or that there is no content in the world. The result of adopting the former would lead to the 'glorious news'. The result of adopting the latter leads to the rejection of the dualism of noumena and phenomena that is central to Idealism. The consequences of rejecting that dualism were explored in the Anti-representationalism of the late Richard Rorty (in particular, 1979).

Anti-representationalism is Rorty's answer to the dichotomies between realist and Idealist, and between the objectivist and the relativist. It is really quite a simple position, though one that is sometimes confused with the latter conjunct of each of those pairs. (Rorty has a reputation as an 'anything goes' relativist, when the point of his position is to build on Davidson's dismissal of Linguistic Idealism to escape from the traditional relaist-realtivist debates.) Anti-representationalism is the thesis that, because there is no worldly content, there's nothing to make our statements about the world true or false. We shouldn't think, like the realist, that there are facts there waiting to be told, that ensure or deny our truth. Nor should we think, like the Idealist, that there are facts there, that in principle can't be told. There's no Idealist gap, because there's nothing to represent. We are – of course – in *causal* contact with the world; but the world provides us with no *justification*.

Rorty's position is partly quietist, and partly radical. It is quietist in that it suggests the deflationary idea that there is nothing substantive to say by way of a theory of why some statements are true, and others false. Truth and justification come together as the constructivist of the previous chapter insisted (though of course what we now think is justified might turn out not to be). Rorty's position, though, does have radical consequences. Given that the world does not constrain what we say about it, it is wrong to suppose that some sorts of subject can represent what is really there, while others cannot. There is, consequently, no divide between subjects that are 'objective' (paradigmatically, physics), and others that are 'subjective' (literary criticism, morality, or aesthetics). Truth is equally applicable to any, since truth is simply a matter of justifying your statements to someone else.

> I do not think of myself as encouraging the pathos of distance by saying 'settle for convincingness to your peers', but rather as saying, in a bracing and uplifting tone 'worry about convincing your peers, and truth and the world will take care of themselves'.
>
> (Rorty, in Brandom (ed.) 2000: 127)

6. Practical relations to the past

One final way to respond to Linguistic Idealism is to suggest that, in attending only to the relation between language and world, it overlooks our practical relation with the world. In emphasizing practical relations, one shifts attention from conceptual knowledge – 'knowing that' – to practical knowledge – 'knowing how'. Aristotle recognized this distinction, with his notion of *phronesis*:

> And so one should attend to the undemonstrable dicta and opinions of the skilful, the old and the Practically-Wise, no less than to those which are based on strict reasoning, because they see aright, having gained their power of moral vision from experience.
>
> (*Nicomachean Ethics*: Book VI Chapter IX)

We find in Heidegger the suggestion that our epistemic and linguistic relation to the world is secondary, built upon a practical relation. knowing- that only makes explicit what we already have in know-how.

> In interpreting, we do not, so to speak, throw a 'signification' over some naked thing which is present-at-hand, we do not stick a value on it; but when something within-the-world is encountered as such, the thing in question already has an involvement which is disclosed in our understanding of the world, and this involvement is something which gets laid out by the interpretation.
>
> (Heidegger 1962, 32: 190–1; as quoted in Mulhall 1996)

That insistence has been used to suggest that the Cartesian method of doubt wrongly presupposes that mind and world are in separate realms, and wrongly attempts to find the resolution to this 'problem' by searching for some belief which can provide a bridgehead into the world. The response is that no such bridgehead is required, for we are embodied minds, and experience the world before we can doubt it. That insistence of 'practical relations first' can be deployed in a similar manner against the Kantian and Linguistic Idealist picture, on the basis that the 'noumenal world' is not hidden from us by conceptual schemes, but experienced.[2]

How might these ideas be applied with regard to the historian's world, the past? At first glance, perhaps not especially well. The standard examples used to illustrate Heidegger's point relate to objects 'present-at-hand'. Heidegger's hammer is perhaps the best known of those examples, demonstrating the idea that use is prior to description. But using and knowing about a hammer is not historical knowledge. The social scientist certainly can make use of the prioritizing of know-how over know-that, and many have (see, in particular, Charles Taylor's 'Social theory as practice', 1999/1985: 91–115). The suggestion there is that we understand social science by its transformation of our practices. An interpretation of democracy as it exists now is judged by the fruits of that interpretation upon those practices; an interpretation of contemporary ethics judged by the fruits of that interpretation upon our ethical practice. This is not the *application* of factual knowledge (as we played with in discussion of history and science, a prediction, on the basis of generalization, that could then be used to guide action), but a much stronger thesis: that the rightness of interpretation is to be judged by its practical effects. Still the historian cannot apply this insight, since we do not understand the past so as to change the past.

I suggest two ways in which our practical activity underpins or otherwise influences our *historical* knowledge: know-how underpinning know-that in the historical domain. One way is in the role of action in sustaining a vision of the past. One creates and shapes a vision of the past in attending a remembrance day service, and in behaving with respect around war memorials. The power of such practical activity can be most clearly seen in divided societies. In Franco's Spain, the Nationalist war graves were honoured, the Republicans' ignored or defaced. Such actions embodied a powerful, and I would say powerfully wrong, vision of the past. Just as a collective vision of the past can be stored in memory and books, so it can be manifest in our activity. One would expect it to be part of the historian's business to make that vision explicit, and to criticize it as necessary. The argument of this paragraph is not that this is impossible, but that the historian's explicit knowledge builds on the implicit, practical knowledge.

Second, historical knowledge is dependent on the past through *open narrative sentences*. This suggestion builds on Danto's notion of narrative sentences (Chapter 11), though as far as I am aware, the extension to 'open' narrative sentences has not been made before. The idea is a familiar one, though. An open narrative sentence is about a past event, but which refers to it in terms of later events, *including events that have not taken place by the time of the speaker*. Such sentences are open to the utterer's future. One example is to utter 'that job interview was a learning experience' the day after failing to achieve a job that you very much wanted.

What makes an open narrative sentence true is, in part, our present attitude: that we mean what we say is part of what it is for the statement to be true, just as with 'performative' utterances such as 'I now pronounce you husband and wife'. But also what is required is an act of will: the will to make that sentence true by your future action. In open narrative sentences, the acting subject and the knowing subject come together. Matters become – politically – more complicated once we consider open narrative sentences that go beyond the autobiographical. A benign, local example would be 'Sheffield's regeneration began in 2002'. A more significant and less benign example would be the nationalist histories of the nineteenth century: 'the battle that marked the birth of our great nation!' And still other examples would rely on metanarratives; narratives that are ostensibly about the past, but that shape our future as well.

Danto implicitly recognized the possibility of open narrative sentences, and resisted them. On those same grounds he rejected speculative philosophies of history: accounts that purport to be historical, but which tacitly shape the present and future as well. The future should be kept open, not closed off. Lydia Goehr, in her recent commentary on Danto, writes that

> What is always at stake for Danto is the presence of openness. To leave the future open is to make no substantive claim upon it; to leave the future open is to leave the present open, as also the past, for only if a past is open does the historian's task make sense when generating historical narratives.
>
> (2007: 17)

I make two replies. First, open narrative sentences are more pervasive than Danto thought. As examples above have demonstrated, they are found well beyond the domain of grand-scale speculative philosophy of history. Second, collective open narrative sentences can indeed be dangerous, but they can also be beneficial. They can be politically dangerous since, as suggested, they are expressions of will which impact on others' lives. It is the philosopher's job to make explicit the existence and function of such devices as open narrative sentences, ways in which the past and present are shaped. Once we have pointed out their existence, philosophy of history will be of no help: it is a matter of choosing the future that we want to have.

Further reading and study questions

Gorman, J. L. (2007) *Historical Judgement*. Stocksfield: Acumen.
Hacking, I. (1999) *The Social Construction of What?* Cambridge, Mass.: Harvard University Press. Chapters 1 and 2 provide typically clear-minded analysis from Ian Hacking.

Rorty, R. (1979) *Philosophy and the Mirror of Nature*. Princeton: Princeton University Press. The classic anti-representationalist text.

(a) What is 'underdetermination', and why is it of any philosophical relevance?
(b) To what extent does a historian have freedom of choice in the history that they write?
(c) To embrace open narrative sentences in a historical work is to combine practicality (perhaps politics) including and historical knowledge. Are there dangers inherent in that combination?

Conclusion

I do not propose to conclude by making a detailed summary of the foregoing material. Neither do I wish to conclude by judging which approach is right and which wrong (critical judgement of that sort has, I hope, already been made apparent; in addition, I shortly explain my reticence in offering that sort of conclusion). Rather, I want to draw the material together in a more oblique way, in order to make three suggestions that I hope are provocative to further enquiry.

(1) The question that philosophers of history asked from the mid-twentieth century until recently concerned the *form* of the historical account: whether it should look like positivist science, or should privilege rationality, or should be narrative. It has been suggested that this obsession with form be dropped, and replaced with a concern with evidence and truth. (A suggestion inspired by a parallel movement in the philosophy of science: Tucker 2004, Introduction.) While the question of historical evidence is a vital one, I don't think that we should abandon enquiry into historiographical form. In Chapter 2, by examining peer reviews, I suggested that historians are particularly concerned with the twin desiderata of producing accounts that are consilient yet of wide scope, and that are precise. That focus has been amply supported in the following chapters. Bayesianism must be supplemented with the explanatory virtues of consilience and precision, if it is to deliver results, and results that do not fly in the face of historical practice (Chapter 3). We can only make sense of interpretation, and the defeasible demand of understanding as rational that is at its heart, by attending to the role of consilience (Chapter 8). To assess historical accounts piece by piece, without attending to the whole, would be to overlook what makes for biased history (Chapter 9), and what is distinctive about historical truth (the last three chapters). To regard historical accounts as a whole requires finding a place for consilience, or its close relation, narrative coherence. To overlook these distinctively historical virtues, which guide the form of the whole account, is to miss out on what makes one history better, another worse; on historiographical debate, and its resolution. Those are issues that the philosopher of history should be very much concerned with. It is to be hoped that both form and evidential support remain on the philosopher of history's agenda.

(2) I have emphasized that we, including historians, relate to the past in different ways. The central relation is that of a critical knower to what is known, *reasoning from the evidence* so as to describe what happened. In Chapter 1 I suggested that artefacts provide a way for us to directly *experience* the past. In Chapter 3 I argued that we *preserve* knowledge from the past; in Chapter 9 that we also *evaluate* the past, and enter into *dialogue* with the past, allowing it to challenge and evaluate us. Then in Chapter 12 I considered our *practical* relations with the past. Of course, we have many relations from the past, and not all will have philosophical interest. These multiple relations are worth attending to because they shape our knowledge of the past, and our descriptions of it. The thesis of multiple relations recalls Oakeshott's talk of different modes of experience. But given that my argument has been that the historian's practice can be fruitfully regarded as a compound of these relations, Oakeshott's demand that the relations not be integrated should be rejected. The thesis of multiple relations also helps to remove the grip of a certain picture as to how the historian and past are related. The idea that there is, in some sense, an unbridgeable gap between the historian and the past, necessitating the imposition of concepts and structure not in the past itself, draws support from Descartes and Kant, as well as more recent Structuralist and Post-Structuralist thought from Barthes and Foucault onwards. Attending to the multiple relations between historian and past shows that thesis to be untenable: one's everyday life, not to mention history itself, would be impossible under such an assumption.

(3) In exploring different historical approaches – as science, as interpretation, as discourse – many of my arguments have been critical. That is not a feature of this Introduction that I regret, for it results from a pernicious assumption still inherent in much philosophical thinking. That assumption is that philosophy should be in the business of providing criteria *that must be the case* for a practice, in this case history, to be successful. Thus, the positivists argued that explanation must presuppose relevant underlying laws. Collingwood argued that historical knowledge must presuppose re-enactment. Winch argued that social knowledge must presuppose that there are rules that can be grasped. White argued that historical understanding must presuppose the imposition of an emplotment upon a past reality that manifested no narrative structure. That common form of argument is unsurprising, given the Kantian roots of modern philosophy of history (in particular, in the work of Dilthey, Rickert, and Windelband in the later nineteenth century). Kant posed the transcendental questions: what must be the case for x (morality, knowledge of space

and time) to exist? I doubt that there are any transcendental presuppositions to be found, at least with regard to history.

But that does not mean that the philosophical suggestions here examined should be regarded as *failures*. Philosophy can be fruitfully regarded by comparison with two other subjects. Philosophy is itself a sort of interpretation. As I argued in Chapters 8 and 9, an interpretation need not be restricted to the terms of those interpreted, or to what is already latent or unconscious in that practice. Similarly, philosophy can interpret a practice, history, without seeking for the necessary presuppositions of that practice. (Winch was right to closely align sociology and philosophy, but picked an overly restrictive philosophy.) Philosophy can also be seen as a sort of art.[1] Philosophy presents a 'way of seeing' the world, but, unlike art, a way of seeing that is distinctively cognitive. That 'cognitive art' can be applied, if fruitful, to other cognitive practice. I would hope that the foregoing philosophical approaches be regarded as tools that *may* be (for who can say in advance of the attempt) fruitfully applied to the historian's enquiries into the past. There is no requirement that the historian align themselves exclusively with one approach rather than another.

Notes

Chapter 1

1 'Critical history' has often been called 'scientific history', for reasons provided in Chapter 3. Yet I will be wary of using the latter term in this context, since I want to keep open the possibility, discussed in Part II, that 'history as science' might locate a distinctive, and probably controversial, form of critical history.

2 The different ways of observing the world that Oakeshott's 'modes of experience' call attention to are nicely captured in a review by Auspitz (1984), which inspires the following example.

3 A philosophical term of art that I shall make liberal use of. An *a priori* judgement is not justified on the basis of empirical evidence. An *a posteriori* judgement is based on empirical evidence. Mathematics is an *a priori* discipline, history an *a posteriori* one. The status of philosophy is contested.

4 It seems that Ranke's famous phrase should be regarded as description of his own work, not an injunction for historians to follow. Fritz Stern, in a letter to the *New York Review of Books* 47 (2000), notes that the phrase was Ranke's 'youthful, modest assertion in his very first book, written when he was still in his twenties, that his work was aspiring not to the "high offices" that had previously been assigned to history: "It wants only to show what actually happened" (*er will blos zeigen, wie es eigentlich gewesen*).'

5 A quote also used by Michael Bentley (1999: 29–30).

6 An example of Edward Gibbon's critical assessment of the value of a historical document can stand in for a proper defence of this general claim. 'It may seem somewhat remarkable that Bernard of Clairvaux, who records so many miracles of his friend St Malachi, never takes any notice of his own, which, in their turn, however, are carefully related by his companions and disciples.' (A passage found in Grafton (1997: 2).)

Chapter 2

1 'Sufficiency' and 'necessity' are much-used philosophical tools which, while they should not be regarded as exhausting philosophical enquiry, can bring clarity. If x is sufficient for y, then whenever x is present, then so is y. If x is not sufficient for y, then it is not the case that y is always present when x is. ('Living in a cottage' is sufficient for 'living in a house', but not vice versa.) If x is necessary for y, then y cannot be present without x. If x is not necessary for y, then y can be present without x. ('Living in a house' is necessary for 'living in a cottage', but not vice versa.)

2 Rules and norms are clearly similar things. They differ in the degree to which they are explicit in the practice in question. It is useful to keep in mind an oft applicable distinction between rules, which are explicitly followed; and norms, which include rules but which also include those implicit demands that constitute the practice without explicitly guiding the practice.

Philosophy is drawn to the constitutive norm: the hidden substructure of the practice that is presupposed but rarely articulated.

3 This comment disguises certain philosophical issues concerning normativity. Take, specifically, the philosophical thesis that one can infer norms from people's sanctioning of other behaviour. The inference of norm from reaction is more plausible than from first-order behaviour, yet is not always the right inference to make. For the reaction might itself be wrong; just as if male A were to criticize female B for writing a history that went beyond the domestic sphere. A general philosophical problem of normative regress looms: how can we know the norms of a practice, when any behaviour (including reaction, reaction to reaction . . .) may or may not correspond to what is *correct*? The (easy) solution that I presume is that we can help ourselves to some level of normativity in the practice described, and need not (indeed should not) attempt to reduce norms to 'mere' behaviour.

4 I have made particular use of Arthur Marwick's *The Nature of History* (1970), John Tosh's *The Pursuit of History* (1991/1984), and Howell and Prevenier's *From Reliable Sources* (2001).

5 Taken from a guide written for history students at the University of Santa Cruz ('How to distinguish between a primary and a secondary source'. http://library.ucsc.edu/ref/howto/primarysecondary.html. Accessed 4 June 2007).

6 Marwick (1970: 133) raises an example that suggests a third foundation for the primacy of evidence: the copy. The copy remains intentionally direct – it is not *about* that which it is copied from. If the copying mechanism is accurate (and such mechanisms have been available to our culture for many centuries), then primacy in the sense of reliability will also be satisfied. Why, then, does Marwick understandably doubt that copies are primary sources? The answer, I think, is that a third notion of primacy derives from the experience gained in objects that are 'from the past'; a phenomenon that I discussed towards the end of Chapter 1.

Chapter 3

1 We do not need to presume at the outset that any historical belief will have the value 1, nor that any will be assigned 0. Neither need we assume that one will be able to allocate very precise quantitative values to historical beliefs. The apparent difficulty of applying to typical historical beliefs a precise number representing the degree to which we hold them typically leads to suspicion with the whole Bayesian approach. Yet, as we shall see, that approach can yield understanding without assuming numerical precision.

2 This criticism is developed at greater length by Peter Achinstein (2001: chapter 4).

3 This example is inspired by Dawid (2002).

4 For simplicity of presentation, I take the hypothesis of pre-1492 contact between Central America and the Mediterranean to be equivalent to the hypothesis that there were Mediterranean visitors to Central America before Columbus. However, the latter is more precisely regarded as a sub-set of the former, given that it is logically possible that there had been Central American visitors to the Mediterranean before Columbus, and more substantively possible that there had been indirect contact between Mediterranean and Central America before Columbus, perhaps via Scandinavia.

5 One who particularly emphasizes this claim in the context of a critique of Bayesianism as a genuine philosophy of science is Alan Chalmers, in the third edition of his *What is This Thing Called Science?* (1999).

6 Including Thomas Bayes' own 'principle of indifference'. For a succinct if fairly technical explanation of the debate in this area, see Richard Swinburne's introduction to Swinburne (ed.) (2002).

7 In keeping with a modest explanationism, I would not insist that there is no difference between explanation and inference. Not all explanation is a matter of inference; sometimes the 'two-step' picture is correct in that we do know what happened, and only want to discover how those things are related. And not every inference implies explanation, a fact which makes the Bayesian model of broader applicability to the explanationist. As I suggested in the previous chapter, inference can run in either temporal direction, or none, while explanation seems more limited to the relation of earlier explaining later.

8 It must be noted that the philosophical propriety of including intentions among causes has been challenged, as will be discussed in Chapter 8. I reject that challenge, though I do not reject the related idea that tracing the causes of actions requires a different methodology to tracing the causes of lumps of matter.

9 Attempts to introduce explanatory considerations of this sort have tended to be resisted by Bayesians, on account of the fact that any modification of the Bayesian equations leaves one open to being 'Dutch Booked'. It is important to realize one should not demand modification of the Bayesian formula, but should rather insist that considerations of explanatory virtue provide a necessary means for specification of the terms in that formula.

10 Deduction, even where available, isn't always a good guide to inference. If it were, then whenever the hypothesis entailed the evidence, then one could infer the former from the latter. Any arbitrary conjunction, say 'Henry XIII had six wives and Louis XVI was beheaded', entails its conjuncts. Therefore, according to the deductive approach, the conjunct 'Louis XVI was beheaded' confirms 'Henry XIII had six wives and Louis XVI was beheaded'. That ridiculous consequence is avoided by an explanationist approach to the evidential likelihood term, on the basis that no sensible theory of explanation should permit a conjunction to be explanatory of one of its conjuncts.

11 See, in particular, Anscombe (1973), Coady (1992), Burge (1993), Owens (2000).

Chapter 4

1 The question is Feyerabend's, the 'anarchist' philosopher of science (see, for example his *Against Method*, 1975). Feyerabend used the question to criticize the assumption that what we usually regard as science is superior to practices not usually regarded as scientific: astrology, black magic and psychoanalysis.

2 A note is needed in order to make explicit the understanding of 'abstract property' that is here implied. I see no fundamental split between abstract scientific properties, and everyday properties. 'Abstract' should not, therefore, be understood to imply a non-empirical property such as one finds in a Platonic metaphysics. Regarding mathematical properties in the same way (as I do later in this section) commits me to a Millian philosophy of

mathematics, wherein numerical properties are a certain kind of abstract empirical property.

3 It is an interesting and more complex question as to what exactly is required to facilitate a quantitative measurement approach. Roughly, one must be able to map entities to be measured to non-negative reals, such that reflexivity, transitivity, connectedness and comparison is entailed. A ratio scale also requires a natural zero (Rawling 2003: 110–11).

4 Taken from his *Cours de Philosophie Positive*, written between 1830 and 1842 (the long span partly explained by a spell during which the author was committed to an asylum).

5 Note the capitalization of the 'variables', or general terms, in this schematic law. By convention, upper case letters are used to stand for general features of the world, the lower case being reserved for particular things.

6 It's clear that this condition, in addition to being rather imprecise, won't be sufficient. One way to demonstrate that is to 'gerrymander' properties that have just as wide scope as our usual terms, yet are intuitively ill-suited to feature in any scientific laws. Nelson Goodman memorably introduced the term 'grue' for that purpose, where an object is grue if it is green up until a certain time, and blue thereafter (Goodman 1965: 73–5).

7 The possibility of a Marxist law of this kind is *suggested* by comments such as these: 'At a certain stage in the development of these means of production and of exchange, the conditions under which feudal society produced and exchanged, the feudal organization of agriculture and manufacturing industry, in one word, the feudal relations of property became no longer compatible with the already developed productive forces; they became so many fetters. They had to be burst asunder; they were burst asunder. Into their place stepped free competition, accompanied by a social and political constitution adapted in it, and the economic and political sway of the bourgeois class.' (Marx and Engels 1848: Part One)

8 The last of these examples is cited by Alasdair MacIntyre (2003: 90).

9 Quine's criticism (1951) of the analytic–synthetic distinction is well known in philosophical circles, and it is not my intention to suggest that this criticism is misplaced. ('Synthetic' truths are those with empirical content, such as scientific laws.) I take the moral of Quine's criticism to be that the designators 'analytic' and 'synthetic' pick out opposite ends of a spectrum within which no clean break can be located: there is no sharp analytic/synthetic divide. If that interpretation is correct, then Quine's criticism supports the current argument.

10 At least, that is the orthodox position; the 'hidden variables' interpretation of quantum mechanics disputes the stochastic irreducibility. At any rate, what is important to the present argument is that the *possibility* of genuinely stochastic laws makes perfect sense.

11 Thomas Kuhn notably drew our attention to the importance of paradigm experiments in scientific teaching and development (1996/1962: 25–30, 187–91). For a good example of experimentation designed to shield one type of cause from others, discussed in detail by Cartwright (1999: 85–93), consider a contemporary attempt to test predictions made by Einsteinian General Theory of Relativity. The 'Gravity B Probe', currently being developed by a team at Stanford University in order to be put into orbit, must be extremely sensitive. It must therefore be correspondingly well shielded, in particular from the Earth's magnetic field, from the effects of high temperature or pressure, and from irrelevant gravitational effects.

Chapter 5

1 This topic has attracted a large psychological literature: begin with the literature review by Rudolf and Fosterling (1997).

2 Consider that the Method of Difference requires us to infer from the fact that {(A,B,C ...) implies E} and from {(not-A,B,C...) implies −E} that A made the difference. Yet that inference only follows if the same set always leads to the same result: the qualified Humean proposal.

3 I have argued that sociological scientific history can and should maintain that individual properties are *irrelevant* in the explanation of the sort of large-scale historical phenomena that those historians typically focus upon. Collins adopts a bolder position: that individual properties are *reduced to* social properties ('ideology follows geopolitics', p.1580). That bolder position is implausible and unnecessary.

4 The following argument has been suggested by Alexander Rosenberg (2001).

5 One example of such a fictional science occurs in Isaac Asimov's *Foundation* trilogy, under the moniker 'psychohistory'.

6 A term that has raised suspicions among certain reviewers of Diamond's *Guns, Germs and Steel*. It is clear that Diamond will have to *operationalize* (Chapter 4) the term to some degree, if his explanandum is not to be the subject of fierce disagreement (in particular, the extent to which development is a matter of meeting economic criteria). Such operationalization is of course possible – one can stipulate what one means for a given word – though I make more critical remarks of that practice in chapters 8 and 9.

7 The situation is even less favourable for a contrastive approach to justification than the above comments suggest. As Mill notes in the quoted passage, the difference is a cause, *or necessary part of the cause*. Even if we were to find two cases, e and f, that differed only in respect of the prior factor C, we could not simply infer that C made the causal difference, only that it was some part – perhaps only some minor and insignificant part – of the causal story. It is as if you ordered pizza while I ordered truffles, the prior difference between us being that you were hungry and I was not. Even if (*per impossible*) there was no other difference than hunger between us, that hunger might only be a small part of the causal story. For perhaps I am not the sort of person who eats pizza when he's hungry, even though you are. In the next chapter I develop this sort of suggestion.

Chapter 6

1 There have been other notable contributions to the question of how general rules relate to particular decisions. Søren Kierkegaard (1985), in his examination of the biblical Abraham's willingness to sacrifice his son, Isaac, strove to make a space for moral, faith-exemplifying action that nonetheless contravened universal ethical rules. 'Faith is just this paradox, that the single individual as the particular is higher than the universal, is justified before the latter, not as subordinate but superior ... [Abraham] acts on the strength of the absurd; for it is precisely the absurd that as the single individual he is higher than the universal. This paradox cannot be mediated; for as soon as he tries Abraham will have to admit that he is in a state

of temptation, and in that case he will never sacrifice Isaac, or if he has done so he must return repentantly to the universal.' (1985: 84–5)

2 For a more detailed version of this argument, see Martin (1972).

Chapter 7

1 It is interesting to note that the association of history with meaning and natural science with non-meaning is not necessary, and might even be wrong. Some, including Hegel, have studied the natural world with the assumption that this world is already meaningful, perhaps as a result of God's meaning or, for Hegel, the meaning of the World Spirit. (Collingwood also considers this possibility, 1994/1946: 217.) On the other hand, one could study the human and social world in a way that avoids the prior imputation of meaning to that object. The latter possibility is quite familiar, carried out in the explanation of human behaviour in terms of neuro-physiology, and in the explanation of societal development in terms of physical environment (recall Diamond's explanation discussed in Chapter 5).

2 Although the foremost anti-naturalist position has been Idealism – so much so that the latter has sometimes been used as a name for the former (as in the so-called 'Positivism vs. Idealism' debates prevalent in the 1950s and 1960s) – it is not a straightforward matter to state what the connection is. Idealism in philosophy is the doctrine that reality is dependent upon our minds, or ideas (more on Idealism in this dense in Chapter 12). (Bishop) George Berkeley espouses a radical version of Idealism: 'to be is to be perceived'. Kant can be regarded as a less radical Idealist: it is not the existence of reality per se that depends on the mind, but the form that reality displays itself to us that so depends. (Still pretty radical though: Kant takes space, time and causality to be forms dependent on the mind, not on the nature of reality itself.)

So defined, how does Idealism relate to anti-naturalism? The trouble (for one who thinks there is such a connection) is that Idealism is a general doctrine, that covers any knowledge whatsoever. Perhaps it is little more than punning, anti-naturalism dependent on a different, more informal notion of 'idealism' as the name of a position that values the importance of ideas. Richard Rorty is one of the few writers that I know of who explicitly considers this issue (1979: 353).

3 For an example of an attempt to draw conclusions about empathy from research into mirror neurons, see Singer et al. (2004).

4 One influential development of this approach to knowledge of self and others can be found in a central part of Wittgenstein's *Philosophical Investigations* (1997/1953). Wittgenstein insists, in what has come to be known as the 'Private Language Argument', that third person ascription of experience is more basic than first person. One could not say that one was in pain, or that one could see a red shape, unless the words 'pain' and 'red' already had a public use in describing the experiences of others. The Cartesian picture is reversed: third person ascription is basic and direct, first person ascription derived and indirect.

5 I should note that an interest in the relation between the experience of the historian and that of the past actor has in recent years started to move back to the centre of concern in the philosophy of history. In particular, see Frank Ankersmit's *Sublime Historical Experience* (2005). The foregoing section has dealt with experience and empathy in a traditional

manner. Ankersmit's approach differs in so far as he regards the historian's experience not as a step towards the goal of producing true statements about the past, but as an end in itself. To the extent that I engage with this idea, it will be in the context of rebutting a certain scepticism about historical truth, at the end of Chapter 12.

Chapter 8

1 See, in particular, Collingwood's essay 'History as re-enactment' in his 1994/1946 and his *Autobiography*: 29–40, which encourage the idea that it is essential to view re-enactment in the context of question and answer.

2 If the action was not rational, then no rational explanation is appropriate. If the action was rational, then we can include that knowledge as a premise in a DN argument, of the form: (i) Person S believes B and desires D; (ii) for all x, if x is rational, then B and D are followed by action A; (iii) S is rational; therefore S A's. Rationality drops out of the picture, as anything other than a way to predict or retrodict other people.

 But premise (ii) – the supposed law of rationality – looks decidedly dodgy. One might be concerned about its lack of universality (perhaps on the basis that in these circumstances it might not be possible to do A). One might, conversely, be concerned about its analyticity (that intentions are, by definition, that which lead to action in the absence of countervailing circumstances). But I want to emphasize a third concern: that the very idea of rationality, as introduced at the start of this chapter, precludes universal connection. It must be possible for agents not to act on their wants, or we would not be acting out of practical rationality but out of compulsion. That is not to say that we have to believe that choice and scientific law are incompatible – that we cannot be free in a deterministic universe – only that *in terms of understanding the behaviour as rational*, no law can be formulated.

3 In particular, we should not restrict the evidence for the reasons, or question, to the action which is the result of that reasoning or questioning. Gadamer (1989/1960: 372) charges Collingwood with doing just that, specifically in the above noted example of Nelson at Trafalgar. If one treats ability to infer questions as being restricted to the basis only of the actions from which they result, then it is plain to see that the method of question and answer would only be applicable to successful action. That can be appreciated by recognizing that an unsuccessful action alone will not inform us what the actor *wanted* to do. We would, therefore, be able to understand Nelson's practical rationality at Trafalgar, but not Villeneuve's. Gadamer is right to condemn any theory of rationality which led to this result; but we are not usually so restricted, and I can see nothing that Collingwood says that would commit him to the unfortunate conclusion.

4 Dray seems to suggest an account of practical rationality of this sort (1957: 125–6.) And Karsten Steuber develops a similar account at greater length (2002).

5 Risjord (2000: 20–7) contains a clear presentation of this debate, which I have found useful in developing the following.

6 It is a contradiction (of an interesting sort) to say 'I believe p, but p isn't true', and another to say 'p is true, but I don't believe it'. For that reason, to ascribe truth to another's beliefs is to have them believe the same as you. Of course, it is no contradiction to claim that 'Carl believes p, but p isn't true': the connection only applies in the first person.

7 For a defence of the related idea that interpretation is a matter of producing a coherent set of explanations, see Risjord (2000: 52–9).

Chapter 9

1 So long as we don't thereby confuse this position with the positivistic approach to explanation described in Chapter 4. That demand for universality implied that history seek scientific laws in which the consequent was universally implied by the antecedent. Universalism here is the thesis that past authors speak to us about common themes, and take part in the same conversation.

2 The organization of these criticisms is mine, not Butterfield's; though it does draw on William Dray's useful paper, 'J. H. Hexter, neo-Whiggism, and early Stuart historiography' (1987).

3 It has sometimes been assumed that there is some logical connection between these two central debates in the philosophy of history: naturalism and anti-naturalism concerning explanation and interpretation, and objectivity versus anti-objectivity. The first of each of those pairs has been connected, and opposed to the second of each of those pairs. But consider that an anti-objectivist naturalism could be the result of applying a Kuhnian understanding of science to history; and an objectivist anti-naturalism is found, in different ways, in both Collingwood and Winch.

4 A warning made more acute by considering that Ranke's explicit notion of objectivity included the belief that the detached and impartial historian would have revealed to them the 'moral energies' and 'spiritual substances' of each age (Ranke 1973: 117, 119). This, itself, can be taken as a useful argument for historicism: Ranke and Weber both believed in objectivity, but there was nonetheless an intellectual gulf between them.

5 The following 'counterfactual model' of historical importance was developed at some length in my PhD thesis: Day (2002).

6 This bald claim is implausible. A more plausible version accepts that counterfactual importance is not the only basis for inclusion in a history, but nonetheless can be presumed unless flagged otherwise. The historian might indeed flag some part of their account as being of anecdotal or personal interest. But in the absence of such an understanding, we are at liberty to presume that those events that are mentioned are more important (with respect to what is being explained) than those which are excluded; and if this condition is not met, then we have grounds to criticize that account. Thus the commitment to include the important and exclude the unimportant is a pragmatic commitment, since it is the hallmark of that sort of commitment it may be explicitly cancelled.

7 An additional relation with the past is worth mentioning in an endnote. Just as we evaluate the past, so, it seems, the past may lay evaluative claim upon us. Consider two examples. The first, from Margalit (2002: 18–19), concerns an army commander who, when asked about a soldier from his unit who had died just a few days before, could not remember the soldier's name. Justified outrage resulted; a justification that I don't think stems only from the hurt caused to the soldier's living relatives, but from a duty to the dead soldier. Second example: if someone that you had been close to had died before completing a project close

to their heart, and it was in your power to complete that project, then it would be ethically praiseworthy to do so. Again, the duty is to the past.

Chapter 10

1 Lamarque (2004), as part of his deflationary approach to questions of narrative, wants philosophers to ignore the narrative and to focus the realism debate on its elements: reference, events, causation, colligatory objects and claims of significance. But if we want to understand the epistemology of history we must pay attention to the *narrative*, on the grounds that the narrative discourse is significant over and above those elements that Lamarque mentions.

2 On its first publication, it was reviewed as a rather eccentric intellectual history, placed in the 'history of ideas' section of the *American Historical Review*, not with the 'historiographical and methodological' works. Indeed it is a history of ideas, but to limit it to that domain is to underestimate its importance.

3 The understanding offered as to *how* these rhetorical techniques are genuinely explanatory is one of the weaker parts of White's treatment. How is any genuinely explanatory information imparted by knowing that a set of events is Tragic? The best suggestion is that shaping the account in that way imparts familiarity, and so explains just as one might explain an unfamiliar electoral system by analogy with one's own. Yet as a *theory* of explanation, familiarity is woefully inadequate, since one can make X familiar without thereby explaining X. By comparing the Jewish Diaspora to a supernova one does not even take the first step to explaining the former. I imagine that White's response would be that his is a descriptive account of historical understanding, and it is not his business to judge the adequacy of that understanding.

4 Psychological experiment has substantiated the claim that narratives *often* distort one's knowledge of the truth. Barbara Tversky (2004) reports that 61 per cent of her experimental sample admit that their own narratives distort, by (highest frequency first) omission, exaggeration, minimisation, invention. She also makes the surprising claim that telling a narrative affects the narrator's understanding more than the audience's. Testing the recall of students both before and after telling a simple narrative, Tversky (2004: 388–9) found the narrator's memories changed radically after being asked to tell deliberately one-sided narratives; she suggests that the audience tend to take distortions as expressive, and quite casually disregard them.

5 This account of how narratives *are* lived as well as told provides the first premise for an account of personal identity in terms of narrative. To argue for that position, one would need to build on that premise by showing how lived narratives make it possible for S at different times to be regarded as the same person.

6 I have already considered one such in Ginzburg (1992/1976). A further well-known example is Natalie Davis' (1973) tale of Martin Guerre.

Chapter 11

1 I do not claim relations of entailment between each position in the pair. What relations obtain between theories of truth, reality and meaning is a subject that has received much

philosophical attention. For an argument *against* lumping questions of truth and realism together, see Michael Devitt (1991/1984: especially 28–33). Nonetheless, there are certain affinities between each of the pair, and as a way to present the landscape of the debate, the grouping has definite advantages.

2 A realization which I owe to correspondence with Jonathan Gorman.

3 The same Laplace whose belief in causal determinism (expressed in the form of a demon that knew all positions and forces, and hence knew all future positions) is so often held up to ridicule in the light of subsequent quantum theory.

4 What relevance, if any, is the metaphysical debate concerning the reality of the past? The debate, largely stemming from McTaggart's argument for the unreality of time, pits detensors – those who regard past, present and future as of no more metaphysical consequence than here, near and far – against tensors, who regard past, present and future as a real feature of the world. The tensor may adopt (and may be forced to adopt on the basis of McTaggart's argument) that only the present is real. I suggest that there is not much relevance in this debate with regard to historical knowledge of the past. That is for the simple reason that the historian doesn't *need* a real past, only a past that was, and now is not. The task is to tell it as it really was, not as it really is. Consequently, it seems that one can be an epistemic realist in history and not be a metaphysical realist, *in the above sense*. At least, that conjunction of positions should not be ruled out without further argument.

Chapter 12

1 Things can get a little more complicated when we focus on social science. Everything is 'socially constructed' in the social sphere, by necessity. Women refugees, to use an example from Ian Hacking (1999), are a result of lamentable social phenomena like war and mass rape. But the social constructivist will want to say something else – that the concept we use to describe them – 'women refugees' – is also constructed. Before that label was applied there was something there, perhaps individual women living hard and sometimes terrible lives, but there were no women refugees. Things are actually a little easier if we consider the social construction of history, for then we could make use of the distinction between the past being a result of social factors contemporary or prior to that past (which all would agree with), and the past being constructed as a result of *our* society (which looks much more contentious).

2 Ian Hacking's claim with regard to scientific understanding is similar (1983: 130): 'By attending only to knowledge as representations of nature, we wonder how we can ever escape from representations and hook up with the world.' Rather, for Hacking, we have realism for x in so far as we can use x.

Conclusion

1 An idea suggested by Jonathan Gorman, in conversation.

References

Achinstein, P. (2001) *The Book of Evidence*. Oxford: Oxford University Press.

Ankersmit, F. (2005) *Sublime Historical Experience*. Stanford: Stanford University Press.

Anscombe, G. E. M. (1973) 'Hume and Julius Caesar', in *Analysis* 34, 1–7.

Aristotle (1966) H. G. Apostle (trans.) *Metaphysics*. Bloomington: Indiana University Press (originally c. 300 BC).

— (1997) S. H. Butcher (trans.) *Poetics*. Toronto: Dover (originally c. 330 BC).

Audi, R. (1998) *Epistemology: A Contemporary Introduction to the Theory of Knowledge*. London: Routledge.

Auspitz, J. L. (1984) 'Review of Oakeshott's "On history and other essays"', in *National Review* 36, 42–8.

Aydelotte, W. O. (1966) 'Quantification in history', in *The American Historical Review* 3, 803–25.

Barnes, B. and D. Bloor (1982) 'Relativism, rationalism, and the sociology of knowledge,' in M. Hollis and S. Lukes (eds) *Rationality and Relativism*. Cambridge, Mass.: MIT Press.

Barraclough, G. (1989) (ed.) *The Times Atlas of World History*. London: Times Books (originally 1978).

Barthes, R. (1981) S. Bann (trans.) 'The discourse of history', in *Comparative Criticism* 3, 7–20 (originally 1967).

Beard, C. A. (1935) 'That Noble Dream', in *The American Historical Review* 41, 74–87.

Beardsley, M. (1981) *Aesthetics: Problems in the Philosophy of Criticism*. Indianapolis: Hackett Publishing Company (originally 1958).

Beardsley, M. and W. K. Wimsatt (1987) 'The intentional fallacy', in J. Margolis (ed.) *Philosophy Looks at the Arts*. Philadelphia: Temple University Press (originally 1946).

Beevor, A. (1999) *Stalingrad*. London: Penguin (originally 1998).

Bentley, M. (1999) *Modern Historiography: An Introduction*. London: Routledge.

Berlin, I. (1960) 'The concept of scientific history', in *History and Theory* 1, 1–31.

Blackburn, S. (1984) *Spreading the Word*. Oxford: Oxford University Press.

Bloch, M. (2004) *The Historian's Craft*. Manchester: Manchester University Press (originally 1954).

Boyle, L. (1981) 'Montaillou revisited: mentalité and methodology', in J. Raftis (ed.) *Pathways to Medieval Peasants*. Toronto: Pontifical Institute of Mediaeval Studies, 119–40.

Brandom, R. B. (1994) *Making it Explicit: Reasoning, Representing, and Discursive Commitment*. Harvard: Harvard University Press.

Brandom, R. B. (ed.) (2000) *Rorty and His Critics*. London: Blackwell.

Browning, C. (1996) 'Daniel Goldhagen's willing executioners', in *History and Memory* 8, 88–110.

Burge, T. (1993) 'Content preservation', in *The Philosophical Review* 102, 457–88.

Burke, P. (1992) 'History of events and the revival of narrative', in P. Burke (ed.) *New Perspectives on Historical Writing*. Cambridge: Polity Press, 93–113.

Butterfield, H. (1931) *The Whig Interpretation of History*. London.

Carlyle, T. (1842) *The French Revolution*. London.

Carroll, N. (1990) 'Interpretation, History and Narrative', in *The Monist* 73.

Cartwright, N. (1989) *Nature's Capacities and Their Measurement*. Oxford: Oxford University Press.

—(1999) *The Dappled World: A Study of the Boundaries of Science*. Cambridge: Cambridge University Press.

Chalmers, A. F. (1999) *What is This Thing Called Science?* (third edition). New York: Open University Press (originally 1978).

Chartier, R. (1991) L. G. Cochrane (trans.) *The Cultural Origins of the French Revolution*. Durham, NC: Duke University Press.

Cioffi, F. (1964) 'Intention and interpretation in criticism', in *Proceedings of the Aristotelian Society* 64, 85–106.

Clark, A. (1997) *Being There: Putting Brain, Body, and World Together Again*. Cambridge, Mass.: MIT Press.

Coady, C. A. J. (1992) *Testimony: A Philosophical Study*. Oxford: Clarendon Press.

Cobban, A. (1964) *The Social Interpretation of the French Revolution*. Cambridge: Cambridge University Press.

Collingwood, R. G. (1942) *The New Leviathan: Or Man, Society, Civilisation, Barbarism*. Oxford: Oxford University Press.

—(1970) *An Autobiography*. Oxford: Oxford University Press (originally 1939).

—(1994) J. Dussen (ed.) *The Idea of History*. Oxford: Oxford University Press (originally 1946).

Collins, R. (1995) 'Prediction in macrosociology: The case of the Soviet collapse', in *American Journal of Sociology* 100, 1552–93.

Comte, A. (1830) *Course of Positive Philosophy*. Widely available.

Cooper, D. (1975) 'Alternative logic in "primitive thought"', in *Man* 10, 238–56.

Croce, B. (1921) *On History*. New York: Harcourt.

Cuff, T. (2005) *The Hidden Cost of Economic Development: The Biological Standard of Living in Antebellum Pennsylvania*. Burlington, Vt.: Ashgate Publishing Company.

Danto, A. C. (1968) *Analytical Philosophy of History*. Cambridge: Cambridge University Press (originally 1965).

Darnton, R. (1986) 'The Symbolic Element in History', in *The Journal of Modern History* 58/1, 218–34.

—(1991) *The Great Cat Massacre and Other Episodes in French Cultural History*. London: Penguin Books (originally 1984).

Davidson, D. (2001a) 'Actions, reasons and causes', in *Essays on Actions and Events*. Oxford: Oxford University Press, 3–20 (paper originally 1963).

—(2001b) 'Radical interpretation', in *Inquiries into Truth and Interpretation*. Oxford: Oxford University Press, 125–39 (paper originally 1973).

—(2001c) 'On the very idea of a conceptual scheme', in *Inquiries into Truth and Interpretation*. Oxford: Oxford University Press, 183–98 (paper originally 1974).

Davis, N. (1973) *The Return of Martin Guerre*. Cambridge, Mass.: Harvard University Press.

Dawid, P. (2002) 'Bayes's theorem and weighing evidence by juries', in R. Swinburne (ed.) *Bayes's theorem: Proceedings of the British Academy*, 71–90. Oxford: Oxford University Press.

Day, M. (2002) 'Competing Explanations: Exclusion and Importance in Historical Accounts', PhD thesis, University of Sheffield, UK.

Day, M. and G. Botterill (2007) 'Contrast, inference, and scientific realism', in *Synthese* (forthcoming).

Devitt, M. (1991) *Realism and Truth*. Princeton: Princeton University Press (originally 1984).

Diamond, J. (1998) *Guns, Germs and Steel: A Short History of Everybody for the Last 13,000 Years*. London: Vintage (originally 1997).

Dray, W. H. (1957) *Laws and Explanation in History*. Oxford: Oxford University Press.

Dray, W. H. (1987) 'J. H. Hexter, neo-Whiggism, and early Stuart historiography', in *History and Theory* 26/2, 133–49.

Dray, W. H. (ed.) (1966) *Philosophical Analysis and History*. New York: Harper and Row.

—(1991) 'Historical explanation of actions reconsidered', in P. Gardiner (ed.) *The Philosophy of History*. Oxford: Oxford University Press (originally 1974).

Dummett, M. (1978) 'The reality of the past', in his *Truth and Other Enigmas*. Cambridge, Mass: Harvard University Press (paper originally 1969).

Elton, G. R. and R. W. Fogel (1983) *Which Road to the Past?: Two Views of History*. New Haven: Yale University Press.

Evans-Pritchard, E. E. (1976) *Witchcraft, Oracles and Magic Among the Azande*. Oxford: Oxford University Press (originally 1937).

Feyerabend, P. (1975) *Against Method*. London: Verso.

Fogel, R. W. (1975) 'The limits of quantitative methods in history', in *The American Historical Review* 80, 329–50.

Fogel, R. W. and S. L. Engerman (1995) *Time on the Cross: The Economics of American Negro Slavery*. New York: Norton (originally 1974).

Foucault, M. (1977) 'Nietzsche, genealogy and history', in D. F. Bouchard (ed.) *Language, Counter-Memory and Practice*. Ithaca: Cornell University Press, 139–64.

—(2002). *The Order of Things*. Paris: Gallimard (1966); reprinted London: Routledge.

—(2005). *The Archaeology of Knowledge*. Paris: Gallimard (1969); reprinted A. M. Sheridan Smith (trans.) London: Routledge.

Gadamer, H. G. (1989) J. Weinsheimer and D. G. Marshal (trans.) *Truth and Method*. London: Sheed and Ward (originally 1960).

Gallie, W. B. (1964) *Philosophy and the Historical Understanding*. London: Chatto.

Garfinkel A. (1981) *Forms of Explanation: Rethinking the Questions in Social Theory*. New Haven: Yale University Press.

Geertz, C. (1973) *The Interpretation of Cultures*. New York: Basic Books.

Gettier, A. L. (1963) 'Is justified true belief knowledge?', in *Analysis* 23, 121–3.

Ginzburg, C. (1992) J. and A. Tedeschi (trans.) *The Cheese and the Worms: The Cosmos of a Sixteenth-Century Miller*. Baltimore: Johns Hopkins University Press (originally 1976).

Goehr, L. (2007) 'Afterwords: An introduction to Arthur Danto's philosophies of history and art', in *History and Theory* 46/1, 1–28.

Goldhagen, D. J. (1996) *Hitler's Willing Executioners: Ordinary Germans and the Holocaust*. New York: Vintage Books.

Goldstein, L. (1972) 'Collingwood and the constitution of the historical past', in M. Krausz (ed.) *Critical Essays on the Philosophy of R. G. Collingwood*. London: Oxford University Press.

—(1976) *Historical Knowing*. Austin: University of Texas Press.

Goodman, N. (1965) *Fact, Fiction, and Forecast*. Indianapolis: Bobbs-Merrill.

—(1978) *Ways of Worldmaking*. Indianapolis: Hackett Publishing Company.

Gorman, J. L. (1974) 'Objectivity and Truth in History', in *Inquiry* 17, 373–397.

—(2007) *Historical Judgement*. Stocksfield: Acumen.

Grafton, A. (1997) *The Footnote: A Curious History*. Harvard: Harvard University Press.

Greer, D. (1935) *The Incidence of the Terror During the French Revolution: A Statistical Interpretation*. Cambridge, Mass.: University of Michigan Press.

Hacking, I. (1983) *Representing and Intervening*. Cambridge: Cambridge University Press.

—(1999) *The Social Construction of What?* Cambridge, Mass.: Harvard University Press.

Hegel, G. W. F. (1956) *The Philosophy of History*, trans. J. Sibree. New York: Dover (originally 1840).

—(1977) *The Phenomenology of Spirit*, trans. A. V. Miller. Oxford: Oxford University Press (originally 1807).

Heidegger, M. (1962) J. Macquarrie and E. Robinson (trans.) *Being and Time*. San Francisco: Harper (originally 1927).

Hempel, C. G. (1942) 'The Function of General Laws in History', in *Journal of Philosophy* 39, 35–47.

Hempel, C. G. and P. Oppenheim (1948) 'Studies in the logic of explanation' in *Philosophy of Science* 15, 135–75.

Hooks, G. (1993) 'The weakness of strong theories: the U.S. state's dominance of the World War II investment process', in *American Sociological Review* 58, 37–53.

Howell, M. C. and W. Prevenier (2001) *From Reliable Sources: An Introduction to Historical Methods*. New York: Cornell University Press.

Howson, C. and P. Urbach (2007) *Scientific Reasoning: The Bayesian Method*. Chicago: Open Court (originally 1989).

Humboldt, W. (1967) 'On the historian's task', in *History and Theory* 6, 57–71 (originally 1822).

Hume, D. (1977) *An Enquiry Concerning Human Understanding*. Indianapolis: Hackett Publishing (originally 1748).

—(2003) *A Treatise of Human Nature*. London: Everyman (originally 1740).

Humphreys, P. (2003) 'Mathematical modelling in the social sciences', in S. P. Turner and P. Roth (eds) *The Blackwell Guide to the Philosophy of the Social Sciences*. Oxford: Blackwell, 166–84.

Iggers, G. G. (1974) 'Historicism', in P. P. Wiener (ed.) *The Dictionary of the History of Ideas*. New York: Scribner, Volume II 456–63.

Jarvie, I. (1978) 'Seeing through movies', in *Philosophy of the Social Sciences* 8, 374–97.

Jenkins, K. (2003) *Re-thinking History*. London: Routledge (originally 1991).

Joll, J. (1992) *The Origins of the First World War*. London: Longman (originally 1984).

Kant, I. (1929) N. Kemp Smith (trans.) *Critique of Pure Reason*. New York: St Martin's Press (originally 1781).

Kates, G. (ed.) (1998) *The French Revolution: Recent Debates and New Controversies*. London: Routledge.

Kellner, H. (1997) 'Language and historical representation', in K. Jenkins (ed.) *The Postmodern History Reader*. London: Routledge, 127–38.

Kershaw, I. (1991) *Hitler: Profiles in Power*. London: Longman.

Kierkegaard, S. (1985) A. Hannay (trans.) *Fear and Trembling*. London: Penguin (originally 1843).

Kipling, R. (1902) *Just So Stories*. Widely available.

Kosso, P. (1993) 'Historical evidence and epistemic justification: Thucydides as a case study', *History and Theory* 32, 1–13.

Kripke, S. A. (1980) *Naming and Necessity*. Cambridge, Mass.: Harvard University Press.

—(1982) *Wittgenstein on Rules and Private Language*. London: Blackwell.

Kuhn, T. (1996) *The Structure of Scientific Revolutions* (3rd edition). Chicago: University of Chicago Press (originally 1962).

Lakatos, I. (1978) J. Worrall and G. Currie (eds) *The Methodology of Scientific Research Programmes*. Cambridge: Cambridge University Press.

Lamarque, P. (2004) 'On not expecting too much from narrative', in *Mind & Language* 19/4, 393–408.

Laplace, P. S. (1951) 'Essai philosophique sur les Probabilités', introduction to *Théorie Analytique des Probabilités* (2nd edition). Paris: V Courcier (1814); reprinted F. W. Truscott and F. L. Emory (trans.) *A Philosophical Essay on Probabilities*, New York: Dover.

Le Roy Ladurie, E. (1990) B. Bray (trans.) *Montaillou: Cathars and Catholics in a French Village*. London: Penguin (originally 1978).

Lefebvre, G. (1947) R. R. Palmer (trans.) *The Coming of the French Revolution*. Princeton: Princeton University Press (originally 1939).

Levi, G. (1992) 'On microhistory', in P. Burke (ed.) *New Perspectives on Historical Writing*. Cambridge: Polity Press, 93–113.

Lewis, D. (1973) *Counterfactuals*. Oxford: Blackwell.

Lipstadt, D. (1993) *Denying the Holocaust: The Growing Assault on Truth and Memory*. New York: Macmillan.

Lipton, P. (2004) *Inference to the Best Explanation*. Second edition. London: Routledge (originally 1991).

Lorenz, C. (1998) 'Can histories be true? Narrativism, positivism, and the "metaphorical turn"', in *History and Theory* 37/3, 309–29.

Lyotard, J. F. (2001) G. Bennington and B. Massumi (trans.) *The Postmodern Condition: A Report on Knowledge*. Manchester: Manchester University Press (originally 1979).

MacIntyre, A. (2003) *After Virtue*. London: Duckworth (originally 1981).

Manicas, P. (1981) 'Review article: Theda Skocpol, states and social revolutions', in *History and Theory* 20, 204–18.

Margalit, A. (2002) *The Ethics of Memory*. Cambridge, Mass.: Harvard University Press.

Martin, R. (1972) 'On weighting causes', in *American Philosophical Quarterly* 9, 291–2.

—(1989) *The Past Within Us: An Empirical Approach to the Philosophy of History*. Princeton: Princeton University Press.

—(1998) 'Progress in historical studies', in *History and Theory* 37/1, 14–39.

Marwick, A. (1970) *The Nature of History*. London: Macmillan.

Marx, K. and F. Engels (1848) *The Communist Manifesto*. Widely available.

McCormick, R. P. (1959) 'Suffrage classes and party alignments: A study in voter behaviour', in *Mississippi Valley Historical Review* 46, 398–403.

McGregor, J. (2006) *So Many Ways to Begin*. London: Bloomsbury Publishing.

McTaggart, J. E. (1908) 'The unreality of time', in *Mind* 17/68, 457–74.

Michelet, J. (1967) C. Cocks (trans.) G. Wright (ed.) *History of the French Revolution*. Chicago: University of Chicago Press (originally 1853).

Mill, J. S. (1973) *A System of Logic Ratiocinative and Inductive Books I-III*, in J. M. Robson (ed.) *Collected Works of John Stuart Mill Volume VII*. Toronto: University of Toronto Press and London: Routledge (originally 1843).

—(1974) *A System of Logic Ratiocinative and Inductive Books IV-VI*, in J. M. Robson (ed.) *Collected Works of John Stuart Mill Volume VIII*. Toronto: University of Toronto Press and London: Routledge (originally 1843).

Milligan, J. D. (1979) 'The treatment of an historical source', in *History and Theory* 18, 177–96.

Mink, L. (1970) 'History and fiction as modes of comprehension', in *New Literary History* 1, 541–58.

Mulhall, S. (1996) *Heidegger and Being and Time*. London: Routledge.

Nash, J. (2002) *John Craige's Mathematical Principles of Christian Theology*. Carbondale, Ill.: Southern Illinois University Press.

Nietzsche, F. (1873) 'On the use and abuse of history for life'. Widely available; originally published as part of his *Untimely Meditations*.

Novick, P. (1999) *That Noble Dream: The 'Objectivity Question' and the American Historical Profession*. Cambridge: Cambridge University Press (originally 1988).

Oakeshott, M. (1933) *Experience and its Modes*. Cambridge: Cambridge University Press.

Obeyesekere, G. (1992) *The Apotheosis of Captain Cook*. Princeton: Princeton University Press.

Owens, D. (2000) *Reason Without Freedom: The Problem of Epistemic Normativity*. London: Routledge.

Pompa, L. (1990) *Human Nature and Historical Knowledge: Hume, Hegel and Vico*. Cambridge: Cambridge University Press.

Popper, K. (1957) *The Poverty of Historicism*. London: Routledge.

—(2004) *The Logic of Scientific Discovery*. London: Routledge (originally 1935).

Porter, R. (1988) 'Seeing the past', in *Past and Present* 118, 186–205.

Quine, W. V. O. (1951) 'Two dogmas of empiricism', in *The Philosophical Review* 60, 20–43.

—(1960) *Word and Object*. Cambridge, Mass.: MIT Press.

Ranke, L. (1824) *Geschichte der romanischen und germanischen Völker von 1494 bis 1514* (History of the Latin and Teutonic Nations from 1494 to 1514). Berlin.

Ranke, L. (1949) W. P. Fuchs (ed.) *Das Briefwerk von Leopold von Ranke*. Hamburg: Hoffmann und Campe Verlag.

Ranke, L. (1973) G. Iggers and K. Moltke (eds) *The Theory and Practice of History*. Indianapolis: Bobbs-Merril.

Rawling, P. (2003) 'Decision theory and degree of belief', in S. P. Turner and P. Roth (eds) *The Blackwell Guide to the Philosophy of the Social Sciences*. Oxford: Blackwell, 110–42.

Ricoeur, P. (1984–1988) 3 volumes. K. McLaughlin and D. Pellauer (trans.) *Time and Narrative*. Chicago: University of Chicago Press.

—(2004) K. Blamey and D. Pellauer (trans.) *Memory, History, Forgetting*. Chicago: University of Chicago Press (originally 2000).

Risjord, M. (2000) *Woodcutters and Witchcraft: Rationality and Interpretive Change in the Social Sciences*. New York: State University of New York Press.

Rorty, R. (1979) *Philosophy and the Mirror of Nature*. Princeton: Princeton University Press.

Rosenberg, A. (2001) 'How is biological explanation possible', in *British Journal for the Philosophy of Science* 52, 735–60.

Rosenstone, R. A. (1988) 'History in images/history in words: reflections on the possibility of really putting history onto film', in *The American Historical Review* 93, 1173–85.

Roth, P. (2003) 'The concept of understanding', in S. P. Turner and P. Roth (eds) *The Blackwell Guide to the Philosophy of the Social Sciences*. Oxford: Blackwell, 311–33.

Rudolph, U. and F. Försterling (1997) 'The psychological causality implicit in verbs: a review', in *Psychological Bulletin* 121, 192–218.

Runia, E. (2006) 'Presence', in *History and Theory* 45, 1–29.

Russell, B. (2004) *The Analysis of Mind*. New York: Cosimo (originally 1921).

Sahlins, M. (1995) *How 'Natives' Think: About Captain Cook, for Example*. Chicago: University of Chicago Press.

de Saussure, F. (1998) R. Harris (trans.) *Course in General Linguistics*. Illinois: Open Court (originally 1916).

Schama, S. (1989) *Citizens: a Chronicle of the French Revolution*. London: Viking.

Singer, T. et al. (2004) 'Empathy for pain involves the affective but not sensory components of pain', in *Science* 303, 1157–62.

Skinner, Q. (1969) 'Meaning and understanding in the history of ideas', in *History and Theory* 8/1, 3–53.

Skocpol, T. (1979) *States and Social Revolutions: A Comparative Analysis of France, Russia and China*. Cambridge: Cambridge University Press.

Steuber, K. R. (2002) 'The psychological basis of historical explanation: Re-enactment, simulation, and the fusion of horizons', in *History and Theory* 41/1, 25–42.

Stockley, D. (1983) 'Empathetic Reconstruction in History and History Teaching', in *History and Theory* 22/4, 50–65.

Stone, L. (1979) 'The revival of narrative: reflections on a new old history', in *Past and Present*, 85, 3–24.

Strawson, P. (1999) 'Truth', in S. Blackburn and K. Simmons (eds) *Truth*. Oxford: Oxford University Press (originally 1950).

Swinburne, R. (ed.) (2002) *Bayes's theorem: Proceedings of the British Academy*. Oxford: Oxford University Press.

Tackett, T. (1998) 'Nobles and the third estate in the revolutionary dynamic of the National Assembly, 1789-90', in G. Kates (ed.) *The French Revolution: Recent Debates and New Controversies*. London: Routledge, 192–235.

Taylor, C. (1999) *Philosophy and the Human Sciences: Philosophical Papers 2*, Cambridge: Cambridge University Press (originally 1985).

Taylor, G. V. (1967) 'Noncapitalist wealth and the origins of the French Revolution', in *American Historical Review* 72, 469–96.

Tolstoy, L. (1991) L. and A. Maude (trans.) *War and Peace*. Oxford: Oxford University Press (originally 1868–9).

Tomlinson, T. (1998) 'Review of Guns, Germs and Steel', in *Institute of Historical Research* online review: www.history.ac.uk/reviews/paper/diamond.html (accessed 1 July 2007).

Tosh, J. (1991) *The Pursuit of History*. London: Longman (originally 1984).

Trevelyan, G. M. (1938) *The English Revolution*. Oxford: Oxford University Press.

Tucker, A. (2004) *Our Knowledge of the Past: A Philosophy of Historiography*. Cambridge: Cambridge University Press.

Tversky, B. (2004) 'Narratives of space, time, and life', in *Mind & Language* 19/4, 380–92.

Van Fraassen, B. C. (1980) *The Scientific Image*. Oxford: Oxford University Press.

Vico, G. (2002) L. Pompa (trans., ed.) *The First New Science*. Cambridge: Cambridge University Press (originally *Scienza nuova* (1725)).

Walsh, W. H. (1970) *An Introduction to the Philosophy of History*. London: Hutchinson (originally 1951).

Weber, M. (1949) '"Objectivity" in social science and social policy', in E. A. Shils and H. A. Finch (trans.) *The Methodology of the Social Sciences*. New York: Glencoe.

Weber, M. (1964) T. Parsons (ed.), A. M. Henderson and T. Parsons (trans.) *The theory of social and economic organization*. London: Macmillan (originally published 1947).

White, H. (1973) *Metahistory*. Baltimore: Johns Hopkins Press.

—(1978) 'The historical text as literary artefact', in *Tropics of Discourse*. Baltimore: John Hopkins Press, 81–100.

—(1980) 'The value of narrativity in the representation of reality', in *Critical Inquiry* 7/1, 5–27.

—(1988) 'Historiography and historiophoty', in *The American Historical Review* 93, 1193–9.

Winch, P. (1958) *The Idea of a Social Science*. London: Routledge.

—(1964) 'Understanding a primitive society', in *American Philosophical Quarterly* 1, 307–24.

Windelband, W. (1980) G. Oakes (trans.) 'History and natural science', in *History and Theory* 19, 169–85 (originally Windelband's 1894 Rectorial address)

Wittgenstein, L. (1922) C. K. Ogden (trans.) *Tractatus Logico-Philosophicus*. London: Routledge (originally 1921).

—(1997) G. E. M. Anscombe (trans.) *Philosophical Investigations*. Oxford: Blackwell (originally 1953).

Index